# MEDITATION

BHAGWAN SHREE RAJNEESH

# MEDITATION
## ∽ THE ART OF ECSTASY ∽

Bhagwan Shree Rajneesh

Edited by Ma Satya Bharti

PERENNIAL LIBRARY
Harper & Row, Publishers
New York, Hagerstown, San Francisco, London

With the exception of chapter 3, chapter 8, and the section on techniques devised by Bhagwan Shree, the material in this book originally appeared in *Dynamics of Meditation,* published by Jeevan Jagriti Kendra (now known as the Rajneesh Foundation). It is published here with their kind permission.

Chapter 3 originally appeared in *Sannyas* 3, no. 1 (January–February 1974), under the title "Modern Man and His Neurosis." It is reprinted here with the kind permission of the publisher, Neo-Sannyas International.

Chapter 8 is an excerpt from a discourse titled "The Occult Mysteries of Initiation" that originally appeared in the book *I Am the Gate.* It is reprinted here with the kind permission of the Rajneesh Foundation.

*Designed by Eve Callahan*

First PERENNIAL LIBRARY edition published 1978

ISBN: 0–06–080394–0

84 85 86 8 7 6

# Contents

# Foreword

There is much talk about meditation these days, but the confusion about what it is and how to "achieve" it is greater than ever. Ask any random group of people if they ever meditate and about half of them will say they do (or have), but, contrary to what is commonly supposed, meditation isn't really something that you can "do." It is something that happens spontaneously when you're not doing *any*thing, when you're in an absolute state of non-doing. What people mean when they say they meditate, then, is that they are practicing some technique that hopefully will create the situation where meditation can happen. No technique is meditation. It is merely to create the situation where meditation can happen spontaneously.

There are a confusing number of meditation techniques to choose from: Zen techniques, tantra techniques, yoga techniques, and Sufi techniques (not to mention Christianity and Hasidic Judaism, which have their own techniques). The technique that is right for any individual can be determined only by experimentation. When something feels right, you know it. When something works for you, you know it. And you know it not because you experience peace or bliss for the twenty to forty minutes every day that you "meditate," but because your whole life has been transformed by it.

In this book, enlightened spiritual master Bhagwan Shree Rajneesh of India talks about meditation and suggests a variety of meditation techniques that are particularly suitable for Westerners. The techniques start out from where man is, not from where he once was, not from where he wants to be. They begin from the beginning to take us from where we are to where we can be. Whether he is devising new meditation techniques that start out from a psychotherapeutic base or revising and updating ancient techniques from a variety of traditions (so that they become pertinent, once again, for the new needs of the modern seeker), Bhagwan Shree's interest is in helping each individual find that path that is right for him. He has no particular philosophy that he wants to "push," no dogma, no doctrines. He says that each individual has to find his own unique path, his own unique yoga.

"To follow in the footsteps of Christ, the footsteps of Buddha, the footsteps of Krishna, will not make you a Christ or a Buddha or a Krishna," he says. "You must find your own path, your own way." The discourses contained in this book, and the techniques they discuss, are an attempt to help you to find that way.[1]

When meditation happens, your whole life will become a meditation, a celebration. You will not have to "practice" awareness. More and more you will find that awareness is there: an awareness of oneself, of others, of the complexity of existence. More and more often you will be "here and now." More and more often you will feel the bliss, the playfulness, the absurdity of existence.

We are all so serious about life, so serious about our attempts to grow beyond that which we have already known, that we miss what is here and now. To live in the moment,

[1] The discourses were spontaneously delivered by Bhagwan Shree from October, 1970, to July, 1972. All the material published by him is from lectures that have been transcribed and edited by his disciples.

unburdened by desires, expectations, longings, is to live in meditation. To take life as a play, to laugh at the dramas that existence creates for us, at the traumas that we create for ourselves, is to know the moment that religious seers have been speaking about for thousands of years. We have not understood their words because they spoke in symbols that are no longer ours. Bhagwan Shree Rajneesh speaks our language. And what he has to say is more than thought-provoking. It is a challenge. It is an invitation to personal transformation.

MA SATYA BHARTI

# Introduction

## Meditation: The Art of Celebration

We train a child to focus his mind—to concentrate—because without concentration he will not be able to cope with life. Life requires it; the mind must be able to concentrate. But the moment the mind becomes able to concentrate, it becomes less aware. **Awareness** means a mind that is conscious but not focused. **Awareness** is a consciousness of all that is happening.

Concentration is a choice. It excludes all except its object of concentration. It is a narrowing. If you are walking on the street, you will have to narrow your consciousness in order to walk. You cannot ordinarily be aware of all that is happening because if you are aware of everything that is happening you will become unfocused. So concentration is a need. Concentration of the mind is a need in order to live—to survive and exist. That is why every culture, in its own way, tries to narrow the mind of the child.

Children, as they are, are never focused. Their consciousness is open from all sides. Everything is coming in; nothing is being excluded. The child is open to every sensation; every sensation is included in his consciousness. And so much is coming in! That is why he is so wavering, so un-

stable. A child's unconditioned mind is a flux—a flux of
sensations—but he will not be able to survive with this type
of mind. He must learn how to narrow his mind, to
concentrate.

The moment you narrow the mind you become particularly conscious of one thing and simultaneously unconscious
of so many other things. The more narrowed the mind is,
the more successful it will be. You will become a spe-
cialist, you will become an expert, but the whole thing
will consist of knowing more and more about less and less.

The narrowing is an existential necessity. No one is
responsible for it. As life exists, it is needed. But it is not
enough. It is utilitarian, but just to survive is not enough;
just to be utilitarian is not enough. So when you become
utilitarian and the consciousness is narrowed, you deny
your mind much of which it was capable. You are not
using the total mind. You are using a very small part of it.
And the remaining—the major portion—will become unconscious.

In fact, there is no boundary between conscious and
unconscious. These are not two minds. "Conscious mind"
means that part of the mind that has been used in the
narrowing process. "Unconscious mind" means that portion
that has been neglected, ignored, closed. This creates a
division, a split. The greater portion of your mind becomes
alien to you. You become alienated from your own self;
you become a stranger to your own totality.

A small part is being identified as your self and the rest
is lost. But the remaining unconscious part is always there
as unused potentiality, unused possibilities, unlived adven-
tures. This unconscious mind (this potential, this unused,
mind) will always be in a fight with the conscious mind.
That is why there is always a conflict within. Everyone is in
conflict because of this split between the unconscious and
the conscious. But only if the potential, the unconscious, is
allowed to flower can you feel the bliss of existence . . .
otherwise not.

If the major portion of your potentialities remains unfulfilled, your life will be a frustration. That is why the more utilitarian a person is, the less he is fulfilled, the less he is blissful. The more utilitarian the approach—the more one is in business life—the less he is living, the less he is ecstatic. The part of the mind that cannot be made useful in the utilitarian world has been denied.

The utilitarian life is necessary but at a great cost. You have lost the festivity of life. Life becomes a festivity, a celebration, if all your potentialities come to a flowering. Then life is a ceremony. That is why I always say that religion means transforming life into a celebration. The dimension of religion is the dimension of the festive, the nonutilitarian.

The utilitarian mind must not be taken as the whole. The remaining . . . the greater . . . the whole mind . . . should not be sacrificed to it. The utilitarian mind must not become the end. It will have to remain there, but as a means. The other—the remaining, the greater, the potential—must become the end. That is what I mean by a religious approach.

With a nonreligious approach, the businesslike mind (the utilitarian) becomes the end. When this becomes the end, there is no possibility of the unconscious actualizing the potential. The unconscious will be denied. If the utilitarian becomes the end, it means that the servant is playing the role of the master.

Intelligence, the narrowing of the mind, is a means toward survival, but not toward life. Survival is not life. Survival is a necessity—to exist in the material world is a necessity—but the end is always to come to a flowering of the potential, of all that is meant by you. If you are fulfilled completely, if nothing remains inside in seed form, if everything becomes actual, if you are a flowering, then and only then can you feel the bliss, the ecstasy, of life.

The denied part of you, the unconscious part, can become active and creative only if you add a new dimension to your life—the dimension of the festive, the dimension of play. So meditation is not a work; it is a play. Praying is not a business; it is a play. Meditation is not something to be done to achieve some goal (peace, bliss . . .) but something to be enjoyed as an end in itself.

The festive dimension is the most important thing to be understood . . . and we have lost it totally. By festive, I mean the capacity to enjoy, moment to moment, all that comes to you.

We have become so conditioned and habits have become so mechanical that even when there is no business to be done, our minds are businesslike. When no narrowing is needed, you are narrowed. Even when you are playing, you are not playing. You are not enjoying it. Even when you are playing cards, you are not enjoying it. You play for the victory, and then the play becomes a work. Then what is going on is not important, only the result.

In business, the result is important. In festivity, the act is important. If you can make any act significant in itself, then you become festive and you can celebrate it.

Whenever you are in celebration, the limits, the narrowing limits, are broken. They are not needed; they are thrown. You come out of your straitjacket, the narrowing jacket of concentration. Now you are not choosing. Everything that comes, you allow. And the moment you allow the total existence to come in, you become one with it. There is a communion.

This communion I call meditation: this celebration, this choiceless awareness, this nonbusinesslike attitude. The festivity is in the moment, in the act—not in bothering about the results, not in achieving something. There is nothing to be achieved, so you can enjoy that which is here and now.

You can explain it in this way: I am talking to you. If I am concerned about the result, then the talk becomes a business; it becomes a work. But if I talk to you without any expectations, without any desire about the result, then the talk becomes a play. The very act, in itself, is the end. Then narrowing is not needed. I can play with the words; I can play with the thoughts. I can play with your question; I can play with my answer. Then it is not serious; then it is lighthearted.

And if you are listening to me without thinking about getting something out of it, then you can be relaxed. Then you can allow me to be in communion with you and your consciousness will not be narrowed. Then it is open: playing, enjoying.

Any moment can be a business moment; any moment can be a meditative moment. The difference is in the attitude. If it is choiceless, if you are playing with it, it is meditative.

There are social needs and there are existential needs that are to be fulfilled. I will not say, "Do not condition children." If you leave them totally unconditioned, they will be barbaric. They will not be able to exist. Survival needs conditioning, but survival is not the end, so you must be able to put your conditioning on and take it off—just like clothes. You can put them on, go out and do your business, and then come home and take them off. Then you ARE.

If you are not identified with your clothes (with your conditioning), if you do not say, for example, "I am my mind," it is not difficult. Then you can change easily. But you become identified with your conditioning. You say, "My conditioning is me," and all that is not your conditioning is denied. You think, "All that is not conditioned is not me; the unconscious is not me. I am the conscious, the focused, mind."

This identification is dangerous. This should not be. A proper education is not conditioned, but is conditioned "with a condition": that conditioning is a utilitarian need; you must be able to take it on and off. When it is needed you put it on, and when you do not need it you can take it off. Until it is possible to educate human beings so that they do not become identified with their conditionings,

human beings are not really human beings. They are robots:
conditioned, narrowed.

To understand this is to become aware of that part of
the mind—the greater part—which has been denied light.
And to become aware of it is to become aware that you are
not the conscious mind. The conscious mind is just a part.
"I" am both, and the greater part is unconditioned. But
it is always there . . . waiting.

My definition of meditation is that it is simply an effort
to jump into the unconscious. You cannot jump by calculation because all calculation is of the conscious and the
conscious mind will not allow it. It will caution: "You will
go mad. Do not do it."

The conscious mind is always afraid of the unconscious
because if the unconscious emerges, all that is calm and
clear in the conscious will be swept away. Then everything
will be dark . . . as in a forest.

It is like this: you have made a garden, a garden with a
boundary. Very little ground has been cleared, but you
have planted some flowers and everything is okay: ordered,
clear. Only, the forest is always nearby. It is unruly, un-
controllable, and the garden is in constant fear of it. At
any moment the forest can enter and then the garden will
disappear.

In the same way, you have cultivated a part of the mind.
You have made everything clear. But the unconscious is
always around, and the conscious mind is always in fear of
it. The conscious mind says, "Don't go into the unconscious.
Don't look at it; don't think about it."

The path of the unconscious is dark and unknown. To
reason, it will look irrational; to logic, it will look illogical.
So if you *think* in order to go into meditation, you will
never go—because the thinking part will not allow you to.

This becomes a dilemma. You cannot do anything without thinking, and *with* thinking you cannot go into meditation. What to do? Even if you think, "I am not going to

think," this is also thinking. It is the thinking part of the mind that is saying, "I shall not allow thinking."

Meditation cannot be done by thinking. This is the dilemma—the greatest dilemma. Every seeker will have to come to this dilemma. Somewhere, sometime, the dilemma will be there. Those who know say, "Jump! Do not think!" But you cannot do anything without thinking. That is why unnecessary devices have been created—unnecessary devices, I say, because if you jump without thinking, no device is needed. But you *cannot* jump without thinking, so a device is needed.

You can think about the device. Your thinking mind can be put at ease about the device, but not about meditation. Meditation will be a jump into the unknown. You can work with a device and the device will automatically push you into the unknown. The device is necessary only because of the training of the mind; otherwise, it is not needed.

Once you have jumped you will say, "The device was not necessary; it was not needed." But this is a retrospective knowing. You will know afterward that the device was not needed (that is what Krishnamurti is saying: "No device is needed; no method is needed." The Zen teachers are saying: "No effort is needed; it is effortless"), but this is absurd for one who has not crossed the barrier. And one is mainly talking with those who have not crossed the barrier.

So I say that a device is artificial. It is just a trick to put your rational mind at ease so that you can be pushed into the unknown.

That is why I use vigorous methods. The more vigorous the method, the less your calculative mind will be needed. The more vigorous it becomes, the more total, because the vitality is not only of the mind—it is of the body, of the emotions. It is of your full being.

Sufi dervishes have used dance as a technique, as a de-

vice. If you go into dance, you cannot remain intellectual
because dance is an arduous phenomenon. Your whole
being is needed in it. And a moment is bound to come
when dance will become mindless. The more vital, the
more vigorous, the more you are in it, the less reason
will be there. So dance was devised as a technique to push.
At some point you will not be dancing, but the dance will
take over, will take *you* over. You will be swept away to
the unknown source.

Zen teachers have used the koan method. Koans are
puzzles that, by their very nature, are absurd. They cannot
be solved by reason. You cannot think about them. Ostensi-
bly, it looks as if something can be thought about them:
that is the catch. It seems as if something can be thought
about koans, so you begin to think. Your rational mind is
put at ease. Something has been given to it to be solved
. . . but the thing given to it is something that *cannot* be
solved. The very nature of it is such that it cannot be
solved because the very nature of it is absurd.

There are hundreds of puzzles. The teacher will say,
"Think about a soundless sound." Verbally, it seems as
though it can be thought about. If you try hard, somehow,
somewhere, a soundless sound can be found. It *may* be
possible. Then, at a certain point (and that point cannot be
predicted; for everyone it is not the same), the mind just
goes flat. It is not there. You *are,* but the mind—with all
its conditioning—is gone. You are just like a child: conditioning is not there. You are just conscious. The narrowing
concentration is not there. Now you know that the device
was not necessary, but this is an afterthought. It should
not be said beforehand.


No method is causal; no method is the cause of meditation. That is why so many methods are possible. Every
method is just a device . . . but every religion says that
*its* method is the way and no other method will do. They
all think in terms of causality.

By heating water, the water evaporates. Heat is the cause: without the heat, the water will not evaporate. This is causal. Heat is a necessity that must precede evaporation. But meditation is not causal, so any method is possible. Every method is just a device; it is just creating a situation for the happening. It is not causing it.

For example, beyond the boundary of this room is the unbound, open sky. You have never seen it. I can talk with you about the sky, about the freshness, about the sea, about all that is beyond this room, but you have not seen it. You do not know about it. You just laugh. You think I am making it up. You say, "It is all fantastic. You are a dreamer." I cannot convince you to go outside because everything that I can talk about is meaningless to you.

Then I say, "The house is on fire!" This is meaningful to you. This is something that you can understand. Now I do not have to give you any explanations. I just run. You follow me. The house is not on fire, but the moment you are outside you don't have to ask me why I lied. The meaning is there. The sky is there. Now you thank me. Any lie will do. The lie was just a device; it was just a device to bring you outside. It did not cause the outside to be there.

Every religion is based on a lie device. All methods are lies; they just create a situation. They are not causal. New devices can be created; new religions can be created. Old devices become flat, an old lie becomes flat, and new ones are needed. So many times you have been told the house is on fire when it is not. The lie has become useless. Now someone has to create a new device.

If something is the cause of something else, it is never useless, but an old device is always useless. New devices are needed. That is why every new prophet will have to struggle with the old prophets. He is doing the same work that they were doing, but he will have to oppose their teachings because he will have to deny old devices that have become flat and meaningless.

All the great ones—Buddha, Christ, Mahavira—have, out of compassion, created great lies just to push you out of the house. If you can be pushed out of your mind through any device, that is all that is needed. Your mind is the imprisonment. Your mind is fatal; it is the slavery.

As I have said, this dilemma is bound to happen. The nature of life is such. You will have to learn to narrow the mind. This narrowing will be helpful when you move outward, but it will be fatal inside. It will be utilitarian with others; it will be suicidal with oneself.

You have to exist with others and with yourself. Any life that is one-sided is crippled. You must exist among others with a conditioned mind, but you must exist with yourself with a totally unconditioned consciousness. Society creates a narrowed consciousness, but consciousness, itself, means expansion. It is unlimited. Both are needs, and both should be fulfilled.

I call a person wise who can fulfill both needs. Either extreme is unwise; either extreme is harmful. So live in the world with the mind, with your conditioning, but live with yourself without mind, without training. Use your mind as a means; do not make it an end. Come out of it the moment you have the opportunity. The moment you are alone, come out of it; take it off. Then celebrate the moment; celebrate the existence itself, Being itself.

Just to BE is such a great celebration if you know how to take the conditioning off. This "taking off" you will learn through Dynamic Meditation.[1] It will not be caused; it will come to you uncaused. Meditation will create a situation in which you will come to the unknown. By and by, you will be pushed from your habitual, mechanical, robotlike personality.

Be courageous. Practice Dynamic Meditation vigorously and all else will follow. It will not be your doing; it will be a happening.

You cannot bring the divine, but you can hinder its coming. You cannot bring the sun into the house, but you can

---

[1] Dynamic Meditation, also known as Chaotic Meditation, will be discussed in detail in chapter 3.

close the door. Negatively, mind can do much; positively, nothing. Everything positive is a gift; everything positive is a blessing. It comes to you, while everything negative is your own doing.

Meditation (and all meditation devices) can do one thing: push you away from your negative hindrances. It can bring you out of the imprisonment that is the mind. And when you have come out, you will laugh. It was so easy to come out! It was right there! Only one step was needed . . . but we go on in a circle and the one step is always missed, the one step that can bring you to the center.

You go on in a circle (on the periphery), repeating the same thing. Somewhere the continuity must be broken. That is all that can be done by any meditation method. If the continuity is broken, if you become discontinuous with your past, then that very moment is the *explosion!* In that very moment you are centered, centered in your being. And then you know all that has always been yours, all that has just been awaiting you.

# PART I

# DYNAMICS OF MEDITATION

# ∽ 1 ∽

# Yoga: The Growth of Consciousness

The purpose of life is to become conscious. It is not only the purpose of yoga. The very evolution of life, itself, is to become more and more conscious. But yoga means something still more.

The evolution of life is to become more and more conscious, but the consciousness is always other oriented: you are conscious of some thing, some object. Yoga means to be evolving in the dimension where there is no object and only consciousness remains. Yoga is the method of evolving toward pure consciousness—not being conscious of *something*, but being consciousness itself.

When you are conscious of something, you are not conscious of being conscious. Your consciousness has become focused on something; your attention is not at the source of consciousness itself. In yoga the effort is to become conscious of both: the object and the source. The consciousness becomes double arrowed. You must be aware of the object, and you must be simultaneously aware of the subject. Consciousness must become a doubled-arrowed bridge. The subject must not be lost, it must not become forgotten when you are focused on the object.

This is the first step in yoga. The second step is to drop both the subject and the object and just be conscious. This pure consciousness is the aim of yoga.

Even without yoga man grows toward becoming more and more conscious, but yoga adds something, contributes something, to this evolution of consciousness. It changes many things and transforms many things. The first transformation is a double-arrowed awareness: remembering yourself at the very moment that there is something else to be conscious of.

The dilemma is this: either you are conscious of some object or you are unconscious. If there are no outside objects, you fall into a sleep: objects are needed in order for you to be conscious. When you are totally unoccupied you feel sleepy—you need some object to be conscious of—but when you have too many objects to be conscious of, you may feel a certain sleeplessness. That is why a person who is too obsessed with thoughts cannot go into sleep. Objects continue to be there; thoughts continue to be there. He cannot become unconscious; thoughts go on demanding his attention. And this is how we exist.

With new objects you become more conscious. That is why there is a lust for the new, a longing for the new. The old becomes boring. The moment you have lived with some object for a while, you become unconscious of it. You have accepted it; now your attention is not needed. You become bored. For example, you may not have been conscious of your wife for years because you have taken her for granted. You no longer see her face; you can't remember the color of her eyes. For years you have not really been attentive. Only when she dies will you again become aware that she was there. That is why wives and husbands become bored. Any object that is not calling your attention continuously creates boredom.

In the same way, a *mantra* (a repeated sound vibration) causes deep sleep. When a particular mantra is being repeated continuously, you are bored. There is nothing mysterious about it. Constantly repeating a particular word bores you; you cannot live with it anymore. Now you will begin to feel sleepy; you will go into a sort of sleep; you will become unconscious. (The whole method of hypnosis, in fact, depends upon boredom. If your mind can be bored with something, then you go into a sleep, sleep can be induced.)

Our whole consciousness depends on new objects. That is why there is so much longing for the new: for new sensations, a new dress, a new house—for anything that is new, even if it's not better. With something different, you feel a sudden upsurge of consciousness.

Because life is an evolution of consciousness, this is good. As far as life is concerned, it is good. If a society is longing for new sensations, life progresses, but if it settles down with the old—not asking for the new—it becomes dead: consciousness cannot evolve.

For example, in the East we try to be content with things as they are. This creates a boredom because nothing is ever new. Then for centuries everything goes on continuously as it is. You are just bored. Of course, you can sleep better (the West cannot sleep; insomnia is bound to exist when you are constantly asking for the new), but there is no evolution. And these are the two things that seem to happen: either the whole society becomes sleepy and dead as has happened in the East, or else the society becomes sleepless as has happened in the West.

Neither is good. You need a mind that can be aware even when there are no new objects. Really, you need a consciousness that is not bound with the new, not bound with the object. If it is bound with the object, it is going to be bound with the new. You need a consciousness that is not bound with the object at all, which is beyond object. Then you have freedom: you can go to sleep when you like, and you can be awake when you like. No object is needed to help you. You become free, really free, from the objective world.

The moment you are beyond object you go beyond subject also, because they both exist co-jointly. Really, subjectivity and objectivity are two poles of one thing. When there is an object you are a subject, but if you can be aware without the object, there is no subject—no self. This is to be understood very deeply: when the object is lost and you can be conscious without objects—just conscious! —then the subject is also lost. It cannot remain there. It cannot! Both are lost, and there is simply consciousness, unbounded consciousness. Now there are no boundaries. Neither the object is the boundary nor the subject.

Buddha used to say that when you are in meditation there is no self (no *atman*) because the very awareness of one's self isolates you from everything else. If you are still there, objects are still there. "I am," but "I" cannot exist in total loneliness: "I" exists in relationship with the outside world; "I" is a *relata*. Then the self (the "I am") is just something inside you that exists in relationship to something outside. But if the outside is not there, this inside dissolves. Then there is simple, spontaneous consciousness.

This is what yoga is for, this is what yoga means. Yoga is the science of freeing yourself from subject and object boundaries, and unless you are free from these boundaries, you will fall into either the unbalance of the East or the unbalance of the West.

If you want contentment—peace of mind, silence, sleep— then it is good to remain with the same objects continuously. For centuries and centuries there should be no visible change. Then you are at ease, you can sleep better . . . but nothing is spiritual; you lose much. The very urge to grow is lost; the very urge for adventure is lost; the very urge to inquire and to find is lost. Really, you begin to vegetate; you become stagnant.

If you change this, then you become dynamic but also diseased: you become dynamic but tense, dynamic but mad. You begin to find the new, to inquire for the new, but you are in a whirlwind. The new begins to happen, but you are lost.

If you lose your objectivity, you become too subjective and dreamy, but if you become too obsessed with objects, you lose the subjective. Both situations are unbalanced.

The East has tried one; the West has tried the other.

And now the East is turning Western and the West is turning Eastern. In the East the attraction is for Western technology, Western science, Western rationalism. Einstein, Aristotle, and Russell have taken hold of the Eastern mind, while in the West quite the opposite is happening: Buddha, Zen, and yoga have become more significant. This is a miracle. The East is turning communist, Marxist, materialist, and the West is beginning to think in terms of expanding consciousness: meditation, spirituality, ecstasy. The wheel can turn and we can change our burdens. It will be illuminating for a moment, but then the whole nonsense will begin again.

The East has failed in one way and the West has failed in another way, because they both tried denying one part of the mind. You have to transcend both parts and not be concerned with one while denying the other. Mind is a totality. You can either transcend it totally or you cannot transcend it. If you go on denying one part, the denied part will take its revenge. And, really, the denied part in the East is taking its revenge in the East, and the denied part in the West is taking its revenge in the West.

You can never go beyond the denied. It is there, and it goes on gathering more and more strength. The very moment when the part you have accepted succeeds is the moment of failure. Nothing fails like success. With any partial success (with the success of one part of you) you are bound to go into deeper failure. That which you have gained becomes unconscious and that which you have lost comes into awareness.

Absence is felt more. If you lose a tooth, your tongue becomes aware of the absence and goes to the absent tooth. It has never gone there before—never!—but now you can't stop it. It continually moves to the vacant place to feel the tooth that is not there.

In the same way, when one part of the mind succeeds, you become aware of the failure of the other part—the part that could have been and is not. Now the East has become conscious of the foolishness of not being scientific: it is the reason why we are poor; it is the reason why we are "no one." This absence is being felt now and the East has begun to turn Western, while the West is feeling their own foolishness, their lack of integration.

Yoga means a *total* science of man. It is not simply religion. It is the total science of man, the total transcendence of all the parts. And when you transcend parts, you become whole. The whole is not just an accumulation of the parts; it is not a mechanical thing in which all the parts are put in alignment and then there is a whole. No, it is more than a mechanical thing; it is like something artistic.

You can divide a poem into words, but then the words mean nothing. And when the whole is there, it is more than words. It has its own identity. It has gaps as well as words. And sometimes gaps are more meaningful than words. A poem becomes poetry only when it says something that has not really been said, when something about it transcends all the parts. If you divide and analyze it, then you have only the parts, and the transcendental flower that was really the thing is lost.

So consciousness is a wholeness. By denying a part you lose something—something that was really significant. And you gain nothing: you gain only extremes. Every extreme becomes a disease; every extreme becomes an illness inside. Then you go on and on in turmoil; there is an inner anarchy.

Yoga is the science of transcending anarchy, the science of making your consciousness whole—and you become whole only when you transcend parts. So yoga is neither religion nor science. It is both. Or, it transcends both. You can say it is a scientific religion or a religious science. That is why yoga can be used by anyone belonging to any religion; it can be used by anyone with any type of mind.

In India, all the religions that have developed have very

different (in fact, antagonistic) philosophies, concepts, perceptions. They have nothing in common. Between Hinduism and Jainism there is nothing in common; between Hinduism and Buddhism there is nothing in common. There is only one common thing that none of these religions can deny: yoga.

Buddha says, "There is no body, there is no soul," but he cannot say, "There is no yoga." Mahavira says, "There is no body, but there is a soul"—but he cannot say, "There is no yoga." Hinduism says: "There is body, there is soul . . . and there is yoga." Yoga remains constant. Even Christianity cannot deny it; even Mohammedanism cannot deny it.

In fact, even someone who is totally atheistically oriented cannot deny yoga because yoga doesn't make it a precondition to believe in God. Yoga has no preconditions; yoga is absolutely experiential. When the concept of God is mentioned (and in the most ancient yoga books it was never mentioned at all), it is mentioned only as a method. It can be used as a hypothesis—if it is helpful to someone it can be used—but it is not an absolute condition. That is why Buddha can be a yogi without God, without the *Vedas,* without any belief. Without any faith (any so-called faith) he can be a yogi.

So for theists, or even for an atheist, yoga can become a common ground. It can become a bridge between science and religion. It is rational and irrational simultaneously. The methodology is totally rational, but through the methodology you move deep into the mystery of the irrational. The whole process is so rational—every step is so rational, so scientific, it is so logical—that you just have to do it, and everything else follows.

Jung mentions that in the nineteenth century no Westerner concerned with psychology could conceive of anything beyond the conscious mind or below the conscious mind, because mind *means* consciousness. So how can there be an unconscious mind? It is absurd, "nonscientific." Then, in the twentieth century, as science

learned more about the unconscious, a theory of the unconscious mind developed. Then, when they went even
deeper, they had to accept the idea of a *collective* unconscious, not only an individual one. It looked absurd—mind
means something individual, so how could there be a collective mind—but now they have even accepted the concept of the collective mind.

These are the first three divisions of Buddhist psychology, of Buddhist yoga—the first three. Then Buddha
goes on dividing into 160 more divisions. Jung says, "Before we denied these three. Now we accept them. It may
be that others also exist. We have only to proceed step by
step; we have only to go into it further." Jung's approach
is very rational, one deeply rooted in the West.

With yoga, you have to proceed rationally—but only in
order to jump into the irrational. The end is bound to be
irrational. That which you can understand—the rational—
cannot be the source because it is finite. The source must
be greater than you. The source from which you have come,
from which everything has come, the whole universe has
come—and where it goes down and disappears again—
must be more than this. *The manifestation must be less
than the source.* A rational mind can feel and understand
the manifested, but the unmanifested remains behind.

Yoga does not insist that one must be rational. It says,
"It is rational to conceive of something irrational. It is
rational, really, to conceive of the boundaries of the rational." A true, authentic mind always knows the limitations of reason, always knows that reason ends somewhere.
Anyone who is authentically rational has to come to a
point where the irrational is felt. If you proceed with reason toward the ultimate, the boundary will be felt.

Einstein felt it; Wittgenstein felt it. Wittgenstein's *Trac-
tatus* is one of the most rational books ever written; he is
one of the most rationalistic minds. He goes on talking
about existence in a very logical way, a very rational way.
His expressions—words, language, everything—is rational,
but then he says, "There are some things about which—

there is a point beyond which—nothing can be said, and
I must remain silent about it." Then he writes, "That
which *cannot* be said *must not* be said."

The whole edifice falls: *the whole edifice!* Wittgenstein
was trying to be rational about the entire phenomenon of
life and existence, and then suddenly a point comes and
he says, "Now, beyond this point, nothing can be said."
This is to say something—something very significant. Something is there now and nothing can be said about it. Now
there is a point that cannot be defined, where all definitions simply fall down.

Whenever there has been an authentic, logical mind, it
comes to this point. Einstein died a mystic . . . and more
of a mystic than your so-called mystics, because if you are
a mystic without ever having tried to follow the path of
reason you can never be deep in mysticism. You have not
really known the boundaries. I have seen mystics who go
on talking about God as a logical concept, as an argument!
There have been Christian mystics who have been trying
to "prove" God. What nonsense! If even God can be proved,
you leave nothing unproved . . . and the unproved is the
source.

One who has experienced something of the divine will
not try to prove it because the very effort to prove shows
that one has never been in contact with the original source
of life (which is unprovable, which cannot be proved).
The whole cannot be proved by the part. For example, my
hand cannot prove my existence. My hand cannot be more
than me; it cannot cover me. It is foolishness to try. But
if the hand can cover itself completely, it is more than
enough—the moment the hand knows itself, it also knows
that it is rooted in something more, that it is constantly
one with something more. It is there because that "more"
is also there.

If I die, my hand will also die. It only existed because
of me. The whole remains unproved; only the parts are
known. We cannot prove the whole, but we can feel it.
The hand cannot prove me, but the hand can feel me. It

can go deep inside itself, and when it reaches the depths, it is me.

The so-called mystics who are annoyed with reason are not real mystics. A real mystic is never annoyed with reason. He can play with it. And he can play with reason because he knows reason cannot destroy the mystery of life. So-called mystics and religious people who are afraid of reason, of logic, of argument, are really afraid of themselves. Any argument against them may create inner doubts; it may help their inner doubts to emerge. They are afraid of themselves.

The Christian mystic Tertullian says, "I believe in God because I cannot prove Him; I believe in God because it is impossible to believe." This is how a real mystic will feel: "It is impossible; that is why I believe." If it is possible, then there is no need to believe. It becomes just a concept, an ordinary concept.

This is what mystics have always meant by faith, by belief. It is not something intellectual; it is not a concept. It is a jump into the impossible. But you can only jump into the mysterious from the edge of reason, never before. How can you do it before? You can jump only when you have stretched reason to its logical extremes.

You have come to a point that reason cannot go beyond . . . and the beyond remains. Now you know that reason cannot take a single step further and yet the "further" remains. Even if you decide to remain with reason, a boundary is created. You know that existence is beyond the boundary of reason, so even if you do not go beyond this boundary, you become a mystic. Even if you do not take the jump you become a mystic because you have known something, you have encountered something that was not rational at all.

All that reason can know you have known. Now something is encountered that reason *cannot* know. If you take the jump, you have to leave reason behind; you cannot take the jump with reason itself. This is what faith is. Faith is not against reason; it is beyond it. It is not antirational; it is *ir*rational.

Yoga is the method of bringing you to the extreme limit of reason—and not only a method to bring you to the extreme, but also a method to take the jump.

How to take the jump? Einstein, for example, would have flowered like a Buddha if he had known something about meditative methods. He was just on the verge: many times in his life he came to the point from which a jump was possible. But again and again he missed. He was entangled, again, in reason. And in the end, he was frustrated by his whole life of reason.

The same thing could have happened with Buddha. He also had a very rational mind, but there was something possible for him, a method that could be used. Not only does reason have its methods: irrationality also has methods. Reason has its own methods; irrationality has its own methods.

Yoga is ultimately concerned with irrational methods. Only in the beginning can rational methods be used. They are just to persuade you, to push you, to persuade your reason to move toward the limit. And if you have come to the limit, you will take the ultimate jump.

Gurdjieff worked with a certain group on some deep, irrational methods. He was working with a group of seekers and using a particular irrational method. He used to call it a Stop Exercise. For example, you would be with him and suddenly he would say, "Stop!" Then everyone had to stop *as he is*—totally stop. If the hand was in a certain place, the hand must stop there. If the eyes were open, they would have to remain open; if the mouth was open—you were just about to say something—the mouth would have to remain as it was. No movement!

This method begins with the body. If there is no movement in the body, suddenly there is no movement in the

mind. The two are associated: you cannot move your body
without some inner movement of the mind, and you cannot
stop your body totally without stopping the inner movement of the mind. Body and mind are not two things; they
are one energy. The energy is more dense in the body than
it is in the mind—the density differs; the frequency of the
wavelength differs—but it is the same wave, the same flow
of energy.

Seekers were practicing this Stop Exercise continuously
for one month. One day Gurdjieff was in his tent and three
seekers were walking through a dry canal that was on the
grounds. It was a dry canal; no water was flowing in it.
Suddenly, from his tent, Gurdjieff cried, "Stop!" Everyone
on the bank of the canal stopped. The three who were in
the canal also stopped. (It was dry, so there was no
problem.)

Then suddenly there was an onrush of water. Someone
had opened the water supply and water rushed into the
canal. When it had come up to the necks of the three, one
of them jumped out of the canal thinking, "Gurdjieff does
not know what is happening. He is in his tent and he is
unaware of the fact that water has come into the canal."
The man thought, "I must jump out. Now it is irrational
to be here," and he jumped out.

The other two remained in the canal as the water became higher and higher. Finally it reached their noses and
the second man thought, "This is the limit! I have not
come here to die. I have come here to know eternal life,
not to lose this one," and he jumped out of the canal.

The third man remained. The same problem faced him,
too, but he decided to remain because Gurdjieff had said
that this was an irrational exercise and if it was done with
reason, the whole thing would be destroyed. He thought,
"Okay, I accept death . . . but I cannot stop this exercise," and he remained there.

Now water was flowing above his head. Gurdjieff
jumped out of his tent and into the canal and brought him
out. He was just on the verge of death. But when he re-

vived, he was a transformed man. He was not the same one who was standing and doing the exercise: he was transformed totally. He had known something; he had taken the jump.

Where is the limit? If you continue with reason, you may miss. You go on falling back. Sometimes one has to suddenly take a step that leads you beyond. That step becomes a transformation: the division is transcended. Whether you say that this division is between the conscious and the unconscious, between reason and nonreason, science and religion, or East and West—division must be transcended. That is what yoga is: a transcendence. Then you can come back to reason, but you will be transformed. You can even reason things out, but *you* will be beyond reason.

# ❧ 2 ❧

## Non-Doing Through Doing

Meditation is always passive; the very essence of it is passive. It cannot be active because the very nature of it is non-doing. If you are doing something, your very doing disturbs the whole thing. Your very doing, your very "activeness," creates the disturbance.

Non-doing is meditation, but when I say non-doing is meditation I do not mean that you need not do anything. Even to achieve this non-doing, one has to do much! But this doing is not meditation. It is only a stepping stone; only a jumping board. All "doing" is just a jumping board —not meditation.

You are just on the door, on the steps. . . . The door is non-doing, but to reach the non-doing state of mind one has to do much. But one should not confuse this doing with meditation.

Life energy works in contradictions. Life exists as a dialectic: it is not a simple movement. It is not flowing like a river; it is dialectical. With each move life creates its own opposite and through the struggle with the opposite, it moves forward. With each new movement the thesis creates the antithesis. And this goes on continuously: thesis creating antithesis, being merged with antithesis, and becoming a synthesis that then becomes the new thesis. Then, again, there is the antithesis. . . .

By a dialectical movement, I mean it is not a simple straight movement: it is a movement divided unto itself, dividing itself, creating the opposite, then meeting with the opposite again. Then, again, dividing into the opposite. And the same thing applies to meditation, because it is the deepest thing in life.

If I say to you, "Just relax," it is impossible because you do not know what to do. So many pseudo teachers of relaxation continue saying, "Just relax. Don't do anything; just relax." Then what are you going to do? You can just lie down, but that is not relaxation. The whole inner turmoil remains . . . and now a new conflict is there: to relax. Something over and above is added. The whole nonsense is there, the whole turmoil is there, with something added—to relax. A new tension is now added to all the old tensions.

So a person who is trying to live a relaxed life is the most tense person possible. He is bound to be because he has not understood the dialectical flow of life. He is thinking that life is a straight flow: you can just tell yourself to relax and you will relax.

It is not possible! So if you come to me, I will never tell you to just relax. First be tense, as utterly tense as possible. Be tense totally! First let your complete organism be tense, and go on being tense to the optimum, to your fullest possibility. And then, suddenly, you will feel a relaxation setting in. You have done whatsoever you could do: now the life energy will create the opposite.

You have brought tension to a peak. Now there is nothing further; you cannot go on. The whole energy has been devoted to tension. But you cannot continue with this tension indefinitely. It has to dissolve; soon it will begin to dissolve. Now be a witness to it.

Through being tense you have come to the verge, to the jumping point. That is why you cannot continue. If you continue further, you may just burst—die. The optimum point has been reached. Now the life energy will relax by itself.

It relaxes. Now be aware, and see this relaxation setting in. Each limb of the body, each muscle of the body, each nerve of the body, is just going to innocently relax without anything being done on your part. You are not doing anything to relax it; it is relaxing. You will begin to feel many points in the organism relaxing. The whole organism will just be a crowd of relaxing points. Just be aware.

This awareness is meditation. But it is a non-doing. You are not doing anything because being aware is not an act. It is not an act at all; it is your nature, a very intrinsic quality of your being. You *are* awareness. It is your un-awareness that is your achievement . . . and you have achieved it with much effort.

So to me, meditation has two steps: first, the active (which is not really meditation at all) and second, the completely nonactive (the passive awareness that is really meditation). Awareness is always passive, and the moment you become active you lose your awareness. It is possible to be active and aware only when awareness has come to such a point that now there is no need of meditation to achieve it, or to know it, or to feel it.

When meditation has become useless, you simply throw meditation. Now you are aware. Only then can you be both aware and active—otherwise not. As long as meditation is still needed, you will not be able to be aware during activity. But when even meditation is not needed . . .

If you have *become* meditation, you will no longer need it. Then you can be active, but even in that activity you are always the passive onlooker. Now you are never the actor: you are always a witnessing consciousness.

Consciousness is passive . . . and meditation is bound to be passive because it is just a door to consciousness— perfect consciousness. So when people talk about "active" meditation, they are wrong. Meditation is passivity. You may need some activity, some doing, to get to it—that can be understood—but this is not because meditation itself is active. Rather, it is because you have been active through so many lives—activity has become so much a part and parcel of your mind—that you will even need activity to reach nonactivity.

You have been so involved in activity that you cannot just drop it. So persons like Krishnamurti may continue to say, "Just drop it," but then you will continue to ask *how* to drop it. Krishnamurti will say, "Do not ask how. I am saying: just drop it! There is no 'how' to it. There is no need for any 'how.' "

And he is right in a way. Passive awareness or passive meditation has no "how" about it. It cannot have, because if there is any "how" then it cannot be passive. But he is wrong, too, because he has not taken the listener into account. He is talking about himself.

Meditation is without any "how," without any technology, without any technique. So Krishnamurti is absolutely correct, but the listener has not been taken into account. The listener has nothing but activity in him: to him, everything is activity. So when you say, "Meditation is passive, nonactive, choiceless. You can just be in it. There is no need of any effort; it is effortless," you are just speaking a language that the listener is unable to understand. He understands the linguistic part of it—that is what makes it so difficult. He says, "Intellectually, I understand completely. Whatever you are saying is completely understood," but he is unable to understand the meaning.

There is nothing mysterious about Krishnamurti's teachings. He is one of the least mystical teachers. Nothing is mysterious! Everything is obviously clear, exact, analyzed, logical, rational, so anyone can understand it. And this has become one of the greatest barriers, because the listener thinks he understands. He understands the linguistic part, but he does not understand the language of passivity.

He understands what is being said to him—the words. He listens to them; he understands them; he knows the meaning of those words. He correlates. A whole correlated picture comes to his mind. What is being said is understood; there is an intellectual communication. But he does not understand the language of passivity. He *cannot* understand. From where he is, he cannot understand. He can understand only the language of action—activity.

So I have to talk about activity. And I have to lead you, through activity, to the point where you can just jump into nonactivity. The activity must come to an extreme point, to a verge point, where it becomes impossible for you to be active (because if activity is still possible, you will continue).

Your activity must be exhausted! Whatever you can do, you must be allowed to do. Whatsoever you can do you must be pushed to do it to the very point where you, yourself, cry, "Now I cannot do anything. Everything has been done. Now nothing is possible; no effort is possible. I am exhausted."

Then I say, "Now, just drop!" This dropping can be communicated. You are on the verge; you are ready to drop. Now you can understand the language of passivity. Before this, you could not understand. You were too full of activity.

You have never been to the extreme point of activity. Things can be dropped only from the extreme, never from the middle. You cannot drop it. You can drop sex—if you have been totally in it, you can just drop it; otherwise not. You can drop everything that you have gone to the very limit of, where there is no further to go and no reason to go backward. You can drop it because you have known it totally.

When you have known something totally, it becomes boring to you. You may want to go into it further, but if there is no further to go, then you will just "stop dead." There is no going back, and there is no possibility of going on further. You are at the point where everything ends. Then you can just drop; you can be passive. And the moment you are passive, meditation happens; it flowers. It comes to you. It is a "dropping dead" into passivity.

So to me, it is effort that leads to "no effort"; it is action that leads to "no action"; it is mind that leads to meditation; it is this very material world that leads to enlightenment. Life is a dialectical process; its opposite is death. It is to be used; you cannot just drop it.

Use it, and you will be thrown into the opposite. And be aware: when you are thrown on the waves, be aware. It is easy. When you come from a tense climax to the point of relaxation, it is very easy to be aware, very easy. It is not difficult then because to be aware you have to just be passive, just be witnessing.

Even the effort of witnessing should not be there. It is not needed. You are so exhausted through activity that you will feel, "Damn it all—*enough*!" Then meditation IS, and you are not. And once tasted, the taste is never lost again. It remains with you wherever you move, wherever you go.

It remains with you. Then it will penetrate your activities also. There will be activity and there—in the very center of your being—there will be a passive silence. On the circumference—the whole world. In the center—the Brahman. On the circumference, every activity; in the center, only silence. But a very pregnant silence, not a dead silence, because out of this silence everything is born, even the activity.

Out of this silence, every creativity comes. It is very pregnant. . . . So whenever I say "silence," I do not mean the silence of a cemetery, the silence of a house when no one is there. No! I mean the silence of a seed; the silence of a mother's womb; the silence of the roots underground. There is much hidden potentiality that will be coming soon.

Activity will be there, but now the actor is no more, the doer is no more. This is the search; this is the seeking.

There are two antagonistic traditions: yoga and *samkhya*. Yoga says that nothing can be achieved without effort. The whole of yoga, the whole of Patanjali's yoga (raja yoga), is nothing but effort. And this has been the main current, because effort can be understood by many. Activity can be understood, so yoga has been the main current. But sometimes there have been freaks who say, "Nothing is to be done." A Nagarjuna, a Krishnamurti, a Huang Po—some freaks! They say, "Nothing is to be done. Do not do anything. Do not ask about the method." This is the tradition of *samkhya*.

There are really only two religions in the world: yoga and *samkhya*. But *samkhya* has always appealed only to a very few individuals here and there, so it is not talked about much. That is why Krishnamurti appears to be very novel and original. He is not, but he seems to be because *samkhya* is so unknown.

Only yoga is known. There are ashrams and training centers and yogis all over the world. Yoga is known: the tradition of effort. And *samkhya* is not known at all. Krishnamurti has not said a single word that is new, but because we are not familiar with the tradition of *samkhya*, it appears to be new. Only because of our blissful ignorance are there revolutionaries.

*Samkhya* means "knowledge," knowing. *Samkhya* says, "Only knowing is enough; only awareness is enough."

But these two traditions are just dialectical. To me, they are not opposed. To me, they are dialectical, and a synthesis is possible. That synthesis I call *effortlessness through effort:* yoga through *samkhya* and *samkhya* through yoga . . . non-doing through doing. In this age, neither of these two opposite, dialectical traditions, by itself, will help. You can use yoga to achieve *samkhya*—and you will *have to* use yoga to achieve *samkhya*.

Non-Doing Through Doing 23

If you can understand Hegelian dialectics, this whole thing will be clear to you. The concept of dialectical movement has not been used by anyone since Marx, and he used it in a very non-Hegelian way. He used it for material evolution, for society, for classes—to show how society progresses through classes, through class struggle. Marx said, "Hegel was standing on his head, and I have put him on his legs again."

But, actually, the contrary is the case. Hegel was standing on his legs; Marx put him on his head. And because of Marx, the very pregnant concept of dialectics became contaminated with communism. But the concept is very beautiful, very meaningful. It has much depth in it. Hegel says, "The progress of an idea, the progress of consciousness, is dialectical. Consciousness progresses through dialectics."

I say any life force progresses through dialectics and meditation is the deepest phenomenon happening, the explosion of the life force. It is deeper than an atomic explosion because in an atomic explosion only a particle of matter explodes, but in meditation a living cell—a living existence, a living being—explodes.

This explosion comes through dialectics. So use action—and remember nonaction. You will have to do much, but remember that all this doing is just to achieve the state in which nothing is done.

*Samkhya* and yoga both appear simple. Krishnamurti is not difficult; neither is Vivekananda. They are simple, because they have chosen one part of the dialectics. Then they appear very consistent. Krishnamurti is very consistent, absolutely consistent. In forty years of talking he has not uttered a single inconsistent word because he has chosen a part of the whole process, the opposite of which is denied. Vivekananda is also consistent: he has chosen the other part.

I may look very inconsistent. Or, you can say, *I am only consistent in my inconsistencies.* Use dialectics: relax through tension . . . meditate through action.

That is why I talk about fasting.[1] It is an action, a very deep action. Taking food is not so great an activity as not taking it. You take it, and then you forget about it. It is not much of an activity. But if you are not taking food, it is a big act. You cannot forget it. The whole body remembers it; each single cell demands it. The whole body gets in a turmoil. It is very active—active to the very core. It is not passive.

Dancing is not passive; it is very active. In the end you *become* movement. The body is forgotten; only movement remains. Really, dancing is a most unearthly thing, a most unearthly art, because it is just rhythm in movement. It is absolutely immaterial, so you cannot hold on to it. You can hold on to the dancer, but never to the dancing. It just withers in the cosmos: it is there, and then it is not there . . . it is not here, and then suddenly it is here. It comes out of nothing and it is here. It comes out of nothing and then, again, goes into nothing.

A dancer is sitting here. There is no dancing in him. But if a poet is sitting here, poetry may be in him. Poetry can exist in the poet. A painter is here: in a very subtle way, painting is present. Before he paints, painting is there. But with a dancer, nothing is present, and if it *is* present, then he is simply a technician and not a dancer. The movement is a new phenomenon coming in. The dancer becomes just a vehicle: the movement takes over.

One of the greatest dancers of this century was Nijinsky. In the end he just went mad . . . and he may have been the greatest dancer in all of history. But the movement became so much for him that the dancer was lost in it. In his last years he was unable to control it. He could begin dancing at any moment—anywhere. And when he was dancing, no one could say when it would end. It might even continue the whole night. . . .

When friends asked him, "What has become of you? You begin, and then there is no end," Nijinsky said, " 'I'

[1] See pages 70–71.

am only in the beginning. Then something takes over, and 'I' am no more . . . and who dances, I do not know."

He went mad. He was in a madhouse; he died in a madhouse.


Take any activity and go to the limit where there is either madness or meditation. Lukewarm search will not do.

## ∽ 3 ∽

## "Chaotic" Meditation . . .

Man is neurotic. It is not that just a few men are neurotic but humanity, itself, is neurotic. It is not a question of correction for a few persons; it is a question of curing humanity as such. Neurosis is the "normal" condition of man because every man passes through a training, a conditioning. He is not allowed to be just whatever he is. He has to be molded into a particular pattern. That pattern creates neurosis.

The society gives you a pattern, a mold. You are cultivated into a certain shape and form. Only a fragment of your being is allowed to be expressed, while the remaining part is repressed. This creates a division, a schizophrenia. And the part that is suppressed goes on fighting for expression.

So every man is schizophrenic, divided . . . divided against himself, fighting against himself. Man, *as such*, is schizophrenic. He cannot be at ease; he cannot be silent; he cannot be blissful. The hell is always there. And unless you become whole, you cannot be freed from this hell.

Something has to be done that releases this neurosis, which brings your divided parts nearer. The unexpressed has to be expressed, and this constant repression of the unconscious by the conscious has to be eliminated.

The old meditation techniques do not take this into consideration. That is why they have been failures. Meditation techniques have been in existence for a long time; they have been known throughout history, but a Buddha, a Jesus, a Mahavira, have all been failures. I don't mean that they themselves didn't realize. They realized, they achieved their own enlightenment, but they couldn't help the greater portion of humanity to reach enlightenment.

Why was religion not more of a help? The reason is this: that man has been taken for granted and meditative techniques have been taught to him *as he is*. These techniques can help only to a certain extent: they can have an effect only on the surface. The inner division remains; nothing has been done to dissolve it.

For example, there are Zen techniques . . . and Mahesh Yogi's Transcendental Meditation . . . and other techniques. They can help you to a certain extent. They can calm you down; your surface can become more peaceful. But nothing happens to your inner being. It *cannot!* And, in a way, that surface calm is dangerous because sooner or later you will explode again. Basically nothing has happened. You have simply trained your conscious mind to be in a more still state.

You can still your mind easily through mantras, through constant chanting, through many things. Anything that creates an inner boredom will help you to calm down. For example, if you constantly repeat *Ram-Ram-Ram*, this constant repetition creates a certain sleepiness, a boredom, and your mind begins to fall asleep. You can feel that sleepiness as calmness, as stillness, but it is not. Really, it is a sort of dullness. But at least you can tolerate your life more because of it. At least on the surface you will feel more contented. And the forces, the neurotic forces, will go on boiling within. Any day they will erupt and disrupt the surface.

Such methods are conciliatory. Very few people can be helped through them. And those who can be helped through them can be helped without any techniques. But they are the rare exceptions, the fortunate few who are not neurotic. Most of humanity is not so fortunate.


That is why my emphasis is first to dissolve your inner division, to make you one—a unity. Unless you are one, nothing can be done. So the first thing is how to dissolve your neurosis.

My technique of Dynamic Meditation accepts your neurosis as it is and tries to release it. The technique basically starts with a catharsis. Whatever is hidden must be released. You must not go on repressing. Rather, choose expression as the path. Do not condemn yourself. Accept what you are, because condemnation only creates division. The moment you accept, you go beyond, because acceptance creates a unity, and when you are united within, you have the energy to go beyond.

When you are divided within, your energy is fighting with itself. Then it cannot be used for any transformation. So let there be an acceptance of what you are. Everything that you have been repressing up until now has to be released. And if you release your neurosis consciously, one day you will come to the point where you are no longer neurotic.

Those who repress their neurosis become more and more neurotic, while those who express it consciously get rid of it. So unless you become "consciously insane," you can never become sane. R. D. Laing is right when he says, "Allow yourself to be insane." He is one of the most sensitive men in the West.

You *are* insane, so something has to be done about it. The old traditions say, "Repress your insanity. Do not allow it to come out or you will begin to act insane," but I say, "Allow it to come out; be conscious of it. That is the only way toward sanity."

Release it! Inside, it will become poisonous. Throw it out; remove it from your system totally. But this catharsis has to be approached in a very systematic, methodical way because it is becoming mad *with a method* . . . consciously mad.

You have to do two things: remain conscious of what you are doing and do not suppress anything. With our minds, consciousness ordinarily means suppression. That is the problem. The moment you become conscious of certain things in yourself, you start suppressing them. So this is what is to be learned: to be conscious and nonsuppressive . . . to be conscious and *expressive*.

My system of Dynamic Meditation[1] begins with breathing, because breathing has deep roots in the being. You may not have observed it, but if you can change your breathing, you can change many things. If you observe your breathing carefully, you will see that when you are angry you have a particular rhythm of breathing. When you are in love, a totally different rhythm comes to you. When you are relaxed you breathe differently; when you are tense you breathe differently. You cannot breathe the way you do when you are relaxed and be angry at the same time. It is impossible.

When you are sexually aroused, your breathing changes. If you do not allow the breathing to change, your sexual arousal will drop automatically. This means that breathing is deeply related to your mental state. If you change your breathing, you can change the state of your mind. Or, if you change the state of your mind, breathing will change.

So I start with breathing and I suggest ten minutes of chaotic breathing in the first stage of the technique. By chaotic breathing I mean deep, fast, vigorous breathing, without any rhythm. Just taking the breath in and throwing it out, taking it in and throwing it out, as vigorously, as deeply, as intensely as possible. Take it in; then throw it out.

This chaotic breathing is to create a chaos within your

[1] Also known as "Chaotic" Meditation.

repressed system. Whatever you are, you are with a certain type of breathing. A child breathes in a particular way. If you are sexually afraid, you breathe in a particular way. You cannot breathe deeply because every deep breath hits the sex center. If you are fearful, you cannot take deep breaths. Fear creates shallow breathing.

This chaotic breathing is to destroy all your past patterns. What you have made out of yourself this chaotic breathing is to destroy. Chaotic breathing creates a chaos within you because unless a chaos is created, you cannot release your repressed emotions. And those emotions have now moved into the body.

You are not body *and* mind: you are body/mind (psycho/somatic). You are both together. So whatever is done with your body reaches to the mind and whatever is done with the mind reaches to the body. Body and mind are two ends of the same entity.

Ten minutes of chaotic breathing is wonderful! But it must be chaotic. It is not a type of *pranayama* ("yogic breathing"). It is simply creating chaos through breathing. And it creates chaos for many reasons.

Deep, fast breathing gives you more oxygen. The more oxygen in the body, the more alive you become, the more animallike. Animals are alive and man is half-dead, half-alive. You have to be made into an animal again. Only then can something higher develop in you.

If you are only half-alive, nothing can be done with you. So this chaotic breathing will make you like an animal: alive, vibrating, vital—with more oxygen in your blood, more energy in your cells. Your body cells will become more alive. This oxygenation helps to create body electricity—or, you can call it "bio-energy." When there is electricity in the body you can move deep within, beyond yourself. The electricity will work within you.

The body has its own electrical sources. If you hammer them with more breathing and more oxygen, they begin to flow. And if you become really alive, then you are no

longer a body. The more alive you become, the more
energy flows in your system and the less you will feel yourself physically. You will feel more like energy and less like
matter.

And whenever it happens that you are more alive, in
those moments you are not body oriented. If sex has so
much appeal, one of the reasons is this: that if you are
really in the act, totally moving, totally alive, then you are
no longer a body—just energy. To feel this energy, to be
alive with this energy, is very necessary if you are to move
beyond.

The second step in my technique of Dynamic Meditation
is a catharsis. I tell you to be *consciously* insane. Whatever
comes to your mind—*whatever*—allow it to express itself;
cooperate with it. No resistance: just a flow of emotions.

If you want to scream, then scream. Cooperate with it.
A deep scream, a total scream in which your whole being
becomes involved, is very therapeutic, deeply therapeutic.
Many things, many diseases, will be released just by the
scream. If the scream is total, your whole being will be
in it.

So for the next ten minutes (this second step is also for
ten minutes) allow yourself expression through crying,
dancing, screaming, weeping, jumping, laughing—"freak-
ing out" as they say. Within a few days, you will come to
feel what it is.

In the beginning it may be forced, an effort, or it may
even be just acting. We have become so false that nothing
real or authentic can be done by us. We have not laughed,
we have not cried, we have not screamed authentically.
Everything is just a facade—a mask. So when you begin to
do this technique—in the beginning—it may be forced. It
may need effort; there may be just acting. But do not
bother about it. Go on. Soon you will touch those sources
where you have repressed many things. You will touch

those sources, and once they are released, you will feel unburdened. A new life will come to you; a new birth will take place.

This unburdening is basic . . . and without it there can be no meditation for man as he is. Again, I am not talking about the exceptions. They are irrelevant.

With this second step—when things are thrown out—you become vacant. And this is what is meant by emptiness: to be empty of all repressions. In this emptiness something can be done. Transformation can happen; meditation can happen.

Then in the third step I use the sound *hoo*. Many sounds have been used in the past. Each sound has something specific to do. For example, Hindus have been using the sound *aum*. This may be familiar to you. But I won't suggest *aum*. *Aum* strikes at the heart center, but man is no longer centered in the heart. *Aum* is striking at a door where no one is home.

Sufis have used *hoo*, and if you say *hoo* loudly, it goes deep to the sex center. So this sound is used just as a hammering within. When you have become empty and vacant, this sound can move within you.

The movement of the sound is possible only when you are empty. If you are filled with repressions, nothing will happen. And sometimes it is even dangerous to use any mantra or sound when you are filled with repressions. Each layer of repression will change the path of the sound and the ultimate result may be something of which you never dreamed, never expected, never wished. You need a vacant mind; only then can a mantra be used.

So I never suggest a mantra to anyone as he is. First there must be a catharsis. This mantra *hoo* should never be done without doing the first two steps. It should *never* be done without them. Only in the third step (for ten minutes) is this *hoo* to be used—used as loudly as possible, bringing your total energy to it. You are to ham-

mer your energy with the sound. And when you are empty
(when you have been emptied by the catharsis of the second
step), this *hoo* goes deep down and hits the sex center.

The sex center can be hit in two ways. The first way is
naturally. Whenever you are attracted to a member of the
opposite sex, the sex center is hit from without. And that
hit is also a subtle vibration.

A man is attracted to a woman or a woman is attracted
to a man. Why? What is there in a man and what is there
in a woman to account for it? A positive or negative electricity hits them: a subtle vibration. It is a sound, really.
For example, you may have observed that birds use sound
for sex appeal. All their singing is sexual. They are re-
peatedly hitting each other with particular sounds. These
sounds hit the sex centers of birds of the opposite sex.

Subtle vibrations of electricity are hitting you from without. When your sex center is hit from without, your energy
begins to flow outward—toward the other. Then there will
be reproduction, birth. Someone else will be born out of
you.

*Hoo* is hitting this same center of energy, but from
within. And when the sex center is hit from within, the
energy starts to flow within. This inner flow of energy
changes you completely. You become transformed: you
give birth to yourself.

You are transformed only when your energy moves in a
totally opposite direction. Right now it is flowing out, but
then it begins to flow within. Now it is flowing down, but
then it flows upward. This upward flow of energy is what is
known as *kundalini*.[2] You will feel it actually flowing in
your spine . . . and the higher it moves, the higher you
will move with it. When this energy reaches the *brahma-
randhra* (the last center in you: the seventh center, located
at the top of the head), you are the highest man possible—
what Gurdjieff calls "man number seven."

You are "man number one" when your energy is just at

---

[2] *Kundalini* will be discussed in greater detail in chapter 6.

the sex center. When some energy comes to your heart center, you are "man number two": the man of emotion. When some energy moves to the intellect, you are "man number three": a man of the intellect. These are ordinary men—all neurotic in their own ways. One man is emotionally neurotic; another is bodily neurotic; another is intellectually neurotic. But these three men are just ordinary men.

"Man number four" is one who is trying to move his energy within: the man who is meditating, the man who is making efforts to dissolve his neurosis, divisions, and schizophrenia. This is "man number four." And as this energy moves upward and inward, a higher man is created. That higher man will be less neurotic, less schizophrenic, more sane.

Then a moment comes when the energy is released from your last center into the cosmos. You become a superman. Or, rather, you are no longer man. And when that moment comes—when you are no longer man—only then are you no longer mad.

Man is bound to be mad somehow or other because he is not a being. He is, rather, a facade. Man is not an end. Rather, he is a process—something midway. He is no longer animal, and he is still not that which he was meant to be. He is just midway between animal and god. This is what creates neurosis.

You are no longer an animal, but the animal is still within you. It goes on pulling you down. There is nothing bad about it; an animal cannot do anything else. It pulls you down to what is natural to it. That is why it goes on pulling you down to the sex center.

Sex is the last center for an animal and the first center for man. So the animal within you cannot do anything else. It goes on pulling you down to the sex center. But that is your first center, not your ultimate possibility. Your ultimate possibility is the superman—going beyond humanity, transcending humanity. This ultimate possibility—this superman, this god within you—goes on pulling you upward.

These two pulls create schizophrenia. One moment you

are pulled to the higher and you are like a saint, and the next moment you are pulled down and you are behaving like an animal. The mind becomes confused. You cannot be an animal wholeheartedly—you cannot be at ease with the animal within you—because the higher possibility, the seed, is there and it goes on challenging you. But you cannot remove the animal. It is there; it is your heritage. So you divide yourself in two. You place the animal part of you in the unconscious, and consciously you identify yourself with your higher possibility, which you are not.

This higher possibility is the ideal, the end. Consciously you identify with the end, but unconsciously you remain with the beginning. These two points create conflict. So unless you go beyond man, you cannot go beyond madness. Man *is* madness.

In the third step, I use *hoo* as a vehicle to bring your energy upward. These first three steps are cathartic. They are not meditation, but just the preparation for it. They are a "getting ready" to take the jump, not the jump itself.

The fourth step is the jump. In the fourth step I tell you to *stop!* When I say, "Stop!" stop completely. Don't do anything at all because anything you do can become a diversion and you will miss the point. Anything—just a cough or a sneeze—and you may miss the whole thing because the mind has become diverted. Then the upward flow will stop immediately because your attention has moved.

Don't do anything. You are not going to die. Even if a sneeze is coming and you do not sneeze for ten minutes, you will not die. If you feel like coughing, if you feel an irritation in the throat and you do not do anything, you are not going to die. Just let your body remain dead so that the energy can move in one upward flow.

When the energy moves upward you become more and more silent. Silence is the by-product of energy moving upward and tension is the by-product of energy moving downward. Now your whole body will become so silent—as if it has disappeared. You will not be able to feel it.

You have become bodiless. And when you are silent, the whole existence is silent because the existence is nothing but a mirror. It reflects you. In thousands and thousands of mirrors, it reflects you. When you are silent, the whole existence has become silent.

In your silence I will tell you to just be a witness—a constant alertness: not doing anything, but just remaining a witness, just remaining with yourself; not doing *anything*— no movement, no desire, no becoming—but just remaining then and there, silently witnessing what is happening.

That remaining in the center, in yourself, is possible because of the first three steps. Unless these three are done, you cannot remain with yourself. You can go on talking about it, thinking about it, dreaming about it, but it will not happen because you are not ready.

These first three steps will make you ready to remain with the moment. They will make you aware. That is meditation. In that meditation something happens that is beyond words. And once it happens you will never be the same again; it is impossible. It is a growth; it is not simply an experience. It is a growth.

That is the difference between false techniques and real techniques. With false techniques you may experience something, but then you will fall back again. It was just a glimpse; it was not a growth. This can happen with LSD. You will have a glimpse. This can happen with other techniques: you can have a glimpse, you can have an experience, but then you will fall down again because you have not grown. The experience has happened *to* you; you have not happened to the experience. You have not grown. When you grow, you cannot fall down.

If a child dreams that he has become a young man, he can have a glimpse of being a young man. But it is a dream. The dream will be broken and he will be a child again because it was not a growth. But if you have grown and become a young man, you cannot fall down and become a child. It is a real growth. So this is the criterion to judge whether a method, a technique, has been real or false.

There are false techniques that are easier to do. They never lead you anywhere. If you are just after experiences you will fall prey to any false technique. A real technique is not concerned with experiences as such. A real technique is concerned with growth. Experiences happen; that is irrelevant. My concern is with growth, not with experiences.

You must grow to become one, to become whole, to become sane. This sanity cannot be forced upon you. Society tries to force it on you, but then you remain insane within and the sanity is just a facade.

I am not going to force sanity upon you. Rather, I am going to bring out your insanity. When it is pulled out completely, thrown into the wind, sanity will happen to you. You will grow. You will be transformed. That is the meaning of meditation.[3]

---

[3] After ten minutes of silence, the Dynamic Meditation concludes with ten minutes of celebration—singing, dancing, and expressing whatever bliss or ecstasy is there. For a step-by-step description of Dynamic Meditation, see pages 232–234.

# ❧ 4 ❧

## . . . Or, Silent Meditation

QUESTION: "Dynamic Meditation is very active, very strenuous. Can one not go into meditation just by sitting silently?"

You can go into meditation just by sitting, but then be *just* sitting. Do not do anything else. If you can be just sitting, it becomes meditation. Be completely in the sitting; non-movement should be your only movement. In fact, the word *Zen* comes from the word *zazen*, which means "just sitting . . . doing nothing." If you can just sit—doing nothing with your body and nothing with your mind—it becomes meditation. But it is difficult.

You can sit very easily when you are doing something else, but the moment you are just sitting and doing nothing, it becomes a problem. Every fiber of the body begins to move inside: every vein, every muscle, begins to move. You will begin to feel a subtle trembling; you will be aware of many points in the body of which you have never been aware before. And the more you try to just sit, the more movement you will feel inside you. So sitting can be used only if you have done other things first.

You can just walk; that is easier. You can just dance; that is even easier. And after you have been doing other things that are easier, then you can sit. Sitting in a Buddha posture is the last thing to do really. It should never be done in the beginning. Only after you have begun to feel identified totally with movement can you begin to feel totally identified with nonmovement.

So I never tell people to begin with just sitting. Begin from where beginning is easy. Otherwise, you will begin to feel many things unnecessarily—things that are not there.

If you begin with sitting, you will feel much disturbance inside. The more you try to just sit, the more disturbance will be felt. You will become aware only of your insane mind and nothing else. It will create depression; you will feel frustrated; you will not feel blissful. Rather, you will begin to feel that you are insane. And sometimes you may really go insane!

If you make a sincere effort to "just sit," you may really go insane. Only because people do not really try sincerely does insanity not happen more often. With a sitting posture you begin to know so much madness inside you that if you are sincere and continue it, you may really go insane. It has happened before, so many times. So I never suggest anything that can create frustration, depression, sadness . . . anything that will allow you to be too aware of your insanity. You may not be ready to be aware of all the insanity that is inside you. You must be allowed to get to know certain things gradually. Knowledge is not always good. It must unfold itself slowly, as your capacity to absorb it grows.

I begin with your insanity, not with a sitting posture. I allow your insanity. If you dance madly, the opposite happens within you. With a mad dance, you begin to be aware of a silent point within you; with sitting silently, you begin to be aware of madness. The opposite is always the point of awareness.

With your dancing madly, chaotically, with crying, with chaotic breathing, I allow your madness. Then you begin to be aware of a subtle point, a deep point inside you, which is silent and still, in contrast to the madness on the periphery. You will feel very blissful; at your center there is an inner silence. But if you are just sitting, then the inner one is the mad one. You are silent on the outside, but inside you are mad.

If you begin with something active—something positive, alive, moving—it will be better. Then you will begin to feel an inner stillness growing. The more it grows, the more it will be possible for you to use a sitting posture or a lying posture—the more silent meditation will be possible. But by then things will be different, totally different.

A meditation technique that begins with movement, action, helps you in other ways, also. It becomes a catharsis. When you are just sitting, you are frustrated: your mind wants to move and you are just sitting. Every muscle turns, every nerve turns. You are trying to force something upon yourself that is not natural for you. Then you have divided yourself into the one who is forcing and the one who is being forced. And, really, the part that is being forced and suppressed is the more authentic part. It is a more major part of your mind than the part that is suppressing, and the major part is bound to win.

That which you are suppressing is really to be thrown, not suppressed. It has become an accumulation within you because you have been constantly suppressing it. The whole upbringing, the civilization, the education, is suppressive. You have been suppressing much that could have been thrown very easily with a different education, with a more conscious education, with a more aware parenthood. With a better awareness of the inner mechanism of the mind, the culture could have allowed you to throw many things.

For example, when a child is angry we tell him, "Do not be angry." He begins to suppress anger. By and by, what was a momentary happening becomes permanent. Now he will not *act* angry, but he will remain angry. We have accumulated so much anger from what were just momentary things. No one can be angry continuously unless anger has been suppressed. Anger is a momentary thing that comes and goes: if it is expressed, then you are no longer angry.

So with me, I would allow the child to be angry more authentically. Be angry, but be deep in it. Do not suppress it.

Of course, there will be problems. If we say, "Be angry," then you are going to be angry *at* someone. But a child can be molded. He can be given a pillow and told, "Be angry with the pillow. Be violent with the pillow." From the very beginning, a child can be brought up in a way in which the anger is just deviated. Some object can be given to him: he can go on throwing the object until his anger goes. Within minutes, within seconds, he will have dissipated his anger and there will be no accumulation of it.

You have accumulated anger, sex, violence, greed—everything! Now this accumulation is a madness within you. It is there, inside you. If you begin with any suppressive meditation (for example, with just sitting), you are suppressing all of this, you are not allowing it to be released. So I begin with a catharsis. First, let the suppressions be thrown into the air. And when you can throw your anger into the air, you have become mature.

If I cannot be loving alone, if I can be loving only with someone I love, then, really, I am not mature yet. Then I am depending on someone even to be loving. Someone must be there; then I can be loving. Then that loving can only be a very superficial thing. It is not my nature. If I am alone in the room I am not loving at all, so the loving quality has not gone deep; it has not become a part of my being.

You become more and more mature when you are less and less dependent. If you can be angry alone, you are more mature. You do not need any object to be angry. So I make a catharsis in the beginning a must. You must throw everything into the sky, into the open space, without being conscious of any object.

Be angry without the person with whom you would like to be angry. Weep without finding any cause. Laugh, just laugh, without anything to laugh at. Then you can just throw the whole accumulated thing. You can just throw it! And once you know the way, you are unburdened of the whole past.

Within moments you can be unburdened of the whole life—of lives even. If you are ready to throw everything, if you can allow your madness to come out, within moments there is a deep cleansing. Now you are cleansed: fresh, innocent. You are a child again. Now, in your innocence, sitting meditation can be done (just sitting . . . or just lying or anything) because now there is no mad one inside to disturb the sitting.

Cleansing must be the first thing—a catharsis. Otherwise, with breathing exercises, with just sitting, with practicing asanas (yogic postures), you are just suppressing something. And a very strange thing happens: when you have allowed everything to be thrown out, sitting will just happen, asanas will just happen. It will be spontaneous.

You may not have known anything about yoga asanas but you begin to do them. Now these postures are authentic, real. They bring much transformation inside your body because now the body itself is doing them. You are not forcing them. For example, when someone has thrown many things out, he may begin to try to stand on his head. He may have never learned to do *shirshasan* (the headstand), but now his whole body is trying to do it. This is a very inner thing now. It comes from his inner body wisdom, not from his mind's intellectual, cerebral information. If his body insists, "Go and stand on your head!" and he allows it, he will feel very refreshed, very changed by it.

You may do any posture, but I allow these postures only when they come by themselves. Someone can sit down and be silent in *siddhasan* (a yogic sitting posture) or in any other posture, but *this siddhasan* is something quite different. The quality differs. He is *trying* to be silent in sitting, but this is a happening. There is no suppression; there is no effort. It is just how your body feels. Your total being feels to sit. In this sitting, there is no divided mind, no suppression. This sitting becomes a flowering.

You must have seen statues of Buddha sitting on a flower—a lotus flower. The lotus is just symbolic. It is symbolic of what is happening inside Buddha. When "just sitting" happens from the inside, you feel just like the opening of a flower. Nothing is being suppressed from the outside; rather, there is a growth, an opening from the inside. Something inside opens and flowers. You can imitate Buddha's posture, but you cannot imitate the flower. You can sit completely Buddha-like—even more Buddha-like than Buddha—but the inside flowering will not be there. It cannot be imitated.

You can use tricks. You can use breathing rhythms that can force you to be still, to suppress your mind. Breath can be used very suppressively because with every rhythm of breath a particular mood arises in your mind. Not that other moods disappear; they just go into hiding.

You can force anything on yourself. If you want to be angry, just breathe the rhythm that happens in anger. Actors do it; when they want to express anger, they change their breathing rhythm. The breathing rhythm must become the same as when there is anger. By making the rhythm fast, they begin to feel anger. The anger part of the mind comes up.

So breathing rhythm can be used to suppress the mind, to suppress anything in the mind. But it is not good; it is not a flowering. The other way is better—when your mind changes and then, as a consequence, your breath changes. The change comes first from the mind.

So I use breathing rhythm as a sign. A person who remains at ease with himself constantly remains in the same breathing rhythm. It never changes because of the mind. It will change because of the body—if you are running it will change—but it never changes because of the mind.

So tantra[1] has used many, many breathing rhythms as

---

[1] Yoga is the path of will; tantra is the path of surrender. Bhagwan Shree has spoken extensively on tantra. The first three of five volumes of these talks have been published under the

secret keys. They even allow sexual intercourse as a meditation, but they allow it only when your breathing rhythm remains constant in intercourse, otherwise not. If the mind is involved, then the breathing rhythm cannot remain the same, and if the breathing rhythm remains the same, the mind is not involved at all. If the mind is not involved even in such a deep, biological thing as sexual intercourse, then the mind will not be involved in anything else.

But you can force. You can sit and force a particular rhythm on your body, you can create a fallacious Buddha-like posture, but you will just be dead! You will become dull, stupid. It has happened to so many monks, so many *sadhus*. They just become stupid! Their eyes have no light of intelligence; their faces are just idiotic, with no inner light, no inner flame. Because they are so afraid of any inner movement, they have suppressed everything—including intelligence. Intelligence is a movement, one of the most subtle movements, so if all inner movement is suppressed, intelligence will be affected.

Awareness is not a static thing. Awareness, too, is movement: a dynamic flow. So if you start from the outside, if you force yourself to sit like a statue, you are killing much. First be concerned with catharsis (with cleaning out your mind, throwing everything out), so that you become empty and vacant—just a passage for something from the beyond to enter. Then sitting becomes helpful, silence becomes helpful, but not before.

To me, silence, in itself, is not something worthwhile. You can create a silence that is a dead silence. Silence must be alive, dynamic. If you "create" silence, you will become more stupid, more dull, more dead. But this is easier in a way, and so many people are doing it now. The whole culture is so suppressive that it is easier to suppress yourself

---

title *The Book of the Secrets* (Poona, India: Rajneesh Foundation, 1: 1974; 2: 1975; 3: 1976; U.S. edition of volume 1 published New York: Harper & Row, Publishers, 1976). Subsequent volumes are to be published soon.

still more. Then you do not have to take any risks; then
you do not have to take a jump.

People come to me and say, "Tell us a meditation technique that we can practice silently." Why this fear? Everyone has a madhouse inside and still they say, "Tell us a
technique that we can do silently." With a silent technique
you can only become more and more mad (silently), and
nothing else.

*The doors of your madhouse must be opened!* Don't be
afraid of what others will say. A person who is concerned
about what others think can never go inward. He will be
too busy worrying about what others are saying, what they
are thinking.

If you just sit silently, closing your eyes, everything will
be okay. Your wife or your husband will say that you have
become a very good person. Everyone wants you to be dead.
Even mothers want their children to be dead: obedient,
silent. The whole society wants you to be dead. So-called
good men are really dead men, so don't be concerned
with what others think, don't be concerned about the image
that others may have of you.

Begin with catharsis and then something good can flower
within you. It will have a different quality, a different
beauty, altogether different. It will be authentic.

When silence comes to you, when it descends on you, it
is not a false thing. You have not been cultivating it. It
comes to you; it happens to you. You begin to feel it growing inside you just like a mother begins to feel a child
growing.

A deep silence is growing inside you; you become pregnant with it. Only then is there transformation; otherwise
it is just self-deception. And one can deceive oneself for
lives and lives. The capacity to do so is infinite.

QUESTION: "But doesn't meditation mean *akarma* (no activity)?"

The fourth stage of Dynamic Meditation is just *akarma* (no activity), but the first three stages are active. The first, second, and third stages are of intense activity. In the first stage, your vital body[2] (your breathing) is in intense movement, in extreme activity. By being in extreme activity in your vital body (in your *prana-sharira,* in your breathing), the second step becomes possible: you become intensely active in your physical body. And in the third stage, after being totally active physiologically, it becomes possible to be active in the mental body.

So in three bodies (the physical, vital, and mental) you create a climax of activity, a climax of tension. You become more and more tense. Your whole existence becomes a whirlwind, a whirlpool. The more intense it becomes, the greater the possibility of being relaxed in the fourth stage.

The fourth stage is total relaxation. It is not a practiced relaxation because, really, no one can practice relaxation. Relaxation can come only as a by-product, as a shadow of intense activity. To practice relaxation is a contradiction in terms. Every practice is a practice of tension. Relaxation means non-doing, and you cannot practice non-doing. You can only come to it, you can only arrive at it.

Only by intense activity is a situation created within you that takes you into a "letting go." So the fourth stage is *akarma.* You are not doing anything: now you *are.* You just exist in it; there is nothing that you are doing. If something is going on, it has just happened. If there is something going on it is through nature, it is not done by you. As far as you are concerned, activity has ceased completely. There is no activity.

In this no-action state (in this *akarmic* state), the cosmic and the individual come nearer. They become intimate: they lose their identities; they overlap each other. Some-

[2] For a discussion of the "seven bodies," see chapter 17.

thing penetrates you from the cosmic and something of
you penetrates into the cosmic. The boundaries become
flexible and liquid. Sometimes there is no boundary and
you feel an absence of consciousness. There are no limits—
no end and no beginning. And sometimes the boundaries
begin to crystallize around you.

This situation goes on flickering back and forth. Sometimes there are boundaries and sometimes there are not.
But the more relaxation is there, the more the boundaries
will be lost. Then a moment comes that can never be predicted. A moment comes that is a moment of happening,
uncaused and unconditioned.

Finally a moment comes when you have lost the boundaries and you never regain them again. Then there begins
to exist a human being without boundaries, a mind without
frontiers, a consciousness without any limitations. That is
the cosmic, that is the divine, that is wholeness.

## ◇ 5 ◇

# Moving Deeply into the Known

### I

I do not believe in fixed methods. I use methods just to push you into a very chaotic consciousness, because the first thing to be done with you, as you are, is to disturb your whole pattern. You have become solid, rigid. You must become more and more liquid and flowing. And unless you become flowing, riverlike, you can never know the divine because it is not a thing: it is an event.

You cannot seek the divine, it cannot be sought after, because you can seek only that which you know already. Seeking means desiring, and you cannot seek something that is unknown. How can you seek something that you have not known at all? The very urge to seek comes only after you have tasted something, known something—even a glimpse. So the divine cannot be sought. But when I say the divine cannot be sought, I do not mean that it cannot be found. It cannot be sought, but it *can* be found.

The more you seek it, the less will be the possibility to find it. Seek, and you will not find at all, because the very seeking, the *very* seeking, becomes the barrier. So do not seek something that is not known to you. Rather, go deep into that which is known to you. Do not long for the unknown; go deep into the known. And if you go deep into the known, you will stumble upon the doors to the unknown, because the known is really the door to the unknown. So go deep.

For example, you cannot seek the divine, but if you have loved, then you have known love. So go deep into love. And as you go deep into love, somewhere, the lover and the beloved are not there and the divine appears.

So rather than to seek the divine, it is better to go into that which is actual to you, that which is known to you, near to you. Do not go far. Begin from the near. We are so anxious to go far that we never take the first step, which can be taken from the near. We ask for the last step first, but you cannot take the last step in the beginning. The first must be taken first. The first is here and now, but we are concerned with there and then.

Seeking means seeking in time. Seeking is a postponement, a deep postponement, because seeking is always in the future. It can never be in the present. How can you seek here and now? There is no space. You can BE here and now, but you cannot seek. So the very mind that seeks creates time, because time is needed; only then can you seek.

That is why those who are seeking *moksha* (liberation, absolute liberation) have had to create the concept of transmigration. More time is needed. One life is not enough; many lives are needed. Only then, within this expanse of time, this space that time creates, can you move. If you have to find the absolute, one moment is not enough. And, of course, one life is also not enough.

Time is really a by-product of desiring. The more you desire, the more time you need. You can deal with this in two ways. One is to conceive of life after life, time not ending at all. This is one way, the Eastern way, to create more space for the desire.

Another is the Western way: to be more conscious of time and to do many things in the allotted time period. There is one life (there is no possibility of further lives; this life is all), so you have to do many things—many, many things. You have to accommodate so many desires in the allotted period. And this is why the West has become so conscious of time. In fact, time consciousness is one of the most common aspects of the Western mind.

But either way, whenever you desire, you create time. Time is a fourth dimension of space: it is a sort of space. Without time your desires cannot move, so any desire creates time and future. And then you can postpone the present moment, which is not really time but existence.

So it is better to go deep into what is known to you, what is life to you. Go deep in it. Whatever it may be, go deep in it. Do not be on the surface; go into it to its ultimate depth. And the moment you begin to go deep, fall deep, you come to a different dimension. It is not a going into the future; it is going deep into the present, into this very moment.

For example, you are hearing me. You can hear very superficially. Then, only your ears are involved. That is the first layer of hearing. You can say, "Of course I am listening," but only the ears are hearing, only the body mechanism. Your mind may be somewhere else. But if you can go deep, you can listen very intently and the mind is also involved. Then you are going deeper into this very moment.

But even if your mind is involved, your being may not be involved. If you are thinking about what I am saying, the mind is involved, but there are still deeper depths. Your being may not be here at all; there may be unconscious currents because of which you are not here. You can go even deeper. That means that the being is involved. Then you are just vacant, not even thinking about it. Your mechanism is here, your mind is here, your being is here— all focused. Then you go deep.

So whatever you are doing at the moment, go deep in it. The more deep you are in it, the nearer you will be to the unknown. And the unknown is not something opposite to the known. It is something hidden in the known. The known is just a screen.

So do not go into the future; do not seek. Just be here

. . . and BE. In seeking you spread yourself out, but in being you are intense, and that intensity, that total intensity in the moment, brings you to a certain crystallization. In that total, intense moment, you ARE. That being, that happening of being, becomes the door. And you have found it without seeking; you can get it without even seeking.

So I say: do not seek it, and find. . . .


All the devices and all the methods I use are just to make you more and more intense here and now, to help you to forget the past and the future. Any movement of your body or mind can be used as a jumping board. The emphasis is that you jump in the here and now.

Even dancing can be used, but then be just the dancing, not the dancer. The moment the dancer comes in, dancing is destroyed. The seeker has come in; the time-oriented has come in. Now the movement is divided. Dancing has become superficial, and you have gone far away.

When you are dancing, then *be* dancing, do not be the dancer. And the moment comes when you are just the movement, when there is no division. This nondivided consciousness is meditation.

And you can use anything. If you are eating then eating can become a meditation—if there is no eater. If you are walking then walking can become a meditation—if there is no walker. If you are loving then love can become a deep meditation—if there is no lover. The lover disappears. Love with a lover becomes poisonous, but love without the lover becomes divine, and something of the unknown suddenly opens.

We are divided, and then we act. The actor is there: that is the problem. Why is the actor there? He is there because of desiring, expectations, past memories, future longings. The actor is there: he is the whole accumulated past and the whole projected future. The actor misses only one thing: the moment, the present. And everything is there in the moment . . . everything of the past, everything of the future. This very moment is just wasted, and this very moment is life. Everything else is just an action of the past or a dream of the future—it is nothing but dreams.

You have a very big, very great accumulation, but it is dead. The actor is the dead point in you. It is rich with many ornaments of the past, much longing for the future— it looks very rich!—but it is dead. And the present moment is just a naked, atomic thing, very poor, poor in the sense that there is no accumulation of the past and no projecting into the future. It is just a naked, bare, existential moment. It looks poor, but it is the only life possible. It is alive! And to be alive and poor is the only richness, while to be dead and rich is the only poverty. That is why it happens that a beggar such as a Buddha or a Christ were the richest possibilities, but a Midas is the poorest happening in the world.

In meditation, only happenings can help, not fake methods. That is why there has always been so much insistence on a living teacher. Books are bound to be fake; they cannot change you; they cannot be in touch with you; they cannot move you. Doctrines cannot be alive, they are bound to be dead, so the East has always insisted on the phenomenon of a teacher, of a master. And the insistence is really for this: that only a master can be liquid. He can change anything. With him, even methods can be no methods, while with scriptures, traditions, even no methods become methods, because the moment something is written, it is dead.

Something is said: it is dead. A master is needed for continuously disturbing his own past assertions so that nowhere does "fixedness" come in. The liquidity of the phenomenon must be there. Only then, happenings can happen.

So to me, a group that is working in meditation is a group that is doing something in the present moment, not seeking anything. And the present doing may be just trivial. An onlooker, an outsider, may not even be aware of

what is being done. He may even think that the meditators
have gone mad! They may be jumping and crying, weeping
and laughing; they may be doing anything. They may be
just sitting silently, or they may be creating mad noises.
But whatever they are doing, they are doing it without a
doer. Really, they are allowing it to happen, not doing it.
They are open to it.

In the beginning it is difficult. You do not want anything
to happen *without* you because you want to be the master.
Nothing should happen of which you are not the master
and the controller! So in the beginning, it is difficult. But,
by and by, the more you feel the freedom that comes with
the death of your controlling mind—the freshness that
comes the moment you have relaxed controlling—the more
you can laugh. And then, at a particular point, you begin
to feel that the mind is the destructive thing in you, that
the owner (the possessor, the controller) is your bondage.

You won't become aware of this by watching someone
else, but just by feeling it, step by step. Then, in a sudden
explosion, *you* are not there: the doer has disappeared, and
the doing alone remains. With that comes freedom, with
that comes awareness, with that you become totally aware.
Rather, now you are only awareness.

This is what I mean by meditation—not seeking, not
seeking for something, but just going deep inside, in the
present. And anything can be used for it. Anything is as
good as anything else. If you understand it, then anything
can be used as a meditational object or as meditation.

That is why I tell you to do Dynamic Meditation and
be in a deep silence . . . in the happening.

## II

QUESTION: "In hatha yoga there is an exercise in which one tenses every muscle in the body and then releases the tension and becomes relaxed. Is this similar to what happens in Dynamic Meditation?"

Relaxation is basically existential. You cannot relax if, existentially, your attitude toward life is tense. Then, even if you try to relax, it is impossible. In fact, to try to relax is absurd. Effort, as such, is inimical to relaxation. You cannot relax: you can only *be* relaxed.

Your very presence is inimical to relaxation. Relaxation means that you are absent, and through no effort on your part can you be absent. Each and every effort will strengthen your presence. It is bound to strengthen it. Whatever you do will be your act: you will be strengthened through it; you will be more condensed through it; you will be more crystallized.

In this sense, you cannot relax. Relaxation can come to you only when you are not. Your very doing will become a part of the ego, your very effort will be a continuity of yourself.

You are relaxed in the moment when you are not. Your very being is the tension. You cannot exist without tension: you *are* the tension.

Tension begins with a desire for that which is not. It is a tension between the past and the future. You are like a bridge between two things, and whenever two things are connected, tension will be there. Man is a bridge—a bridge of desires—but it is a "rainbow bridge," not a steel bridge. It can evaporate.

When I say relaxation is existential, I mean by this: understand the tension; don't do anything with it, just understand it.

You can understand tension, but you cannot understand relaxation. That is impossible. You can only understand tension, so understand what it is, how it is, from where it comes; how it exists, by what means it exists. Understand tension totally, and the minute you understand it, a moment is created in which there is no tension. Then it is not only the body which is relaxed. The whole being is relaxed.

To relax the body is really not very difficult, but it has become more difficult with the advance of civilization because the contact with the body is lost. We do not exist in the body. Our existence has become basically cerebral, mental.

You do not even love with your body; you love with your mind. The body follows just like a dead weight. When you touch someone, it is not the body you touch. The sensitivity is not there. The mind touches, but since minds cannot really touch, two bodies meet but there is no communion. The bodies are dead, so you can embrace, but it is only two dead bodies embracing. They come near, but they are not really near. Nearness can only be there if you exist in the body, if you are inside the body.

We are outside our bodies, just like ghosts. Around and around, but never inside. The more man has become civilized, the less he is in contact with his own body. The contact is lost: that is why the body is tense.

Body has its own automatic mechanism to relax. The body is tired, it is on the bed. But because you are not there, it cannot relax. You must be in it; otherwise, the automatic mechanism becomes ineffective. It cannot work without your presence. It needs you; it cannot go to sleep by itself. Sleep is lost, relaxation is lost, because the contact with the body is lost.

You are not in your body, so your body cannot function adequately. It cannot function with its own wisdom. It has a genetic, inborn wisdom of centuries, but because you are not in it, there is tension. Otherwise, the physical body is basically automatic: it works automatically; you only have to be there. Your presence is needed. Then it starts working.

Our minds are also full of tension. They need not be. The mind is tense because you are always creating confusion. For example, a person who is thinking about sex is creating confusion because sex is not something to be thought about. The mind center is not made for that. Sex has its own center, but you are doing the work of the sex center through your mind. Even when you are in love you think about it, you do not feel it. The feeling center is not working.

The more civilized man is, the more the center of the intellect is overburdened. Other centers are not working, not functioning. This, too, creates a tension because a center that *should* work, and has a particular energy to work with, is left without anything to do. It then creates its own tensions. It becomes overburdened by its own unused energy.

The mind center is overburdened by work. It is being made to feel, which it cannot do. Mind cannot feel; it can only think. The categories of thinking are quite different from the categories of feeling, and not only different, but diametrically opposite. The logic of the heart is not the logic of the mind.

Love has its own way of thinking, but it is not a mental way, so mind has to do things that it is not meant to do. It becomes overburdened and there is tension. The situation is like this: the father is doing the work of the child, and the child is doing the work of the father. This is the sort of confusion that is created by a mental existence.

If every center does its own work, there is relaxation. Mind is not the only center. Because we function as if it is, we have destroyed the whole silence, the whole relaxed attitude, the whole tuning of humanity with the universe.

Mind has to work; it has a function, but a very limited one. It is overburdened. Your whole education is concerned with only one center. You are being educated as if you have only one center: the mind, the mathematical, the rational.

Life is not only rational. On the contrary, the greater part of life is irrational. Reason is just like a small lighted island in the vast, dark, and mysterious ocean of irrationality. And this island is rooted in the ocean of mystery—the great ocean of mystery.

This lighted part is just a part. It is not the whole and must not be taken as the whole, otherwise tension will be the result. The mysterious will take its revenge; the irrational will take its revenge.

You can see the results of this in the West. The West has overdone, overworked, one center: the rational. And now the irrational is taking revenge. Revenge is there; it is disrupting the whole order. The anarchic, the undisciplined, the rebellious, the illogical, are erupting. It may be in music, painting, or anything. The irrational is taking its revenge and the established order is being put in its place.

Reason is not the totality. When it is made to be so, the whole culture becomes tense. The same laws that apply to the individual apply to the whole culture, to the whole society.

These laws must be understood. And the very understanding will begin to effect a change in you: the very understanding will become a transformation.

Body has become tense because you are not in it and mind has become tense because you have overburdened it. But your spiritual being is never tense. I divide you into body, mind, and spirit as a method only. You are not divided—these boundaries do not, in fact, exist—but in order to help you to understand things, the division will be useful.

The spiritual realm is never tense, but you are not in contact with it. A person who is not even in contact with his body can never be in contact with the spirit because it is a deeper realm. If you are not even in contact with your outer boundaries, you cannot be in contact with your inner centers.

The third realm, the spiritual, is relaxed. Even this minute it is relaxed. In fact, it would be more accurate to say that the spiritual realm is the realm of relaxation. There is no tension there because the reasons for tension cannot exist in the third realm.

You cannot exist without the third realm. You can be forgetful of it, but you can never be without it because you *are* it. It is your Being. It is pure existence.

You are not aware of the spiritual because you have so much tension in the body, so much tension in the mind. But if you are not tense in the physical and mental realms, you will automatically know the bliss of the spiritual, the relaxation of the spiritual. It comes to you; it has been waiting for you. Your whole attention is so absorbed by the physical and the mental that there is no attention left to divert to the spiritual. Only if the body and the mind are not tense can you delve into the spiritual, can you know the bliss of it. The spiritual is never tense; it cannot be. There is no spiritual tension, only bodily tension, only mental tension.

Bodily tension has been created by those who—in the name of religion—have been preaching anti-body attitudes. In the West, Christianity has been emphatically antagonistic toward the body. A false division, a gulf, has been created between you and your body. Then your total attitude becomes tension creating. You cannot eat in a relaxed way, you cannot sleep in a relaxed way. Every bodily act becomes a tension. The body is the enemy, but you cannot exist without it. You must remain with it, you must live with your enemy, so there is constant tension. You can never relax.

Body is not your enemy nor is it in any way unfriendly or even indifferent to you. The very existence of the body is bliss. And the moment you take the body as a gift, as a divine gift, you will come back to the body. You will love it, you will feel it, and subtle are the ways of its feeling!

You cannot feel another's body if you have not felt your own; you cannot love another's body if you have not loved your own. It is impossible. You cannot care for another person's body if you have not cared for your own . . . and no one cares! You may say that you care, but I insist: no one cares! Even if you seem to care, you do not really care. You are caring for some other reason—for the opinion of others, for the look in someone else's eyes. You never care for your body for yourself; you do not love your body. And if you cannot love it, you cannot be in it.

Love your body, and you will feel a relaxation such as you have never felt before. Love is relaxing. When there is love, there is relaxation. If you love someone—if, between you and him or you and her, there is love—then with love comes the music of relaxation. Then relaxation is there.

When you are relaxed with someone that is the only sign of love. If you cannot be relaxed with someone, you are not in love; the other, the enemy, is always there. That is why Sartre has said, "The other is hell." Hell is there for Sartre, it is bound to be. When there is no love flowing between the two, the other is hell, but if there is love flowing in between, the other is heaven. So whether the other is heaven or hell depends on whether there is love flowing in between.

Whenever you are in love, a silence comes. Language is lost; words become meaningless. You have much to say and nothing to say at the same time. The silence will envelop you, and in that silence, love flowers.

You are relaxed. There is no future in love; there is no past. Only when love has died is there a past. You only remember a dead love; a living love is never remembered. It is living; there is no gap to remember it; there is no space to remember it. Love is in the present. There is no future and no past.

If you love someone, you do not have to pretend. Then you can be what you are. You can put off your mask and be relaxed. When you are not in love, you have to wear a mask. You are tense every moment because the other is there. You have to pretend; you have to be on guard. You have to be either aggressive or defensive: it is a fight, a battle. You cannot be relaxed.

The bliss of love is more or less the bliss of relaxation. You feel relaxed; you can be what you are. You can be nude in a sense, as you are. You need not be bothered about yourself, you need not pretend. You can be open, vulnerable. And in that opening, you are relaxed.

This same phenomenon happens if you love your body. You become relaxed; you care about it. It is not wrong, it is not narcissistic, to be in love with your own body. In fact, it is the first step toward spirituality.

That is why Dynamic Meditation begins with the body. Through vigorous breathing the mind expands, the consciousness expands. The whole body becomes a vibrating, living existence. Now the jump will be easier. Now you can jump; thinking will be less of a barrier. You have become a child again: jumping, vibrating, alive. The conditioning, the mental conditioning, is not there.

Your body is not so conditioned as your mind. Remember this: your mind is conditioned, but your body is still a part of nature. All religions and religious thinkers (who have been basically cerebral) are against the body because with the body, with the senses, the mind and its conditioning are lost. That is why they all have been afraid of sex. With sex, the conditioning mind is lost. You again become part of the greater biological sphere, the biosphere. You become one with it.

Mind is always against sex because sex is the only thing in ordinary life that can rebel against the mind. You have controlled the whole thing; only one thing remains uncontrolled. So mind is very much against sex because it is the only remaining link between the body and you. If it can be denied completely, then you can become totally cerebral, and you are not a body at all.

The fear of sex is basically the fear of the body because with sex, the whole body becomes vibrating, vital, living. The moment sex takes over the body, the whole mind is pushed back. It is not there. Breathing takes it over; the breathing becomes vigorous, vital.

That is why I begin my meditation with breathing. With breathing, you begin to feel your whole body, every corner of it. The body is flooded; you become one with it. Now it is possible for you to take a jump.

The jump that is taken in sex is a very small jump, while the jump that is taken in meditation is a very great jump. In sex, you "jump" into someone else. Before that jump you need to be one with your body, and in that jump you need to expand still more: to another's body. Your consciousness spreads beyond your body. In meditation you jump from your body to the whole body of the universe; you become one with it.

The second step of Dynamic Meditation is cathartic. Not only will you be one with your body, but all the tensions that have been accumulated in the body must be thrown. The body must become light, unburdened, so the movements are to be vigorous, as vigorous as possible. Then the same thing that is possible in dervish dancing (in Sufi dancing) becomes possible. If your movements are vital and vigorous, a moment will come when you will lose control.

And that moment is needed! *You* must not be in control because your control is the barrier, *you* are the barrier. Your controlling faculty—your mind—is the barrier.

Go on moving! Of course, you will have to begin, but a moment will come when you will be taken over. You will feel that the control is lost. You are on the brink; now you can take the jump.

Now you have again become a child. You have come back; all the conditioning is thrown. You do not care for anything; you do not care for what others think. Now everything that has been put into you by society is thrown. You have become just a dancing particle in the universe.

When you have thrown everything in the second stage of Dynamic Meditation, only then is the third stage possible. Your identity will be lost, your image will be broken, because whatever you know about yourself is not about yourself but only a labeling. You have been told you are "this" or "that," and you have become identified with it. But with vigorous movement, with the cosmic dance, all identifications will be lost. You will be, for the first time, as you must have been when you were born. And with this new birth, you will be a new person.

## ~ 6 ~

### *Kundalini:* The Awakening of the Life Force

#### I

No theoretical knowledge ever helps and no anatomical
visualization of *kundalini* is really meaningful for meditation.[1] When I say this I do not mean that there is nothing
like *kundalini* or chakras. *Kundalini* is there, chakras are

[1] *Kundalini,* Bhagwan Shree explains, is the passage through
which the life force moves. It is, however, commonly thought
to be the life force itself, (Bhagwan Shree speaks about this
common misunderstanding on pages 76–77) and is visualized as
a coiled serpent residing in the lowest chakra (or center) in
the body, the *muladhar* chakra, located at the base of the spine.
As energy awakens through meditation, the *kundalini* moves
through the chakras and ultimately, when enlightenment happens, it is released through the *sahasrar,* the last chakra, which
is located at the top of the head. The release of energy through
the *sahasrar* is often visualized as the opening of a thousand-
petaled lotus. The seven chakras through which the *kundalini*
passes correspond physically to at (1) the base of the spine, (2)
beneath the navel, (3) above the navel, (4) the heart, (5) the
throat (the thyroid), (6) the middle eye (the pineal gland),
and (7) the top of the head.

People talk about *kundalini,* they talk "knowingly" about the
seven chakras, but Bhagwan Shree warns against theoretical
knowledge of these things. In this discourse he clears up many
of the misconceptions that occur through knowledge—not
knowing.

there, but no knowledge helps in any way. Rather, it can hinder. It can become a barrier for so many reasons.

One reason is that any knowledge about *kundalini* or about esoteric paths of bioenergy—the inner paths of *élan vital*—is generalized. It differs from individual to individual; the root is not going to be the same. With "A" it will be different; with "B" it will be different; with "C" it will be different. Your inner life has an individuality, so when you acquire something through theoretical knowledge it is not going to help—it may hinder—because it is not about you. It *cannot* be about you. You will only know about yourself when you go within.

There are chakras, but the number differs with each individual. One may have seven; one may have nine; one may have more; one may have less. That is the reason why so many different traditions have developed. Buddhists talk of nine chakras, Hindus talk of seven, Tibetans talk of four—and they are all right!

The root of *kundalini,* the passage through which *kundalini* passes, is also different with each individual. The more you go in, the more individual you are.

For instance, in your body your face is the most individual part, and on the face the eyes are even more individual. The face is more alive than any other part of the body; that is why it takes on an individuality. You may not have noticed that with a particular age—particularly with sexual maturity—your face begins to assume a shape that will continue, more or less, for the whole life. Before sexual maturity the face changes much, but with sexual maturity your individuality is fixed and given a pattern, and now the face will be more or less the same.

The eyes are even more alive than the face, and they are so individual that every moment they change. Unless one attains enlightenment, the eyes are never fixed. Enlightenment is another kind of maturity.

With sexual maturity the face becomes fixed, but there is another maturity where the eyes become fixed. You cannot see any change in Buddha's eyes: his body will grow old, he will die, but his eyes will continue to be the same. That has been one of the indications. When someone attains nirvana, the eyes are the only door by which outsiders can know whether the man has really attained it. Now the eyes never change. Everything changes, but the eyes remain the same. Eyes are expressive of the inner world.

But *kundalini* is still deeper.

No theoretical knowledge is helpful. When you have some theoretical knowledge, you begin to impose it on yourself. You begin to visualize things to be the way you have been taught, but they may not correspond to your individual situation. Then much confusion is created.

One has to feel the chakras, not know "about" them. You have to feel; you have to send feelers inside yourself. Only when you feel your chakras—and your *kundalini* and its passage—is it helpful. Otherwise, it is not helpful. In fact, knowledge has been very destructive as far as the inner world is concerned. The more knowledge gained, the less the possibility of feeling the real, the authentic, things.

You begin to impose what you know upon yourself. If someone says, "Here is the chakra, here is the center," then you begin to visualize your chakra at that spot. And it may not be there at all! Then you will create imaginary chakras. You can create. The mind has the capacity. You can create imaginary chakras, and then, because of your imagination, a flow will begin that will not be *kundalini* but will be simple imagination—a completely illusory, dreamlike phenomenon.

Once you can visualize centers and can create an imaginary *kundalini*, then you can create everything. Then imaginary experiences will follow, and you will develop a very false world inside you. The world that is without is illusory, but not so illusory as the one you can create inside.

All that is within is not necessarily real or true because imagination is also within, dreams are also within. The mind has a faculty—a very powerful faculty—to dream, to create illusions, to project.

That is why it is good to proceed in meditation completely unaware of *kundalini,* of chakras. If you stumble upon them, then it is good. You may come to feel something. Only then, ask. You may begin to feel a chakra working, but let the feeling come first. You may feel energy rising up, but let the feeling come first. Do not imagine, do not think about it, do not make any intellectual effort to understand beforehand. No prenotion is needed. Not only is it not needed, but it is positively harmful.

And another thing: *kundalini* and the chakras do not belong to your anatomy, to your physiology. Chakras and *kundalini* belong to your subtle body (to your *sukshma sharira*),[2] not to this body, the gross body. Of course, there are corresponding spots. The chakras are part of your *sukshma sharira,* but your physiology and anatomy have spots that correspond to them. If you feel an inner chakra, only then can you feel the corresponding spot. Otherwise, you can dissect the whole body, but nothing like chakras will be found.

All the talk and all the so-called evidence and all the scientific claims that your gross body has something like *kundalini* and chakras is nonsense, absolute nonsense. There are corresponding spots, but those spots can only be felt when you feel the real chakras. With the dissection of your gross body nothing can be found. There is nothing. So the question is not of anatomy.

One thing more: it is not necessary to pass through chakras. It is not necessary! One can just bypass them. It is also not necessary that you will feel *kundalini* before enlightenment. The phenomenon is very different from what you may think. *Kundalini* is not felt because it is rising. *Kundalini* is only felt if you do not have a very clear

[2] Your *sukshma sharira* is your etheric body. Bhagwan Shree talks about the seven bodies in chapter 17.

passage. If the passage is completely clearcut, then the energy flows but you cannot feel it.

You feel it when there is something there that resists the flow. If the energy flows upward and you have blocks in the passage, only then do you feel it. So the person who feels more *kundalini* is really blocked: there are many blocks in the passage, so the *kundalini* cannot flow.

When there is resistance, then the *kundalini* is felt. You cannot feel energy directly unless there is resistance. If I move my hand and there is no resistance, the movement will not be felt. The movement is felt because the air resists, but it is not felt as much as when a stone resists. Then I will feel the movement more. And in a vacuum I will not feel the movement at all. So it is relative.

Buddha never talked about *kundalini*. It is not that there was no *kundalini* in his body, but the passage was so clear that there was no resistance. Thus, he never felt it.

Mahavira never talked about *kundalini*. Because of this, a very false notion was created, and then Jains (who followed Mahavira) thought that *kundalini* was all nonsense, that there was nothing like it. Thus, because Mahavira, himself, did not feel *kundalini*, twenty-five centuries of Jain tradition has continued to deny it, claiming, "It does not exist." But Mahavira's reason for not talking about it was very different. Because there were no blocks in his body, he never felt it.

So it is not necessary for you to feel *kundalini*. You may not feel it at all. And if you do not feel *kundalini*, then you will bypass chakras, because the working of the chakras is needed only to break the blocks. Otherwise, they are not needed.

When there is a block, and the *kundalini* is blocked, then the nearby chakra begins to move because of the blocked *kundalini*. It becomes dynamic. The chakra begins to move because of the blocked *kundalini* and it moves so fast that, because of the movement, a particular energy is created, which breaks the block.

If the passage is clear no chakra is needed, and you will

never feel anything. Really, the existence of chakras is just to help you. If *kundalini* is blocked, then the help is just nearby. Some chakra will take the energy that is being blocked. If the energy cannot move further, it will fall back. Before it falls back, the chakra will absorb the energy completely, and the *kundalini* will move in the chakra. Through movement the energy becomes more vital, it becomes more alive, and when it again comes to the block, it can break it. So it is just an arrangement, a help.

If *kundalini* moves and there are no blocks, then you will never feel any chakras. That is why someone may feel nine chakras, someone else may feel ten chakras and someone else may feel only three or four, or one, or none. It depends. In actual fact, there are infinite chakras and at every movement (every step of the *kundalini*) a chakra is by the side to help. If the help is needed, it can be given.

That is why I insist that a theoretical acquaintance is not helpful. And meditation, as such, is not really concerned with *kundalini* at all. If *kundalini* comes, that is another thing—but meditation has nothing to do with it. Meditation can be explained without even mentioning *kundalini*. There is no need. And by mentioning *kundalini* it creates even more conflicts, to explain the thing.

Meditation can be explained directly; you need not bother about chakras. You begin with meditation. If the passage is blocked you may come to feel *kundalini*, and chakras will be there, but that is completely nonvoluntary. You must remember that it is nonvoluntary; your volition is not needed at all.

The deeper the path, the more nonvoluntary. I can move my hand—this is a voluntary path—but I cannot move my blood. I can try. Years and years of training can make a person capable of making blood circulation voluntary (hatha yoga can do that: it has been done; it is not impossible), but it is futile. Thirty years of training just to control the movement of the blood is meaningless and stupid because with the control comes nothing. The blood circulation is nonvoluntary; your will is not needed. You take food and the moment it goes in, your will is not needed: the body machinery, the body mechanism, has taken over, and it goes on doing whatever is needed. Your sleep is not voluntary, your birth is not voluntary, your death is not voluntary. These are nonvoluntary mechanisms.

*Kundalini* is still deeper, deeper than your death, deeper than your birth, deeper than your blood, because *kundalini* is a circulation of your second body.[3] Blood is the circulation of your physiological body; *kundalini* is the circulation of your etheric body. It is absolutely nonvoluntary. Even a hatha yogi cannot do anything with it voluntarily.

One has to go into meditation; then the energy begins to move. The part that is to be done by you is meditation. If you are deep in it, then the inner energy begins to move upward. And you will feel the change of flow. It will be felt in so many ways: even physiologically the change can be known.

For example, ordinarily, biologically, it is a sign of good health for your feet to be warm and your head to be cool. Biologically it is a healthy sign. When the reverse occurs— the feet become cool and the head becomes warm—a person is ill. But the same thing happens when the *kundalini* flows upward: the feet become cool.

Really, the warmth in the feet is nothing but sex energy flowing downward. The moment the vital energy (the *kundalini*) begins to flow upward, sex energy follows. It begins to flow upward: the feet become cool and the head becomes warm. Biologically it is better for the feet to be warmer than the head, but spiritually it is healthier for the feet to be cooler because this is a sign that the energy is flowing upward.

Many diseases may begin to occur once the energy begins to flow upward because, biologically, you have dis-

[3] See chapter 17 on the seven bodies.

turbed the whole organism. Buddha died very ill; Mahavira died very ill; Raman Maharshi died with cancer; Ramakrishna died with cancer. And the reason is that the whole biological system is disturbed. Many other reasons are given, but they are nonsense.

Jains have created many stories because they could not conceive that Mahavira could have been ill. For me, the contrary is the case; I cannot conceive how he could have been completely healthy. He couldn't be, because this was going to be his last birth, and the whole biological system had to break down. A system that had been continuous for millennia had to break down. He could not be healthy; in the end he had to be very ill. And he was! But it was very difficult for his followers to conceive that Mahavira was ill.

There was only one explanation for illness in those days. If you were suffering from a particular disease, it meant your *karmas* (your past deeds) had been bad. If Mahavira was suffering from a disease, then, it would have meant that he was still under his karmic influence. This could not be so, so an ingenious story was invented: that Goshalak, a competitor of Mahavira, was using evil forces against him. But this was not the case at all.

The biological, natural flow is downward; the spiritual flow is upward. And the whole organism is meant for the downward flow.

You may begin to feel many changes in the body, but the first changes will come in the subtle body. Meditation is just the means to create a bridge from the gross to the subtle. When I say "meditation" I mean only that. If you can jump out of your gross body, that is what is meant by meditation. But to take this jump you will need the help of your gross body: you will have to use it as a stepping stone.

From any extreme point, you can take the jump. Fasting has been used to take one to an extreme. With long, continuous fasting, you come to the verge. The human body can ordinarily sustain a ninety-day fast, but then, the moment the body is completely exhausted, the moment the reservoir that has been accumulated for emergencies has been depleted—at that moment, one of two things is possible. If you do nothing, death may occur, but if you use this moment for meditation, the jump may occur.

If you do not do anything—if you just go on fasting—death may occur. Then it will be a suicide. Mahavira, who experimented more deeply with fasting than anyone else in the whole history of human evolution, is the only man who allowed his followers a spiritual suicide. He called it *santhara:* that on-the-verge point when both things are possible. In a single moment, you may either die or you can jump. If you use some technique, you can jump. Then, Mahavira says, it is not suicide, but a very great spiritual explosion. Mahavira was the only man—the only one—who has said that if you have the courage, even suicide can be used for your spiritual progress.

From any verge point, the jump is possible. Sufis have used dancing. A moment comes in dancing when you begin to feel unearthly. With a real Sufi dancer, even the audience begins to feel unearthly. Through body movements, rhythmic movements, the dancer soon begins to feel that he is different from the body, separate from the body. One has to begin the movement, but soon a nonvoluntary mechanism of the body takes over.

You begin, but if the end is also yours, then the dancing was just ordinary dancing. But if you begin and by the end you feel as if somewhere in between the dancing was taken over by a nonvoluntary mechanism, then it has become a dervish dance. You move so fast that the body shakes and becomes nonvoluntary.

That is the point where you can go crazy or you can jump. You may go mad because a nonvoluntary mechanism has taken over your body movement. It is beyond your control; you cannot do anything. You may just go mad and never be able to come back again from this nonvoluntary movement. This is the point where there is either madness or, if you know the technique to jump, meditation.

That is why Sufis have always been known as mad people. They have been known as mad! Ordinarily, they are mad! There is also a sect in Bengal that is just like the Sufis: *Baul* fakirs. They move from village to village, dancing and singing. The very word *baul* means *bawla* ("mad"). They are people who are mad.

Madness happens many times, but if you know the technique, then meditation can happen. It always happens on the verge. That is why mystics have always used the term "the sword's edge." Either madness may happen or meditation may happen, and every method uses your body as a sword's edge from which either one or the other is possible.

Then what is the technique to jump into meditation? I have talked about two: fasting and dancing. All techniques of meditation are to push you to the verge where you can take the jump, but the jump, itself, can be taken only through a very simple, very nonmethodical method.

If you can *be aware* at the very moment when fasting has led you to the precipice of death, if you can *be aware* at the moment when death is going to set in, if you can *be aware*, then there is no death. And not only is there no death this time. Then there is no death forever. You have jumped! When the moment is so intense that you know in one second it will be beyond you, when you know that should a second be lost, you will not be able to come back again, *be aware* . . . and then jump! Awareness is the method. And because awareness is the method, Zen people say that there is no method. Awareness is not a method at all. That is why Krishnamurti will go on saying that there is no method.

Of course, awareness is not really a method at all. But I still call it a method because if you cannot be aware, then at the exact moment that the jump is possible, you will be lost. So if someone says, "Only awareness will do," that may be true for one out of ten thousand people, but that one will be one who has come to the point where either madness is possible or death is possible. He has come to that point anyway. And with the others—the majority of people—just talking about awareness will not do. First, they must be trained.

To be aware in ordinary situations will not do. And you *cannot* be aware in ordinary situations. The mind's stupidity has such a long history—the lethargy of it, the laziness of it, the unconsciousness of it, has been going on for so long —that just by hearing Krishnamurti or me or anyone else you can never hope to be aware. And it will be difficult to be aware of those same things that you have done without awareness so many times.

You have come to your office, completely unaware that you have been moving: you have turned, you have walked, you have opened the door. For your whole life you have been doing it. Now it has become a nonvoluntary mechanism. It has been removed from your consciousness completely. Then Krishnamurti says, "Be aware when you are walking." But you have been walking without ever being aware. The habit has set in so deeply; it has become a part of the bones and blood. Now it is very difficult.

You can only be aware in emergencies, in sudden emergencies. Someone puts a gun on your chest. You can be aware because it is a situation that you have never practiced. But if you are familiar with the situation, you will not be aware at all.

Fasting is to create an emergency, and such an emergency as you have never known. So one who has been practicing fasting may not be helped through it. He will need longer periods to fast. Or, if you have never danced, you can be helped easily through dancing. But if you are an expert dancer, Sufi dervish dancing will not do. It will not do at all because you are so perfect, so efficient, and efficiency means that the thing is now being done by the nonvoluntary part of the mind. Efficiency always means that.

That is why 112 methods of meditation have been developed.[4] One may not do for you; another may. And the one which will be most helpful is the one which is completely unknown to you. If you have never been trained in a particular method at all, then an emergency is created very soon. And in that emergency, *be aware!*

So be concerned with meditation and not with *kundalini*. And when you are aware, things will begin to happen in you. For the first time you will become aware of an inner world that is greater, vaster, more extensive than the universe. Energies unknown, completely unknown, will begin to flow in you. Phenomena never heard of, never imagined or dreamed of, will begin to happen. But with each person they differ, so it is good not to talk about them.

They differ. That is why the old traditional emphasis on a guru is there. Scriptures will not do; only the guru will do. And gurus have always been against the scriptures, although the scriptures talk about gurus and praise gurus. The very concept of the guru is in opposition to the scriptures. The well-known proverb *"Guru bin gnana nahee"* ("Without the guru there will be no knowledge") does not really mean that without the guru there will be no knowledge. It means, "With *only* the scriptures there is no knowledge."

A living guru is needed, not a dead book. A book cannot know what type of individual you are. A book is always generalized, it cannot be particular. That is impossible; the very possibility is not there. Only a living person can be aware of your needs, of things which are going to happen to you.

This is really very paradoxical: scriptures talk about

[4] These 112 methods (along with all of their present and past derivations) have been discussed by Bhagwan Shree in a series of 80 discourses on the Vigyan Bhairava Tantra. The first series of these lectures has been published by Harper & Row, Publishers under the title *The Book of the Secrets*.

gurus, *"Guru bin gnana nahee"* ("No knowledge without the guru"), but gurus are symbolically against scriptures. The very concept that the guru will give you knowledge does not mean that he will *provide knowledge*. Rather, it means that only a living person can be of any help. Why? Because he can know the individual.

No book can know the individual. Books are meant for no one in particular; they are meant for everyone. And when a method is to be given, your individuality has to be taken into account, very, very exactly, scientifically.

This knowledge that the guru has to transfer has always been transferred secretly, privately, from guru to disciple. Why the secrecy? Secrecy is the only means for transference of knowledge. The disciple is ordered not to talk about it to anyone. The mind wants to talk. If you know something, it is very difficult to keep it a secret: this is one of the most difficult things. But it has always been the way of the gurus, the way of the teachers. They will give you something with the condition that it is not to be talked about. Why? Why this secrecy?

So many people say that Truth needs no secrecy; it needs no privacy. This is nonsense! Truth needs more privacy than nontruth because it can prove fatal to just anybody; it can prove dangerous. It has been given to a particular individual. It is meant only for him and for no one else. He should not give it to anyone else until he, himself, comes to the point where his individuality is lost. This must be understood.

A guru is a person whose individuality is lost. Only then can he look deeply into your individuality. If he, himself, is an individual, he can interpret you, but he will never be able to know you. For example, if I am here and I say something about you, it is I who am talking about you. It is not about you; rather, it is about me. I cannot help you because I cannot really know you at all. Whenever I know you, it is in a roundabout way, by knowing myself.

This point of *my being here* must disappear. I must be just an absence. Only then can I go deep inside you, without any interpretation. Only then can I know you *as you are*, not according to me. And only then can I help.

Hence, the secrecy.

So it is good not to talk about *kundalini* and chakras. Only meditation is to be taught and to be listened to and to be understood. Then, everything else will just follow.

## II

*Kundalini* is not, itself, a life force. Rather, it is a particular passage for the life force, a way. But the life force can take other ways also, so it is not necessary to pass through *kundalini*. It is possible that one may reach enlightenment without passing through *kundalini*—but *kundalini* is the easiest passage, the shortest one.

If the life force passes through *kundalini*, then the *brahma-randhra*[5] will be the terminal point. But if the life force takes another route—and infinite routes are possible—then the *brahma-randhra* will not be the terminus. So the flowering of the *brahma-randhra* is only a possibility, a potentiality, if the life force passes through *kundalini*.

There are yogas that will not even mention *kundalini*. Then there is nothing like the *brahma-randhra*. But this is the easiest route, so ordinarily 90 percent of the persons who realize pass through *kundalini*.

*Kundalini* and the chakras are not located in the physical body. They belong to the etheric body, but they have corresponding points within the physical body. It is like when you feel love and you put your hand on your heart. Nothing like "love" is there, but your heart (your physical heart) is a corresponding point. When you put your hand

---

[5] The *brahma-randhra* is the middle point of the *sahasrar*, the last chakra in the body, located at the top of the head.

on your heart, you are putting your hand at the chakra that belongs to the etheric body, and this point is approximately parallel to your physical heart.

*Kundalini* is part of the etheric body, so whatever you achieve as progress on the path of *kundalini* does not die with your physical body. It goes with you. Whatever is achieved will remain with you because it is not a part of your physical body. If it *were* a part of your physical body, then with each death it would be lost and you would have to begin from the very beginning. But if someone reaches the third chakra, this progress will remain with him in his next life. It will go with him; it is stored in the etheric body.

When I say that the life energy goes through *kundalini*, I mean *kundalini* as a passage—the whole passage connecting the seven chakras.[6] These chakras are not in the physical body, so everything that can be said about *kundalini* is being said about the etheric body.

When the life force passes through *kundalini*, the chakras will begin to vibrate and flower. The moment energy comes to them, they become alive. It is just like when hydroelectricity is created. The force and pressure of the water rotate the dynamo. If there were no pressure and no water, the dynamo would stop; it would not work. The dynamo rotates because of the pressure. In the same way, the chakras are there, but they are dead until the moment the life force penetrates them. Only then do they begin to rotate.

That is why they are called "chakras." "Chakra" is not exactly translated by the word "center" because center means something static and chakra means something moving. So the right translation would be "wheel," not "center." Or, a dynamic center . . . or a rotating center . . . a moving center.

Chakras are centers until the life force comes to them.

---

[6] Or nine or four or infinite chakras. See page 68.

The moment the life force comes to them, they begin to be chakras. Now they are not centers: they are wheels, rotating. And each wheel, by rotating, creates a new sort of energy. This energy is used again to rotate further chakras. So as the life force passes through each chakra, it becomes more vital, more alive.

*Kundalini* is the passage through which the life force moves. The life force is located in the sex center, stored in the sex center (the *muladhar*). It can be used as sex energy. Then it generates a particular life, a biological life. Then, too, it creates movements; then, too, it creates more energy. But this is biological. If this same energy moves upward, the passage of *kundalini* is opened.

The sex center (the *muladhar*) is the first to open. It can open either toward biological generation or it can open toward spiritual generation. The *muladhar* has two openings, a lower one and an upper one. In the passage of *kundalini*, the highest center is the *sahasrar*, of which the *brahma-randhra* is the middle point. The opening of the *brahma-randhra* is one way toward self-realization.

Other ways are also possible in which the passage of *kundalini* is not used. But they are more arduous. In these other methods there is no question of *kundalini*. Then there is no movement through this passage. There are Hindu methods: raja yoga, mantra yoga, and all the many techniques of tantra. There are Christian methods, Buddhist methods, Zen methods, Tao methods. They are not concerned with *kundalini* awakening. That passage is not used. They use other passages, passages that do not even belong to the etheric body. Astral passages can be used. The astral body (the third body) has its own passage,[7] the mental body (the fourth body) has its own passage. All of the seven bodies have their own passages.

There are many yogas that have nothing to do with *kundalini*. Only hatha yoga uses *kundalini* as a passage. But it is the most scientific and the least difficult. It is an

[7] Again, see chapter 17.

easier step-by-step method for gradual awakening than the other yogas.

Even if the *kundalini* passage is not used, there are sometimes sudden awakenings of the *kundalini*. Sometimes things happen that are beyond your capacity, sometimes things happen that you cannot conceive. Then you are completely shattered. Other passages have their own preparations. Tantric or occult methods are not *kundalini* yoga.[8] *Kundalini* yoga is only one of so many methods. But it is better to be concerned with just one.

The Dynamic Meditation method that I am using is concerned with *kundalini*. It is easier to work with *kundalini* because it is the second body that you are concerned with. The more deeply you go—with the third or the fourth body—the more difficult it becomes. The second body is the nearest one to your physical body and there are corresponding points in your physical body, so it is easier.

If you work with the third body, the corresponding points are in the second body. If you work with the fourth, the corresponding points are in the third. Then your physical body is not concerned. You cannot feel anything at all in your physical body. But with *kundalini* you can feel each step accurately, and you know where you are. Then you are more confident. With the other methods you will have to learn techniques that will help you to feel the corresponding points in the second body or in the third body, and that takes its own time.

The other methods will deny *kundalini,* but their denial is not correct. They deny it because they are not concerned with it. *Kundalini* has its own methodology. If you are working with a Zen method, you should not be concerned with *kundalini*.

---

[8] By "*kundalini* yoga" is meant all those methods that deal directly with *kundalini*. This is not to be confused with the specific teachings of Yogi Bhajan (and the 3HO organization), which are called "*Kundalini* Yoga."

But sometimes, even in working with another method, *kundalini* comes because the seven bodies penetrate one another; they are interlinked. So if you are working with the astral body (the third body), the second body may begin to work. It may get a spark from the third.

The opposite is not possible. If you are working with the second body, the third body will not get ignited because the second is lower than the third. But if you are working with the third, you are creating energy that can come to the second without any effort on your part. Energy flows to lower fields. Your second body is lower than the third, so energy generated in the third may sometimes flow to it.

*Kundalini* may be felt through other methods, but those who teach methods that are not concerned with *kundalini* will not allow you to pay attention to it. If you pay attention to it, more and more energy will come. The whole method that was not concerned with *kundalini* will be shattered. They do not know anything about *kundalini*, so they do not know how to work with it.

Teachers of other methods will deny *kundalini* completely. They will say, "It is nonsense"; they will say, "It is imagination"; they will say, "You are just projecting. Do not be concerned with it; do not be attentive to it." And if you are not attentive to it and you go on working on the third body, by and by the *kundalini* will stop. Energy will no longer come to the second body. Then it is better.

So if you are concerned with any method, be concerned with it totally. Don't be involved in any other method, don't even think about any other method, because then it will become confusing. And the passage of *kundalini* is so subtle and so unknown that confusion will be harmful.

My method of Dynamic Meditation is concerned with *kundalini*. Even if you just go on watching your breath, it will be helpful to *kundalini* because breath, accompanied by *prana* (the life energy) is concerned with the etheric body, the second body. It, too, is not concerned with your physical body. It is being taken from your physical body, it is being drawn from your physical body, but your physical body is just the door.

Prana is concerned with the etheric body. The lungs are doing the breathing, but doing it for the etheric body. Your physical body (the first body) is working for the etheric (the second body). In the same way, the etheric works for the astral (the third body) and the astral works for the mental (the fourth body).

Your physical body is the door for the second body. The second body is so subtle that it cannot be concerned with the material world directly, so, first, your physical body transmutes every material into vital forms. Then these can become food for the second body.

Everything taken from the senses gets transformed into vital forms. This then becomes food for the second body. Then the second body transforms this into even more subtle forms, and this becomes food for the third body.

It is like this: you cannot eat mud, but, in vegetables, the elements of the mud are transformed. Then it can be eaten. The vegetable world transforms the mud into a living, subtle form. Now you can take it in. You cannot eat grass. A cow does it for you. It goes into the cow, and the cow transforms it into milk. Then, you can take it, you can drink the milk.

Just like this, your first body takes matter into it, transforming it into vital forms. Then the second body takes it. Breath is being taken by your lungs: the lungs are machines, working for the second body. If the second body dies, the lungs remain all right, but there is no breathing. Breath has gone. The second body is the master of the first body, and the third body is the master of the second body. Every lower body is a servant to the upper one.

So awareness of breathing is helpful in *kundalini* practice. It generates energy; it conserves energy and helps the life force to go upward. My whole method is concerned with *kundalini*. Once the method has been grasped, everything can be done by it. Now, nothing more is needed.

The last chakra (the *sahasrar*) can be reached through any method. *Sahasrar* and *brahma-randhra* are the names given to the seventh chakra in *kundalini* yoga. If you do not work on *kundalini*, if you work on the third body, then, too, you will reach this point, but it will not be known as *brahma-randhra*, and the first six chakras will not be there. You have gone through another passage. So the milestones will be different, but the end will be the same. All the seven bodies are connected with the seventh chakra, so from anywhere, one can reach it.

One must not be concerned with two passages, with two methods. Otherwise, confusion will be created and the inner energy will be diverted into two channels. Any method should channel the whole energy into one dimension. That is what my method of Dynamic Meditation does, and that is why it begins with ten minutes of deep, fast breathing.

## III

QUESTION: "Is the feeling of *kundalini* similar to the movement of a serpent?"

No, it is different. There may be a person who has never seen a snake. If his *kundalini* awakens, he cannot conceive of it as "serpent power." It is impossible because the symbol is not there. Then he will feel it in different ways. This has to be understood.

In the West they cannot conceive of *kundalini* as serpent power because the serpent is not a reality in their ordinary lives. It *was* in ancient India: the serpent was your neighbor, your day-to-day neighbor. And it was one of the most powerful things perceived, with the most beautiful movements. So the serpent symbol was chosen to represent the phenomenon of *kundalini*. But elsewhere, the serpent cannot be the symbol. It becomes unnatural. Snakes are not known. Then you cannot conceive of it; you cannot even imagine it.

Symbols are there . . . and they are meaningful as far as your personality is concerned, but a particular symbol is meaningful only if it is real to you, only if it fits into your mental makeup.

QUESTION: "Is *kundalini* a psychic phenomenon?"

When you ask, "Is it psychic?" the fear is there that if it is psychic it is unreal. The psychic has its own reality! Psychic means another realm of reality: the nonmaterial. In the mind, reality and materiality have become synonymous, but they are not. Reality is much greater than materiality. Materiality is only one dimension of reality. Even a dream has its own reality. It is nonmaterial, but it is not unreal; it is psychic, but do not take it as unreal. It is just another dimension of reality.

Even a thought has its own reality, though it is not material. Everything has its own reality, and there are realms of reality and grades of reality and different dimensions of reality. But in our minds materiality has become the only reality, so when we say "psychic," when we say "mental," the thing is condemned as unreal.

I am saying that *kundalini* is symbolic, it is psychic; the reality is psychic. But the symbol is something that you have given to it. It is not inherent in it.

The phenomenon is psychic. Something rises in you: there is a very forceful rising. Something goes from below toward your mind. It is a forceful penetration. You feel it, but whenever you are to express it, a symbol comes. Even if you begin to understand it, you use a symbol. And you do not only use a symbol when you express the phenomenon to others. You, yourself, cannot understand it without any symbol.

When we say "rising," this, too, is a symbol. When we say "four," this, too, is a symbol. When we say "up" and "down," these are symbols; in reality nothing is up and nothing is down.

In reality there are existential feelings, but no symbols by which to understand and express these feelings. So when you understand, a metaphor comes in. You say, "It is just like a serpent." Then it becomes just like a serpent. It assumes the form of your symbol; it begins to look like your conception. You mold it into a particular pattern; otherwise you cannot understand it.

When it comes to your mind that something has begun to open and flower, you will have to conceive of what is happening in some way. The moment thought comes in, thought brings its own category. So you will say "flowering," you will say "opening," you will say "penetration." The thing itself can be understood through so many metaphors. The metaphor depends on you; it depends on your mind. And what it depends on, depends on so many things—for example, your life experiences.

Two hundred, three hundred years from now, it is possible that there will be no snakes on earth because man kills everything that proves antagonistic to him. Then "snake" will just be a historical word, a word in books. It will not be a reality. It is not even a reality to most of the world today. Then the force will be lost; the beauty will not be there. The symbol will be dead, and you will have to conceive of *kundalini* in a new way.

It may become "an upsurge of electricity." "Electricity" will be more congenial, more appropriate to the mind than "snake." It may become "just like a jet going upward, a jet going to the moon." The speed will be more appropriate; it will be like a jet. If you can feel it, and your whole mind can conceive of it just like a jet, it will become just like a jet. The reality is something else, but the metaphor is given by you. You have chosen it because of your experiences, because it is meaningful to you.


Because yoga developed in an agricultural society, it has agricultural symbols: a flower, a snake, etc. But they are just symbols. Buddha did not even talk about *kundalini*, but if he had, he would not have talked about serpent power. Nor would Mahavira have talked about it. They came from royal families: the symbols that were congenial to other people were not congenial to them. They used other symbols.

Buddha and Mahavira came from royal palaces: the snake was not a reality there. But to the peasants it was a great reality. One could not remain unacquainted with it. And it was dangerous, too. One had to be aware of it. But to Buddha and Mahavira it was not a reality at all.

Buddha could not talk of snakes; he talked of flowers. Flowers were known to him, more known to him than to anybody else. He had seen many flowers, but only living ones. The palace gardeners were instructed by his father to see that no dying flower would be seen by him (Gautama). He was to see only young flowers, so the whole night the gardens were prepared for him. In the morning when he came, not a dead leaf, not a dead flower, could be seen, only flowers coming to life.

So flowering was a reality to him in a way in which it is not to us. Then when he came to his realization, he spoke about it as a process of flowers and flowers, opening and opening. The reality is something else, but the metaphor comes from Buddha.

These metaphors are not unreal. They are not just poetry. They correspond to your nature: you belong to them; they belong to you. The denial of symbols has proved drastic and dangerous. You have denied and denied everything that is not materially real, and rituals and symbols have taken their revenge. They come back again; they get through. They are there in your clothes, in your temples, in your poetries, your deeds. The symbols will have their revenge; they will come back. They cannot be denied because they belong to your nature.

The human mind cannot think in relative, purely abstract, terms. It cannot. Reality cannot be conceived of in terms of pure mathematics: we can only conceive of it in symbols. The connection with symbols is basic to the human character. In fact, it is only the human mind that creates symbols; animals cannot create them.

A symbol is a living picture. Whenever something inward happens you have to use outward symbols. Whenever you begin to feel something, the symbol comes automatically, and the moment the symbol comes, the force is molded into that particular symbol. In this way, *kundalini* becomes just like a snake: it becomes a serpent. You will feel it and see it. And it will be even more alive than a living snake. You will feel the *kundalini* as a snake because you cannot feel an abstraction. You cannot!

We have created idols of God because we cannot perceive an abstraction. God becomes meaningless as an abstraction. He becomes just mathematical. We know that the word "god" is not God, but we have to use the word. The word is a symbol. We know that the word "god" is a symbol, a term, and not actually God, but we will have to use it. And this is the paradox: when you know that something is not a fact, but also know that it is not a fiction (that it is a necessity, and a real one), then you must transcend the symbol. Then you must be beyond it, and you must know the beyond also.

But the mind cannot conceive of the beyond. And the mind is the only instrument you have. Through it, every conception must come to you. So you will feel the symbol: it will become real. And to another person another symbol may become as real as your symbol has become to you. Then there is controversy. To every person his symbol is authentic, real, but we are obsessed with concrete reality. It must be real to *us*, otherwise it cannot be real.

We can say, "This tape recorder is real," because it is real to us all. It has an objective reality. But yoga is concerned with *subjective* reality. Subjective reality is not as real as objective reality, but it is real in its own way.

The obsession with the objective must go. Subjective reality is as real as objective reality, but the moment you conceive of it, you give it a fragrance of your own. You give it a name of your own, you give it a metaphor of your own. And this way of perceiving it is bound to be individual. Even if someone experiences the same thing, the records will differ. Even two snakes will differ because the metaphor has come from two different individuals.

So these metaphors (i.e., that the feeling of *kundalini* is like the movement of a serpent) are just symbolic. But they correspond with reality. The same movement is there, the subtle movement, just like a snake, is there. The force is there; the golden appearance is there. And all of this corresponds to the symbol of the snake. So if that symbol is congenial to you, it is all right.

But it may not be congenial. So never say to anybody that what has happened to you is bound to happen to him. Never say that to anyone! It may be, or it may not be. The symbol is appropriate for you; it may not be for him. If this much can be understood, there is no reason for dissension.

Differences have come about because of symbols. A Mohammed cannot conceive of a Buddha's symbol. It is impossible! The environments of the two were so different. Even the word "god" can be a burden if it is not conceived of as a symbol that corresponds to your individuality.

For example, Mohammed could not conceive of God as "compassion." Compassion did not exist anywhere in his environment. Everything was so terrifying, so dangerous, that God had to be conceived of differently. Crossing from one country to the next, slaughtering; the people in Mohammed's environment could not conceive of a God that was not cruel. An uncruel God, a compassionate God, would have been unreal to them because the concept wouldn't have corresponded to their reality.

To a Hindu, God is seen through the environment. The nature is beautiful, the soil is fertile. The race is deeply rooted in the earth. Everything is flowing and flowing in a particular direction, and the movement is very slow, just like the Ganges. It is not terrifying and dangerous. So the Hindu god is bound to be a Krishna, dancing and playing on his flute. This image comes from the environment and from the racial mind and its experiences.

Everything subjective is bound to be translated, but whatever name and symbol we give to it is not unreal. It is real to us. So one must defend one's own symbol, but one must not impose one's own symbol on others. One must say, "Even if all the others are against this symbol, it is congenial to me. It comes to me naturally and spontaneously. God comes to me in this way. I do not know how He comes to others."

So there have been many ways to indicate these things, thousands and thousands of ways. But when I say it is subjective, psychic, I do not mean it is just a name. It is not just a name. To you it is a reality. It comes to you in this way, and it cannot come to you otherwise. If we do not confuse materiality with reality, and do not confuse objectivity with reality, then everything will become clear. But if you confuse them, then things become difficult to understand.

## ❧ 7 ❧

# Enlightenment: An Endless Beginning

Meditation is going inward. And the journey is endless, endless in the sense that the door opens and goes on opening . . . until the door, itself, becomes the universe. Meditation flowers, and it goes on flowering until the flowering, itself, becomes the cosmos. The journey is endless: it begins, but it never ends.

There are no degrees of enlightenment. Once it is, it is there. It is just like jumping into an ocean of feeling. You jump, you become one with it, like a drop dropping into the ocean becomes one with it. But that doesn't mean that you have known the whole ocean.

The moment is total: the moment of dropping the ego—the moment of ego elimination, the moment of egolessness—is total. It is complete. As far as you are concerned, it is perfect. But as far as the ocean is concerned (as far as the divine is concerned) it is just a beginning, and there will be no end to it.

One thing to remember: ignorance has no beginning, but it has an end. You cannot know from what point your ignorance begins. You always find it there; you are always in the midst of it. You never know the beginning: there *is* no beginning.

Ignorance has no beginning, but it ends. Enlightenment has a beginning, but it *never* ends. And both of these become one; they both *are* one. The beginning of enlightenment and the end of ignorance is a single point. It is one point, a dangerous point with two faces: one face looking toward beginningless ignorance and the other face looking at the beginning of endless enlightenment.

So you reach enlightenment, but yet you *never* reach it. You come to it, you drop into it, you become one with it, but, still, a vast unknown remains. And that is the beauty of it. That is the mystery of it.

If everything was known in enlightenment, there would be no mystery. If everything became known, the whole thing would become ugly. Then there would be no mystery; everything would be dead. So enlightenment is not "knowing" in this sense. It is not knowing as a suicide. It is knowing in the sense that it is an opening into greater mysteries. "Knowing" then means that you have known the mystery, you have become aware of the mystery. It is not that you have solved it: it is not that there is a mathematical formula and now everything is known. Rather, the knowing of enlightenment means that you have come to a point where the mystery has become ultimate.

You have known that this is the ultimate mystery; you have known it as a mystery. Now it has become so mysterious that you cannot hope to solve it. Now you leave all hope. But it is not despair; it is not hopelessness. It is just understanding the nature of the mystery.

The mystery is such that it is insoluble; the mystery is such that the very effort to solve it is absurd. The mystery is such that to try to solve it through the intellect is meaningless. You have come to the limit of your thinking. Now there is no thinking at all. And knowing begins.

But this is something very different from the knowing of science. The very word "science" means knowing, but knowing in the sense of making a mystery demystified. Religious knowing means something quite the contrary. It is not demystifying reality. Rather, all that was known before becomes mysterious again, even ordinary things about which you were confident, absolutely confident, that you knew. Now even that gate is lost. Everything, in a way, becomes gateless—endless and unsolvable.

Knowing must be conceived of in this sense: it is participating in the exclusive mystery of existence; it is saying *yes* to the mystery of life. The intellect—intellectual theory —is not there now. You are face to face with it. It is an existential encounter—not through the mind, but through *you*, the totality of you. Now you feel it from everywhere: from your body, from your eyes, from your hands, from your heart. The total personality comes in contact with the total mystery.

This is just a beginning. And the end will never be, because the end would mean demystifying it.

This is the beginning of enlightenment. There is no end to it, but this is the beginning. You can conceive of the end of ignorance, but there will be no end to this enlightened state of mind. Now you have jumped into a bottomless abyss.

You can conceive of it from so many points of view. If one comes to this state of mind through *kundalini*, it will be an endless flowering. The one thousand petals of the *sahasrar*[1] do not mean exactly one thousand: the "one thousand" simply means the greatest number. It is symbolic. This means that the petals of *kundalini* that are flowering are endless. They will go on opening and opening and opening. So you will know the first opening, but the last will never be there, because there is no limit to it.

One can come to this point through *kundalini* or one can come to it through other ways. *Kundalini* is not indispensable.

Those who reach enlightenment by other paths come to this same point, but the name will be different, the symbol will be different. You will conceive of it differently because

---

[1] The last chakra, symbolized as a thousand-petaled lotus.

what is happening cannot be described, and what is being described is not exactly what is happening.

The description is an allegory, the description is metaphoric. You can say, "It is like the flowering of a flower—though there is no flower at all. But the feeling is just as if you are a flower that is beginning to open. The same feeling of opening is there." But someone else can conceive of it differently. He can say, "It is like the opening of a door—a door that leads to the infinite, a door which goes on opening." So one can use anything.

Tantra uses sex symbols. They can use them! They say, "It is a meeting, an endless union." When Tantra says, "It is just like *maithuna* (intercourse)," what is meant is: "a meeting of individuals with the infinite—but endless, eternal."

It can be conceived of in this way, but any conception is bound to be just a metaphor.

It is symbolic; it is bound to be. But when I say "symbolic," I do not mean that a symbol has no meaning.

A symbol has meaning as far as your individuality is concerned because you conceived of it in this way. You cannot conceive of it otherwise. A person who has not loved flowers, who has not known flowering, who has passed by flowers but remained unacquainted with them, whose whole life is not concerned with the "realm of flowering," cannot feel it as a flowering. But if you feel it as a flowering, it means so many things. It means that the symbol is natural to you. It corresponds somehow to your personality.

QUESTION: "How does one *feel* after the *sahasrar* begins to open?"

After the *sahasrar* opens, there should be no feeling but inner silence and void. The feeling will be acute in the beginning—when you feel it for the first time it will be very acute—but the more you know it, the less acute it will become. The more you become one with it, the more it will lose its acuteness. Then a moment comes—and it must come—when you will not feel it at all.

Feeling is always of the new. You feel that which is strange; you do not feel that which is not strange. The strangeness is felt. If it becomes one with you and you have known it, you won't feel it, but that doesn't mean that it will not be there. It will be there, even more than before. It will go on intensifying more and more, but the feeling will be there less and less. And the moment will come when there will be no feeling. There will be no sense of "otherness," so the feeling will not be there.

When the flowering of the *sahasrar* comes for the first time, it is something other than you. It is unknown to you and you are unacquainted with it. It is something penetrating into you, or you are penetrating into it. There is a gap between you and it. But the gap will gradually drop, and you will become one with it. Now you will not see it as something happening to you. You will *become* the happening. It will go on expanding and you will become one with it.

Then you will not feel it. You will notice it, but will not feel it any more than you feel your breathing. You feel your breathing only when something new (or wrong) has happened to you, otherwise you do not feel it. You do not even feel your body unless some disease has crept in, unless you are ill. If you are completely healthy, you do not feel it: you just have it. Really, your body is more alive when you are healthy, but you do not feel it. You need not feel it; you are one with it.

QUESTION: "What happens to religious visions and other manifestations of deep meditation when the *sahasrar* opens?"

All these things will drop. All pictures will drop—visions, everything, will drop—because these things come only in the beginning. They are good signs, but they will drop away.

Before the opening of the *sahasrar* comes, many visions will come to you. These are not unreal; visions are real. But with the opening of the *sahasrar* there will be no more visions. They will not come because this "flowering experience" is the peak experience for the mind. It is the last experience for the mind; beyond this, there will be no mind.

All that is happening beforehand is happening to the mind, but the moment you transcend mind, there will be nothing. When the mind ceases, there will be neither *mudras* (outward expressions of psychic transformation) nor visions, neither flowers nor serpents. There will be nothing at all, because beyond mind there is no metaphor. Beyond mind the reality is so pure that there is no otherness; beyond mind the reality is so total that it cannot be divided into the experiencer and the experienced.

Within the mind, everything is divided into two. You experience something (you may call it anything; the name doesn't matter), but the division between the experiencer and the experienced, the knower and the known, remains. The duality remains.

But these visions are good signs because they come only in the last stages. They come only when the mind is to drop; they come only when the mind is to die. Particular *mudras* and visions are symbolic only, symbolic in the sense that they indicate a coming death for the mind. When the mind dies there will be nothing left. Or, everything will be left, but the divisions between the experiencer and the experienced will not be there.

*Mudras,* visions—particularly visions—are experiences. They indicate certain stages. It is just like when you say, "I was dreaming." We can take it for granted that you were asleep because dreaming indicates sleep. And if you say, "I was daydreaming," then, too, you have dropped into a sort of sleep because dreaming is possible only when the mind, the conscious mind, has gone to sleep. So dreaming is indicative of sleep. In the same way, *mudras* and visions are indicative of a particular state.

You may see visions of certain figures. You can identify

them. And these figures, too, will be different for different
individuals. The figure of Shiva cannot come to a Christian
mind. It cannot: there is no possibility of it coming. But
Jesus will come. That will be the last vision for a Christian
mind. And it is very valuable!

The last vision to be seen is of a central religious figure.
This central figure will be the last vision. To a Christian
(and by Christian I mean one who has imbibed the language of Christianity, the symbols of Christianity, one
whose Christianity has entered his blood and bones from
his very childhood), the figure of Jesus on the cross will be
the last. The knower, the experiencer, is still present, but
at the very end there will be the Savior. It has been experienced; you cannot deny it. In the last moment of the mind
(of the dying mind), in the end, Jesus is there.

But to a Jain, Jesus cannot come; to a Buddhist, Jesus
cannot come. To a Buddhist, the figure of Buddha will be
there. The moment the *sahasrar* opens—with the opening
of the *sahasrar*—Buddha will be there.

That is why Buddha is visualized on a flower. The flower
was never placed there for the real Buddha—under his
feet the flower was not there—but the flower is placed
there in statues because statues are not real replicas of
Gautama Buddha. They are the representation of the last
vision to come into the mind. When the mind drops into the
eternal, Buddha is seen in this way: on the flower.

That is why Vishnu is placed on a flower. This flower is
symbolic of the *sahasrar,* and Vishnu is the last figure to be
seen by a Hindu mind. Buddha, Vishnu, Jesus, are archetypes—what Jung calls "archetypes."

The mind cannot conceive of anything abstractly, so the
last effort of the mind to understand reality will be through
the symbol that has been most important to it. This peak
experience of the mind is the mind's last experience. The
peak is always the end; the peak means the beginning of
the end. The peak is the death, so the opening of the
*sahasrar* is the peak experience of the mind, the utmost
that is possible with the mind, the last that is possible with

the mind. The last figure—the centralmost figure: the deepest one, the archetype—will come.

And it will be real! When I say "vision" many will deny that it is real. They will say that it cannot be real because they think the word "vision" means illusionary, but it will be more real than reality itself.

Even if the whole world denies it, you will not be ready to accept the denial. You will say, "It is more real to me than the whole world. A stone is not so real as the figure I have seen. It is real. It is perfectly real." But the reality is subjective; the reality is colored by your mind. The experience is real, but the metaphor is given by you, so Christians will give one metaphor, Buddhists will give another, Hindus will give another.

QUESTION: "Does transcendence come with the opening of the *sahasrar*?"

No, transcendence is beyond the opening. But enlightenment has two connotations. One, the dying mind (the ending mind, the mind that is going to die, the mind that has come to its peak, the mind that has come to its last) conceives of the enlightenment. But a barrier has come and now the mind will not go beyond this. The mind knows that it is ending, and with its ending the mind also knows the end of suffering. The mind also knows the end of division, the mind also knows the end of the conflict that was there. All this ends, and the mind conceives of this as enlightenment. But it is still the mind that is conceiving of it. So this is enlightenment conceived of by the mind.

When the mind has gone, then the real enlightenment comes. Now you have transcended, but you cannot talk about it, you cannot say anything about it. That is why Lao-tzu says, "All that can be said cannot be true. That which can be said will not be true, and the Truth cannot be said. Only this much can be said, and only this much is true."

And this is the last statement of the mind. This last statement has meaning, much meaning, but it is not transcendental. The meaning is still a limitation of the mind. It is still mental; it is still conceived of through the mind.

It is just like a flame, a flame in a lamp that is just going to die. Darkness is descending: the darkness is coming, it is encircling nearer and nearer. And the flame is dying, the flame has come to the very end of its existence. It says, "Now there is darkness," and it goes out of existence. Now the darkness has become full and complete. But the last statement of the dying flame was known by the flame: the darkness was not complete because the flame was there, the light was there. The darkness was conceived of by the light.

The light cannot really conceive of darkness. The light can only conceive of its own limitations, and beyond that is darkness. The darkness was coming nearer and nearer, and the light was going to die. It could make its last statement, "I am going to die," and then the darkness was there. The darkness had been coming and coming and coming. Then the light made its last statement and dropped, and the darkness was complete. So the statement was true, but not the Truth.

There is a difference between true and Truth. Truth is not a statement. The flame has gone, and darkness is there. This is Truth. Now there is no statement: darkness is there. The statement was true, it was not untrue. It was true: darkness was coming, enclosing, encircling. But, still, the statement was made by light. And a statement made by light about darkness can, at the most, be true—*not* Truth.

When the mind is not there, the Truth is known: when the mind is not, the Truth is. And when the mind is, you can be more true, but not Truth; you can be less untrue, but not Truth. The last statement that the mind can make will be the least untrue, but that is all that can be said.

So between enlightenment as conceived of by the mind and enlightenment as such, there is much difference, though it is not great. With a dying flame, there is not a single moment before it will die. Then the flame dies, and simultaneously the darkness comes. There is not a single moment between the two conditions, but the difference between them is great.

A dying mind will see visions in the end—visions of that which is coming. But these will be visions conceived of through metaphors, pictures, archetypes. The mind cannot conceive of anything else. The mind is trained in symbols, nothing else. There are religious symbols, artistic symbols, aesthetic, mathematical, and scientific symbols, but these are all symbols. This is how the mind is trained.

A Christian will see Jesus, but a mathematician who is dying, a mind that has been trained nonreligiously, may see nothing in the last moment but a mathematical formula. It may be a zero or it may be a symbol of infinity, but it will not be Jesus, not be Buddha. And a Picasso dying may just see an abstract flow of colors at the last moment. That will be the divine to him. He cannot conceive of the divine otherwise.

So the end of the mind is the end of symbols and at the end the mind will use the most significant symbol that it knows. And after that, because there is no mind, there will be no symbols.

This is one reason why neither Buddha nor Mahavira talked about symbols. They said that there was no use talking about them since they are all below enlightenment. Buddha would not talk about symbols, and because of this he said that there were eleven questions that should not be asked to him. It was declared that no one should ask these eleven questions. And they should not be asked because they could not be truly answered: a metaphor would have to be used.

Buddha used to say, "I would not like to use any metaphor. But if you ask and I do not reply, you will not feel good. It will not be gentlemanly; it will not be courteous. So, please, do not ask these questions. If I reply to you it will be courteous, but untrue. So do not put me in this dilemma. As far as the Truth is concerned, I cannot use a symbol; I can use symbols only to approximate non-Truth or approximate Truth."

So there will be persons who will not use any metaphors, any visions. They will deny everything because Truth conceived of by the mind cannot be enlightenment itself. These are two different things. The conceptions of the mind will go when the mind goes, and then enlightenment will be there, but without mind.

So the enlightened personality is without mind—a "no mind" personality: living, but without any conceptions; doing, but not thinking about it; loving, but without the concept of love; breathing, but without any meditation. So living will be moment to moment and one with the Total, but mind will not be there in between. The mind divides, and now there will be no division.

## ∽ 8 ∽

## Initiation to a Master:
## The Ultimate Technique

Man exists as if in sleep. Man *is* asleep. Whatever is known as waking is also a sleep. Initiation means to be in intimate contact with one who is awakened.[1] Unless you are in intimate contact with one who is awakened, it is impossible to come out of your sleep because the mind is even capable of dreaming that it is awake. The mind can dream that now there is no more sleep.

When I say that man is asleep, this has to be understood. We are dreaming continuously, twenty-four hours a day. In the night we are closed to the outward world, dreaming inside. In the day our senses are opened toward the outside world, but the dream continues inside. Close your eyes

---

[1] Although there are hundreds of meditation techniques in existence and although Bhagwan Shree, himself, is constantly devising new techniques, it seems as though the major "function" of techniques is to open one up to the point where initiation to a master becomes possible. Then, many things can happen. Life, itself, becomes a technique; the world, itself, becomes an esoteric school.

The concept of initiation and surrender to a master is a difficult one for the Western mind to accept or understand. In this discourse, Bhagwan Shree explains what initiation means and why it is the "ultimate technique."

for a moment, and you can again be in a dream. It is a continuity inside. You are aware of the outside world, but that awareness is not without the dreaming mind. It is imposed on the dreaming mind, but, inside, the dream continues. That is why we are not seeing what is real even when we are "supposedly" awake. We impose our dreams on reality. We never see what *is;* we always see our projections.

If I look at you and there is a dream in me, you will become an object of projection. I will project my dream on you, and whatever I understand about you will be mixed with my dream, with my projection. When I love you, you appear to me something quite different; when I do not love you, you appear to me completely different. You are not the same because I have just used you as a screen and projected my dreaming mind on you.

When I love you, the dream is different, so you appear different. When I do not love you, you are the same—the screen is the same—but the projection is different. Now I am using you as a screen for another dream of mine. Again, the dream can change; again I can love you. Then you will appear different to me. We never see what is; we are always seeing our own dream projected on what is.

I am not the same to each one of you. Each one projects onto me something else. I am one only as far as I, myself, am concerned. And if I myself am dreaming, then, even for me, I am different each moment because for each moment my interpretation will differ.

But if I am awakened, then I am the same. Buddha said that the test of an enlightened one is that he is always the same, just like the sea water. Anywhere, everywhere, it is salty.

You have around yourself a filmy enclosure of projections, ideas, notions, conceptions, interpretations. You are a projector going on and on, projecting things that are nowhere, only inside you, and the whole becomes a screen. So you can never be aware, by yourself, that you are in a deep sleep.

There was a Sufi saint, Hijira. An angel appeared in his dream and told him that he should save as much water as possible from the well because the following morning all the water in the world was going to be poisoned by the devil and everyone who would drink it would become mad.

So the whole night the fakir saved as much water as possible. And the phenomenon really happened! Everyone became mad the next morning. But no one knew the whole city had become mad. Only the fakir was not mad, but the whole city talked as if he had gone mad. He knew what had happened, but no one believed him, so he went on drinking his water and remained alone.

But he could not continue that way. The whole city was living in an altogether different world. No one listened to him, and finally there was a rumor that he would be caught and sent to prison. They said that he was mad!

One morning they came to get hold of him. Either he would be treated as if he was ill, or he would have to go to prison, but he could not be allowed freedom. He had become absolutely mad! What he said could not be understood; he spoke a different language.

The fakir was at a loss to understand. He tried to help the others to remember their past, but they had forgotten everything. They did not know anything of the past, anything about what existed before that maddening morning. They could not understand. The fakir had become incomprehensible to them.

They surrounded his house and caught hold of him. Then the fakir said, "Give me one moment more. I shall treat myself." He ran to the common well, drank the water, and became all right. Now the whole city was happy: the fakir was okay now; now he was not mad. Really, he had gone mad, but now he was part and parcel of a common world.

If everyone else is asleep, you will never even be aware that you are asleep. If everyone is mad, and you are mad, you will never be aware of it.

By initiation it is meant that you have surrendered to someone who is awakened. You say, "I do not understand, I cannot understand, I am part of the world that is mad and asleep. I am dreaming all the time." This feeling can come even from a sleepy person because the sleep is not always deep. It wavers, becoming very deep at times and then coming up and becoming very shallow. Just like ordinary sleep is a fluctuation of so many levels, so many planes, the metaphysical sleep that I am talking about also fluctuates. Sometimes you are just on the border line, very near to the Buddha. Then you can understand something of what Buddha is talking about, what he is saying. It will never be exactly what was said, but at least you have had a glimpse of the Truth.

So a person who is on the border of metaphysical sleep will want to be initiated. He can hear something, he can understand something, he sees something. Everything is as if in a mist, but, still, he feels something. So he can approach a person who is awakened and surrender himself. This much can be done by a sleepy person. This surrendering means he understands that something quite different from his sleep is happening. Somewhere he feels it. He cannot know it correctly, but he feels it.

Whenever a Buddha passes, those who are on the border line of sleep can recognize that there is something different about this man. He behaves differently, he speaks differently, he lives differently, he walks differently. Something has happened to him. Those who are on the border line can feel it. But they are asleep, and this borderline awareness is not permanent. They may fall back into sleep at any moment. . . .

So before they fall into a deeper unconsciousness, they can surrender to the awakened one. This is initiation from the side of the initiated. He says, "I cannot do anything myself. I am helpless. And I know that if I do not surrender this moment, I may again go into deep sleep. Then it will be impossible to surrender." So there are moments that cannot be lost, and one who loses those moments may not be able to get them again for centuries, for lifetimes, because it is not in one's hands when one will come again to the border line. It happens for so many reasons that are beyond your control.

On the part of the initiated, initiation is a total letting go: a complete trust, a complete surrender. It can never be partial. If you surrender partially, you are not surrendering; you are deceiving yourself. There can be no partial surrender because in partial surrender you are withholding something and that withholding may push you again into a deep sleep. That nonsurrendering part will prove fatal. Any moment you may again be in deep sleep.

Surrender is always total. That is why faith was required and always will be required in initiation. Faith is required as a total condition, as a total requirement. And the moment you surrender totally, things begin to change. Now you cannot go back to your dream life. This surrendering shatters the whole projection, the whole projecting mind, because this projecting mind is tethered to the ego, it cannot live without the ego. The ego is the main center of it, the base. If you surrender, you have surrendered the very base. You have given up completely.

Initiation is just a person who is asleep asking for help to be awakened. He surrenders to one who is awake. It is very simple; the thing is not very complex. When you go to a Buddha, to a Jesus, or to a Mohammed and surrender yourself, what you are surrending is your sleep, your dreams. You cannot surrender anything more, because you *are* nothing more. You surrender this. Your sleep, your dreaming, your whole nonsense of the past you surrender.

So from the initiated it is a surrendering of the past, and from the one who initiates you it is a responsibility for the future. He becomes responsible . . . and only he *can* be responsible. You can never be responsible: how can one who is asleep be responsible? Responsibility comes with awakening. This is really a fundamental law of life: one who is asleep is not responsible even for himself, and one who is awakened is responsible even for others.

If you come to him and surrender to him, then he becomes particularly responsible for you. So Krishna could say to Arjuna, "Leave everything. Come to me; surrender at my feet," and Jesus could say, "I am the Truth, I am the door, I am the gate. Come to me; pass through me. I will be the witness on the last day of your judgment. I will answer for you."

This is all analogical. Every day is the day of judgment, and every moment is the moment of judgment. There is not going to be any last day. These are just the terms that could be understood by the people to whom Jesus was speaking. He was saying, "I will be responsible for you, and I will answer for you when the divine asks. I will be there as a witness. Surrender to me; I will be your witness."

This is a great responsibility. No one who is asleep can take it because even to be responsible for yourself becomes difficult in sleep. You can be responsible for others only when you no longer need to be responsible for yourself, when you are unburdened completely, when you are no more. So, only one who is "no more" can initiate you; otherwise, no one can initiate you. No particular individual can initiate anyone, and if that happens (and it happens so many times, it is happening every day—those who are themselves asleep initiate others who are asleep—the blind leading the blind), both fall into the ditch.

No one who is asleep can initiate anyone, but the ego wants to initiate. This egoistic attitude has proved fatal and very dangerous. The whole initiation, the whole mystery of it, the whole beauty of it, became ugly because of those who were not entitled to initiate. Only one who has no ego inside, who has no sleep inside, who has no dream inside, can initiate. Otherwise, initiation is the greatest sin.

In the old days, to take initiation was not easy. It was the most difficult thing. One had to wait for years to be initiated. Even for his whole life one might wait. This waiting was a testing ground; it was a discipline.

For example, Sufis would only initiate you when you had waited for a particular period. You had to wait—without questioning—for the moment when the teacher, himself, would say that it was time. The teacher might be a shoemaker. If you wanted to be initiated, you would have to help him for years in shoemaking. And not even the relevance of the shoemaking could be questioned! So for five years you would just be waiting, helping the teacher in shoemaking. He would never talk of prayer or meditation, he would never talk of anything except shoemaking. You have waited for five years . . . but this is a meditation! And it is no ordinary meditation. You would be cleansed through it.

This simple waiting, this unquestioned waiting, would make the ground ready for complete surrender. Only after a long waiting could initiation happen, but then surrender was easy and the master could take responsibility for the disciple.

Now the whole thing has become different. No one is ready to wait. We have become so time conscious that we cannot wait for a single moment. And because of this time consciousness, initiation has become impossible. You cannot be initiated. You run past Buddha and you ask him, "Will you initiate me?" You are running; you meet Buddha on the street while running. Even during this utterance of four or five words you have been running.

This whole running of the modern mind is because of the fear of death. For the first time man is so fearful of death because for the first time man has become absolutely unaware of the deathless. We are only conscious of the body that is going to die; we are not conscious of the inner consciousness that is deathless.

In ancient days there were people who were conscious of the deathless and because of their consciousness, their deathlessness, they created an atmosphere in which there was no hurry. Then initiation was easy. Then waiting was easy. Then surrender was easy. Then for the master to assume responsibility for the disciple was easy. These things have all become difficult now but, still, there is no alternative: initiation is needed.

If you are in a hurry, I will give initiation to you in your running state because otherwise there will be no initiation. I cannot ask you to wait as a precondition. I must initiate you first and then prolong your waiting in so many ways. Through so many devices, I will persuade you to wait. If I tell you first, "Wait five years and then I will initiate you," you cannot wait, but if I initiate you this very moment then I will be able to create devices for your waiting.

So let it be like this; it makes no difference. The process will be the same. Because you cannot wait, I change. I will allow you to wait afterward. I will create so many devices, so many techniques, just to make you wait. Because you cannot wait unoccupied, I will create techniques for you, I will give you something to play with. You can play with these techniques. It will become a waiting. Then you will be ready for a second initiation, which would have been the first in the old days. The first initiation is a formal one; the second one will be informal. It will be like a happening. You will not ask me, I will not give you. It will happen; in the innermost being it will happen. And you will know it when it happens.

Surrender from the disciple, responsibility from the teacher: that is the bridge. And whenever you are able to surrender, the teacher will come. The teacher is there. Teachers have always been in existence. The world has never lacked teachers; it has always lacked disciples. But no teacher can begin anything unless someone surrenders. So whenever you have a moment to surrender, do not lose it. Even if you do not find anyone to whom to surrender, then just surrender to existence. But whenever there is a moment to surrender, do not lose it, because then you are on the border line, you are in between sleep and waking. Just surrender!

If you can find someone to whom to surrender that is good, but if you cannot find anyone, just surrender to the universe. And the teacher will appear; he will come. He comes whenever there is surrender. You become vacant, you become empty, and the spiritual force rushes toward you and fills you.

So always remember that whenever you feel like surrendering, do not lose the moment. It may not come again or it may come only after centuries and lives have been unnecessarily wasted. Whenever the moment comes, just surrender.

Surrender to the divine, to anything—even to a tree— because the real thing is not to whom you surrender: the real thing is surrendering. Surrender to a tree, and the tree will become a teacher to you. Surrender to a stone, and the stone will become a god. The real thing is surrendering. And whenever there is surrendering, one always appears who becomes responsible for you. This is what is meant by initiation.

# ∿ 9 ∿

## *Sannyas:* Dying to the Past

### I

To me, *sannyas* is not something very serious. Life, it-self, is not very serious, and one who is serious is always dead. Life is just an overflowing energy without any pur-pose, so to me, *sannyas* is to lead life purposelessly. Live life as a play and not as a work. If you can take this whole life just as a play, you are a *sannyasin;* then you have re-nounced. Renunciation is not leaving the world, but chang-ing the attitude.[1]

That is why I can initiate anyone into *sannyas*. To me, initiation, itself, is a play. And I will not ask for any qualifications—whether you are qualified or not—because qualifications are asked when something serious is done.

---

[1] Bhagwan Shree initiates his disciples into the ancient tradi-tion of *sannyas*. But his *sannyas,* unlike the traditional, is not a social renunciation; it is not a renunciation of the world. Rather, it is a renunciation of one's attachment to the world. A new name, new clothes, and a *mala* (a string of beads with a locket containing Bhagwan Shree's picture attached to it) are given to the disciple to remind him that now he is no longer the old. He has begun a fresh life, he has been reborn.

Whoever is ready to take the jump, Bhagwan Shree is ready to push. He says, "The miracle is not that someone achieves. The miracle is that he begins."

Just by existing everyone is qualified enough to play, and
even if he is unqualified to be a *sannyasin* it makes no
difference—because the whole thing is just a play!

So I will not ask for any qualifications. And my *sannyas*
does not involve any obligation either. The moment you
are a *sannyasin* (or a *sannyasini*) you are totally at freedom. It means that you have taken a decision, and this is
the last decision: to live in indecision, to live in freedom.

The moment you are initiated into *sannyas*, you are
initiated into an uncharted, unplanned, future. Now you
are not tethered by the past. You are free to live! So a
*sannyasin*, to me, is a person who decides to live to the
utmost, to the optimum, to the maximum. Moment to
moment you live. Moment to moment you act. Each moment is complete in itself. You do not decide how to act.
The moment comes to you, and you act. There is no pre-
determination; there is no preplan.

*Sannyas* means living moment to moment, with no com-
mitments to the past. If I give you a *mala* and if I give you
new clothes, this is only for your remembrance: to remind
you that now you do not have to make any decisions, now
you are no longer the old. When this awareness becomes
so deep that you do not need to remember it, then throw
the robe, then throw the *mala*. But not until the awareness
becomes so deep that now, even in sleep, you know that
you are a *sannyasin*. So a new name, a new robe, a *mala*—
these are just devices to help you, to help you toward
freedom, to help you toward total being, to help you toward
total action.

*Sannyas* means that you have come to realize that you
are a seed, a potentiality. Now you have taken the decision
to grow . . . and this is the last decision. To decide to
grow is a great renunciation—renunciation of the security
of the seed, renunciation of the "wholeness" of the seed.
But this security is at a very great cost. The seed is dead;
it is only potentially living. Unless it becomes a tree, unless
it grows, it is dead—only potentially living. And as far as
I know, human beings, unless they decide to grow, unless

they take a jump into the unknown, are like seeds: dead, closed.

To be a *sannyasin* is to take a decision to grow, to take a decision to move into the unknown, to take a decision to live in indecision. It is a jump into the unknown. It is not a religion and it is not bound to any religion. It is religiousness itself.

## II

QUESTION: "At first sight, *sannyas* appears to be something that limits one's activities. Why does one have to change one's clothes to orange, why should one have to change his appearance, since *sannyas* is something that is within rather than without?"

*Sannyas* is not negative. The very word denotes negativity, but it is not a pure negativity. It means to leave something, but it is only leaving something because you have gained something else.

Something has to be left. It is not that leaving anything is meaningful in itself, but that it creates a space for something new to come in. Negativity is just creating a space . . . and if you are to grow, you need space.

As we are, we have no space within. We are so filled with unnecessary things and thoughts. *Sannyas,* in its negative aspect, means just creating a space—throwing aside the trivial, the useless, the meaningless, so you can grow inside.

Growth is decay, but growth is positive also. And I say emphatically that *sannyas* is positive! Negativity is just the clearing: it is just clearing the ground for the growth to come in. Negativity is only something without—something outside—and the growth is inside. The positivity is at the center, and the negativity is at the periphery.

And, really, nothing can exist that is simply negative or simply positive. That is impossible because these are two polarities. Existence exists in between: these are the two banks between which existence flows. No river can exist with one bank, and neither can existence. When emphasis is given to only one side or to one bank or to one pole, it becomes fallacious. But when you accept the total, then there is no emphasis on anything. You just accept the two polarities, and then you grow within. And you use both of them as a dialectic within which to move.

*Sannyas* is understood as being negative. Its connotation has become negative because you have to begin with the negative, you have to begin from the periphery. This must be understood because *sannyas* is inner. Something is to grow on the inside, so why must you begin from the outside? When you have to grow inside, why not begin from the inside?

But you cannot begin from the inside because, as you are, you are on the periphery, on the outside. You have to begin from the point where you are; you cannot begin from somewhere where you are not.

For example, health is something inner; it grows. But you are diseased and ill, so we have to begin with your disease, not with your health. We have to negate the disease. By negating disease we are only creating space for the health to grow in. But the beginning is negative.

Medical science has no definition of health. They cannot have it. All that they can have is a definition of what disease is and a science of how to negate it. Health remains indefinable and disease is negatively defined because you have to begin with disease. You cannot begin with health. When there is health, you need not begin at all.

So if you have the inner space, you do not need *sannyas*. *Sannyas* is to negate the *samsar* (the world), the disease. When I say *samsar*, I do not mean that the world is diseased. Rather, I mean the world that you have created around you. Everyone is living in a world of his own making.

I do not deny the world that exists outside. It cannot be denied; it is there. But you have a fantasy world, a dream world, around you and that dream world has become you.

The periphery has become your center and you have forgotten the center completely. So when one begins, one has to deny this dreaming world, since this denial is the beginning.

This becomes negative, and *sannyas* then appears to be negative. We give it a negative connotation because it means to negate this dream world. So *sannyas* is really medicinal: it is just a medicine to deny the disease. When the disease is negated, the possibility arises for the inner to grow. So *sannyas* is just to create a situation.

You must understand clearly that when I say "to deny the world," I do not mean the world that exists, but, rather, the world that every individual creates around him. Because of this dream world, we cannot know the world that really exists. This constant dreaming becomes a barrier. It becomes a double barrier: you cannot go inside (there is something existential there); you cannot go outside (there is something existential there also). You are stuck to your dreaming mind and you cannot proceed either way.

A miracle happens when this dreaming barrier is annihilated. There is no longer any disease. You begin to exist in two worlds simultaneously, only now they are no longer two because the barrier was the thing that divided them. You become existential inside, and you become existential outside. So this is why a negative approach is chosen.

How does this—the taking of *sannyas*—affect your behavior? There are two possibilities: one is to change your behavior *consciously* and the other is to change your consciousness consciously. Behavior is nothing but consciousness expressed, but if you start with behavior, you may continue with the old consciousness. You can adjust any new behavior to the old consciousness and then behavior changes outwardly, but nothing really changes.

For example, your consciousness can continue to be violent, but you can be nonviolent in your behavior. You can be nonviolent in your behavior, but your consciousness continues to be the same as it was when your behavior was violent. Now you begin to suppress your consciousness.

You *have* to suppress it because you have to pose a behavior that is not in the consciousness. The consciousness has to be suppressed, and when you suppress consciousness, you create the unconscious in yourself.

When you begin to behave in ways that your consciousness is not ready to behave in, then you are denying part of your consciousness, putting it off. This part becomes your unconscious, and it becomes more powerful than your consciousness because you have to continue denying your behavior. You become false; a false personality is created. This false personality exists only up to the point where the unconscious exists. So if you try to change your behavior directly, you will become less and less conscious and more and more unconscious.

A person who has become completely behavior oriented will just be automatic. Only the very small consciousness that is needed to work automatically will be there. Otherwise, the whole mind will become unconscious. And this unconscious mind is the disease of your consciousness.

You can begin by changing your behavior as more or less "ethical" persons ordinarily do. The so-called religions begin with changing your behavior. But I do not begin with changing your behavior; I begin with changing your consciousness. Because, really, consciousness is the behavior. That is the behavior; this outward behavior is meaningless. So begin with changing your consciousness.


That is why my emphasis is on meditation and not on behavior. Meditation changes your consciousness. First, it destroys the barrier between your conscious and unconscious. You become more fluid; you begin to move in a less fixed way; you become one with your consciousness. So meditation first has to destroy the barrier inside. And the destruction of the barrier means the expansion of your consciousness.

You must become more conscious. So the first thing is to be more conscious in whatsoever you are doing. I am not interested in the content of your doing, but with the consciousness of your doing. Be more conscious in doing it!

For example, if you are violent, the so-called moralists and religious people will say, "Be nonviolent, cultivate nonviolence." I will not say this. I will say: Be violent, but now be *consciously* violent. Do not change your behavior. Be conscious about your violence and you will find that you cannot be consciously violent, because the more you become conscious, the less is the possibility of being violent.

Violence has a built-in process. It can exist only when you are not aware. Your very awareness changes the whole thing: you cannot be violent if you are aware. Unawareness is a must for violence to exist or for anger or for sex or for anything that one wants to change in the behavior.

The greater the built-in mechanism, the more you are unaware of what you are doing and the more you can do things that are evil. When I say a thing is evil, I do not mean the content of it. I say a thing is evil when it creates unconsciousness unnecessarily: that is my definition. I do not say violence is bad because you will kill someone. I say violence is bad because you cannot be violent without·unconsciousness. That unconsciousness is the evil because that unconsciousness is the background, the basis, of all ignorance, of all dreams, of all illusions, of all the nonsense that we can create. Evil is nothing more than an unconscious mind.

So for one who is a *sannyasin*—for one who has taken *sannyas*—I emphasize that you do whatever you are doing. Do not change your behavior; change your consciousness. Do whatever you are doing consciously. Be angry; anger is no cause for worry. But be angry *consciously*. This consciousness becomes transformation and your whole behavior is changed. You cannot remain the same. And now this change is not just a change in behavior. It becomes a change of your being also, not only of your doing.

You do not have to create a false personality—a mask. You can be completely at ease with yourself. But this "being at ease with yourself" can come only when you have become totally conscious. Tension is there because you are living with masks: you are violent and you have to be nonviolent; you are angry and you have to be non-angry; you are sexual and you have to be nonsexual. This creates tensions, this creates anxieties. This is the anguish—the whole anguish. You have to be something which you are not, so you are bound to be in a deep anxiety constantly. This "being something which you are not" is withering and dissipating your whole life energy in tensions, in conflicts. Really, conflict is never with someone else. It is always with yourself.

So I emphasize *being at ease with yourself*. And you can only be at ease when your behavior is conscious. So be conscious: meditate and be conscious in your behavior. Then things will begin to change without your knowing it. You will be different because of your different consciousness.

You ask why I emphasize the changing of dress, the changing of name—these outward things. They are so outward, the most outward things.

As I know man to be—as man exists—he is clothes. As man is, clothes are very significant. You give a military uniform to a person and his very face changes, his very attitude. Something different arises within him. Look at a policeman when he is in civilian dress and when he is in his uniform. He is not the same man at all. Why?

Outward things create a change inside because you are nothing *but* the outside. There is no such thing as "inside" right now. Gurdjieff used to say a very meaningful thing: that as you are now, you have no soul. He was both right and wrong. You have a soul, but you do not know about it.

You are the outside, and so clothes are very meaningful. Because of clothes a person becomes beautiful and because of clothes a person becomes ugly. Because of clothes he becomes respected; because of clothes he is *not* respected. A judge has to wear certain clothes—a Supreme

Court justice has to use a particular robe—and no one asks why. With that robe he is a Supreme Court justice; without that robe he is no one.

This is how man is. When I look at a man he is more his clothes than his mind. And this is as it should be because we belong to the body; we are identified with the body. This identification with the body becomes an identification with the clothes.

If I ask a man to wear a woman's dress and walk down the street, do you think that this is just going to be a change of clothes? It is not! Firstly, he will not be ready to do it. No man will be ready to do it. Why this unreadiness, why this resistance? It is only a change of clothes and clothes are neither male nor female. How can clothes be male or female?

But, in fact, clothes are not simply clothes. Psychologically they have become identified as either male or female. What type of minds do we have that even *clothes* have gender?

If you move in a female dress, you will feel feminine. Your gestures will be different; your walking will be different; your eyes will be different; your very awareness of what is happening on the street will be different. You will be aware of things that you have never been aware of before even though you may have walked down the same street your whole life. Because everything about you will be different, others will look at you differently . . . and you will react differently to their looking. You won't be the same person.

So when I say that clothes are our outside, they only *appear* to be outside. They have gone deeply inward; they have penetrated inside. So I emphasize a change of clothes. A readiness to change the clothes is a readiness to throw the old mind, which was associated with the clothes. A readiness to make this change is a readiness to change your identity.

When someone resists the change in clothes I know why he is resisting. He goes on asking, "Why do you emphasize the clothes?" But I am not emphasizing them. *He* is emphasizing them. He keeps saying, "Why must you emphasize the clothes? They are just the outside. What is the difference if I continue wearing my old things?"

I am not emphasizing the clothes at all; he is emphasizing them. And he is not even aware that he is resisting. Then I ask him, "Why are you resisting?" If someone comes to me and is not at all resistant, I may not even ask him to change his clothes. If I ask him to change his clothes and he says "Okay," then I may not tell him to change his clothes because he is not identified with clothes really.

So I may tell you to change your clothes: to use a particular type of robe, a particular color. The moment you change your clothes, *you* change. Sometimes you are this color, sometimes that color. If I just ask you to change your type of clothes without specifying any particular color, that may not be a change at all because you have changed your type of clothing so continuously. So the change can happen only with an unchanging robe. Then there is really a change. If I give you an unchanging robe, then the change in you can happen.

Why do we change clothes really? It is a deep thing, not just an outward one. Why are we bored with one style, one color, one type of cloth? Why are we bored? The mind is always asking for something new, something different. We go on asking how to stop our mind from running continuously and yet we go on always feeding it the new. We go on asking how to stop our constant, wavering mind—how to bring it to a standstill, how to be silent—but we go on feeding it in subtle ways. We go on changing clothes, we go on changing things—we go on changing everything. We are bored with anything that remains constant. But the more the mind is fed changes, the more the mind is fed.

With a nonchanging robe, for the first time your mind has to fight daily (every moment) with the identity that it wants to change. And if you are at ease with a nonchanging robe, soon you will be at ease with a nonchanging world. This is just a beginning. The more you are at ease with something nonchanging, the more the mind will be able to stop.

So the emphasis is to become more and more at ease with the nonchanging. Only then can you come to the eternal. With a mind that is asking for constant change, how can you come to the eternal? You have to begin with the nonchanging.

Somewhere, with this nonchanging of your clothes, you will become unaware of clothes. When you use the same robe and the same color, you will soon become unaware of clothing. Moving on the streets you will become unaware of the clothing shops. Your consciousness of these things will just drop because it is the mind that notices them. And if your mind is again looking at clothes and at the shops, be aware of it. What is your mind asking for?

We feel this constant changing of clothes to be something beautiful. But, in a nonchanging robe you can attain a graceful beauty that can never be attained with a changing robe. With a changing robe you are hiding ugliness, nothing else, but with a nonchanging robe everything about you *as you are* is revealed.

When you change your clothes, others become aware of your clothes. That is why everyone always asks about your new clothes. But when you are constantly in one robe, no one asks about your clothes. The asking drops. Then one looks at *you*, not at your clothes.

This is a fact that every woman knows. If she wears ornaments and nice clothes, you become aware of the ornaments and clothes and forget the woman. This is hiding. Clothes are not expressers, but hiders. And the more precious the ornament the more deeply you can hide because others become more attentive to the ornament.

With a diamond on my finger, my finger is hidden. The diamond has so much appeal and the luster of it somehow becomes associated with my finger, but it is not part of the finger at all. A bare or naked finger is exposed as it is. If it is beautiful, then it is beautiful; if it is ugly, then it is ugly.

A person who is not hiding his ugliness has a beauty of his own. A person who is not hiding anything has a certain grace . . . and this grace comes only when you are totally naked. When you are at ease a certain grace comes, and even an ugly face becomes beautiful. But with hiding, even a beautiful face becomes ugly.

To me, beauty is to be as you really are: to be *as you are* and totally relaxed in it. If you are ugly, you are ugly and at ease with it. Then a subtle beauty begins to come to your face. With relaxation and ease, a subtle flow begins to manifest. It is not coming from the diamond; now it is coming from your inner self.

One who is not at ease with himself cannot be at ease with anyone else. And one who does not love himself, who is hiding himself, cannot be loved by anyone else. He is deceiving others, and others are deceiving him. Then we never really meet. Only faces are meeting—far-off faces. I have come with a made-up face and you have also come with a made-up face. I am hiding myself and you are hiding yourself. Two faces are meeting in this room, but nowhere is there an encounter, nowhere is there an authentic meeting and communion between these faces.

But why do you change your faces? You change them because if you do not, you will not pay enough attention to the face that you are showing and the real may be exposed. That is why a beloved is someone altogether different when she becomes your wife. She is not the same now because she cannot put on a new face. She is so much with you that the real is bound to show up. In the morning she will be just as she is, and now she is ugly! On the beach you were just fascinated, but in the morning (in bed, after the whole night) she will be just as she is. And once you have known your wife in the morning when she is just getting out of bed, you have known her ugly face. But her face is not ugly because she is ugly. It is ugly because now nothing is hidden. You see everything; she sees everything.

So when I say that a *sannyasin* should remain in one robe, this means to be free from the changing clothes and the changing identities—to remain as you are and to be expressive as you are. To just accept yourself. The moment you accept yourself, others will begin to accept you, but that is irrelevant. Whether they accept you or not, it is irrelevant. If you think about people accepting you, then you will create another false face. There is nothing to think about: it just happens.

So I change the name, I change the clothes just to help a person who is living on the periphery.[2]

---

[2] For more on initiation in general and *sannyas* in particular, see the book *I Am the Gate* by Bhagwan Shree, available through the Rajneesh centers or from Shree Rajneesh Ashram, 17 Koregaon Park, Poona, Maharastra, India.

## ◦ 10 ◦

## Total Desire: The Path to Desirelessness

Death is more important than life. Life is just the trivial, just the superficial. Death is deeper. Through death you grow to the real life . . . and through life you only reach death and nothing else.

Whatever we say and mean by life is just a journey toward death. If you can understand that your whole life is just a journey and nothing else, then you are less interested in life and more interested in death. And once someone becomes more interested in death, he can go deep into the very depths of life. Otherwise, he is just going to remain on the surface.

But we are not interested in death at all. Rather, we escape the facts; we are continuously escaping the facts. Death is there, and every moment we are dying. Death is not something far away; it is here and now. We are dying. But while we are dying we go on being concerned about life. This concern with life, this overconcern with life, is just an escape, just a fear. Death is there, deep inside—growing.

Change the emphasis: turn your attention around. If you become concerned with death, your life comes to be revealed to you for the first time because the moment you become at ease with death you have gained a life that cannot die. The moment you have known death, you have know that life which is eternal.

Death is the door from the superficial life, the so-called life, the trivial. There *is* a door. If you pass through the door you reach another life (deeper . . . eternal), without death, deathless. So from so-called life, which is really nothing but dying, one has to pass through the door of death. Only then does one achieve a life that is really existential and active—without death in it.

But one should pass this door very consciously. We have been dying so many times. But whenever someone dies, he becomes unconscious. You are so afraid of death that the moment death comes to you, you become unconscious. You pass through the door in an unconscious state of mind. Then you are born again, and the whole nonsense begins again. And, again, you are not concerned with death.

One who is concerned with death rather than with life begins to pass the door consciously. This is what is meant by meditation: to pass the door of death consciously. To die consciously *is* meditation. But you cannot wait for death. You need not, because death is always there. It is a door that exists inside you. It is not something that is going to happen in the future, it is not something outside of you that you have to reach, it is inside you, a door.

The moment you accept the fact of death and begin to feel it, to live it, to be aware of it, you begin to drop through the inner door. The door opens, and through the door of death you begin to have glimpses of an eternal life. Only through death can one have glimpses of eternal life; there is no other way. So really, all that is known as meditation is just a voluntary death, just a deepening inside, a drowning inside, a sinking inside, just a going away from the surface toward the depths.

Of course, the depths are dark. The moment you leave the surface you will feel you are dying because you have identified the surface of life with yourself. It is not that the surface waves are just surface waves. You have become identified with them; you *are* the surface. So when you leave the surface, it is not only that you leave the surface. You leave yourself, your identity: the past, the mind, the memory. All that you were, you have to leave. That is why meditation appears to be a death. You are dying. . . . And only if you are ready to die this voluntary death—to go deep beyond yourself, to leave the self and transcend the surface—do you come to the reality, which is eternal.

So for one who is ready to die, this very readiness becomes the transcendence; this very readiness is the religiousness. When we say someone is worldly, it means he is more concerned with life than with death. Rather, that he is absolutely concerned with life and not at all concerned with death. A worldly person is one to whom death comes in the end. And when it comes, he is unconscious.

A religious man is one who is dying every moment. Death is not in the end; it is the very process of life. A religious man is one who is more concerned with death than with life because he feels that whatever is known as life is going to be taken away. It is being taken away; every moment you are losing it. Life is just like sand in an hourglass. Every moment the sand is being lost, and you cannot do anything about it. The process is natural. Nothing can be done; it is irreversible.

Time is something which cannot be retained, which cannot be prevented, which cannot be reversed. It is one-dimensional: there is no going back. And, ultimately, the very process of time *is* death. Because you are losing time, you are dying. One day all the sand is lost, and you are empty—just an empty self with no time left. So you die. . . .

Be more concerned with death (and time). It is right here and now, by the corner . . . present every moment. Once you begin to look for it, you become aware of it. It is here; you were just overlooking the fact. Not even overlooking the fact, escaping it. So enter into death; jump into it. This is the arduousness of meditation, this is the austerity of it: one has to jump into death.

To go on loving life is a deep lust, and to be ready to die somehow looks unnatural. Of course, death is one of the most natural things . . . but it looks unnatural to be ready to die.

This is how the paradox, how the dialectics, of existence works: if you are ready to die, this very readiness makes you undying—but if you are not ready to die, this very unreadiness, this overattachment and lust for living, makes you a dying phenomenon.

When we assume any attitude, we always reach the opposite. This is the deep dialectics of existence. The expected never comes; the longed-for is never achieved; the desire is never fulfilled. The more you desire it, the more you lose it. Whatever the dimension may be, it makes no difference: the law remains the same. If you ask too much of anything, by the very asking, you lose it.

If someone asks for love, he will not get love because the very asking makes him unlovely, ugly. The very fact of asking becomes the barrier. No one can love you if you are asking for love. No one can love you! You can be loved only when there is no asking. The very fact of "not asking" makes you beautiful, makes you relaxed.

It is just like when you close your fist and you lose the air that was in the open fist. In an open fist all the air is there, but the moment you close your fist, in the very closing, you are losing the air. You may think that when you have closed your fist you will have possessed the air, but the moment you try to possess it, you lose it. With an open fist all the air is there and you are the master. With a closed fist you are the loser: you have lost everything; you have no air in your hand at all.

And the more closed the fist, the less is the possibility of air being there. But this is how the mind works, this is the absurdity of the mind. If you feel that the air is not there, you close your fist even more. Logic says, "Close it better; you have lost all the air. You have lost it because you did not close your fist so well. You have not really closed your fist as you should; somewhere *you* are at fault.

You have closed your fist wrong. That is why air has escaped. So close it more, close it more," and in the very closing you are losing. But this is how it happens.

If I love someone, I become possessive. I begin to close in. The more I close in, the more love is lost. The mind says, "Arrange to be even closer," and it makes more arrangements, but somewhere there is a leakage. That is why love is being lost. The more I close in, the more I lose. Only with an open hand can love be possessed; only with an open hand, only with a nonclosing mind, can love become a flowering. And this happens with everything. . . .

If you love life too much, you become closed. You become like a dead person even while you are alive. So a person who is filled with lust for life is a dead person. He is already dead, just a corpse. The more he feels to be just a corpse, the more he yearns to be alive, but he does not know the dialectics. The very longing is poisonous. A person who does not long for life at all—a person like Buddha, with no lust for life—lives ardently. He flowers into aliveness perfectly, totally.

The day Buddha died someone said to him, "Now you are dying. We will be missing you so much, for ages and ages, for lives and lives."

Buddha said, "But I died a long time ago. For forty years I have not been aware that I am alive. The day I achieved knowing, enlightenment, I died."

But he was so alive! And he was really alive only after he "died." The day he achieved inner enlightenment he died outwardly, but then he became very alive. Then he was so relaxed and so spontaneous. Then he was without fear, without fear of death.

Fear of death is the only fear. It may take any shape, but that is the basic fear. Once you are ready—once you have died—there is no fear. And only in a nonfearing existence can life come to its total flowering.

Even then, death comes. Buddha dies. But death happens only to us, not to him, because one who has passed death's door has an eternal continuity, a timeless continuity.

So do not be concerned with life at all, not even your own life. And if you are not interested in life, then you cannot desire even death because desire *is* life. If you become interested in (and desirous of) death, you are again desiring life because you *cannot* desire death really. To desire death is an impossibility. How can you desire death? Desire, itself, means life.

So when I say, "Do not be interested in life too much," I do not mean, "Be interested in death." When I say, "Do not be interested in life," then you become aware of a fact . . . which is death. But you cannot desire it. It is not a desire really.

When I talk about an open fist, it will be good to understand: you have to close your fist, but you do not have to open it. Opening is not an effort at all. You just do not close it, and it opens. Opening is not an effort; it is not something positive that has to be done. In fact, if you are making an effort to open your fist it will just be a closing in reverse. It may look like an opening, but it is simply the reverse of closing.

Real opening only means "no closing," simply "no closing." It is a negative phenomenon. If you are not closing your fist, then the fist is open. Now, even if it is closed, it is open. The internal closing has dropped, so even if it is closed now—half-closed or whatever—it is open because the internal closing is not there.

In the same way, a life that is not desiring is not desiring the opposite. Nondesiring is not the opposite of desiring. If it is the opposite, then you have begun to desire again. Rather, nondesiring is just the absence of desiring.

You must feel the distinction. When we say "nondesiring" in words, it becomes the opposite. But nondesiring is not the opposite of desiring. It is simply the absence of desiring, not the opposite. If you make it the opposite, you begin to desire again (you are desiring nondesire), and when this happens, you are back in the same circle.

But this is what happens. A person who has become frustrated in life begins to desire death. It again becomes

a desire. He is not desiring death; he is desiring something
else other than his life. So even a person who is filled with
a lust for life can commit suicide, but this suicide is not
nondesiring. It is really desiring something else. This is a
very interesting point, one of the ultimate points of the
whole search. If you turn to the opposite thing, then you
are in the wheel again, in the vicious circle again. And
you will never be out of it. But this happens. . . .

A person renounces life, goes to the forest or in search
of the divine or in search of liberation or whatever. But
now, again, desire is there. He has simply changed the
object of desire, not desire itself. The object now is not
wealth; it has become God. The object is not this world;
it has become that world. But the object remains. The desiring is the same, the thirst is the same . . . and the tension and the anguish will be the same. The whole process
will simply be repeated again with a new object. You can
go on changing the objects of your desire for lives and
lives, but you will remain the same because the desiring
will be the same.

So when I say "nondesiring," I mean the *absence* of
desiring—not the futility of the object, but the futility of
desiring itself. It is not the realization that this world is
nonsense because then you will desire the other world. It
is not that life is useless so now you must desire death,
annihilation, cessation, nirvana. No, I mean the futility of
desiring itself! The very desiring drops. No object is replaced, substituted. Desire just becomes absent. And this
absence, this very absence, becomes life eternal.

But that is a happening: it is not because of your desire.
It is a spontaneous outcome of nondesiring; it is not a
consequential result. This happens . . . but you cannot
make this happening your desire. If you do, you miss the
point.

When the hand is open (the fist is open), all the air is
there and you are the master of it all. But if you want to
open your fist in order to become the master of the air,
you will not be able to open it because the very effort, in

an inner sense, will be a closing. This mastery of the air is not really a result of your effort, but, rather, a natural happening when there is no effort.

If I simply try not to possess you so that love can flower, this "trying not to possess" will become an effort. An effort can *only* possess: even in nonpossession it will be a possession. I will constantly be aware that I do not possess you. In essence I am saying, "Love me more because I am not trying to possess you." Then I wonder why the love is not coming.

Someone was here. He had been making every effort toward meditation for at least ten years, but was reaching nowhere. I told him, "You have made enough effort—sincerely, seriously. Now do not make *any* effort. Just sit down, without any effort."

Then he asked me, "Can I reach meditation with this method, with 'no effort'?"

I told him: "If you are still asking for the result, then a very subtle effort will continuously be there. You will not be just sitting. You cannot just sit if there are any desires. The desire will be a subtle movement in you . . . and the movement will continue. You may be sitting like a stone or like a Buddha, but still, within, the stone will be moving. Desire is movement."

You cannot remain "just sitting" if there is a desire. It may appear as if you are—everyone may say that you are just sitting—but you cannot be just sitting. You can *just sit* only when desiring is absent. To "just sit" is not a new desire, just an absence. All desiring has become a futility.

You are not frustrated with life because of objects. Religious people go on telling others that there is nothing in women, there is nothing in the world, there is nothing in sex, there is nothing in power. But these are all objects. They are still saying: there is nothing in these *objects*. They are not saying there is nothing in desiring itself.

You can change objects and you can create new objects of desire. Even eternal life can become an object. Again, the circle sets in: the fact of desiring. You have desired everything, you have desired too much.

If you can feel this very fact of desiring—that desiring is futile, meaningless—then you will not create another object to desire. Then desiring ceases. Become aware of it, and it ceases. Then there is an absence, and this absence is silent because there is no desire.

With desire, you cannot be silent. Desire is the real noise. Even if you have no thoughts—if you have a controlled mind and you can stop thinking—a deeper desire will continue because you are stopping this very thinking only to achieve something. A subtle noise will be there. Somewhere inside someone will be looking and asking whether the desired something has been achieved or not. "Thoughts have been stopped. Where is divine realization, where is God, where is enlightenment?" But desiring, itself, will become futile if you can become aware of this.

The whole trick of the mind is that you always become aware that some *object* has become futile. Then you change the object, and in changing the object, the desire continues to take hold of your consciousness. It always happens that when this house becomes useless then another house becomes attractive; when this man becomes unattractive, repulsive, then another man becomes attractive. This goes on. . . . And the moment you become aware of the futility of what you are desiring, the mind goes on to some other object.

When this happens, the gap is lost. When something becomes futile, useless, unattractive, *remain in the gap*. Be aware of whether the object has become futile or whether it is desiring itself that is futile. And if you can feel the very futility of desire, suddenly something drops in you. Suddenly you are transformed to a new level of consciousness. This is a nothingness, an absence, a negativity. No new circle begins.

In this moment, you are out of the wheel of *samsar*

(the world). But you cannot make it an object of your desire to be out of the wheel. Do you feel the distinction? You *cannot* make desirelessness an object.

QUESTION: "Wasn't Buddha's desire for realization a desire?"

Yes, it was a desire; Buddha had the desire. When Buddha said, "I will not leave this place. I am not going to leave unless I achieve enlightenment," it was a desire. And with this desire, a vicious circle set in. Even for Buddha it set in.

Buddha could not achieve enlightenment for a long time because of this desire. Because of it, he searched and searched for six years. He did everything that was possible to be done, that could be done. He did *everything,* but he did not get even an inch nearer. He remained the same, even *more* frustrated. He had left the world, renounced everything, for the sake of realization, and nothing had come of it. For six years continuously, every effort was made, but nothing came of it.

Then one day, near Bodh Gaya, he came to take a bath in the Niranjana (the river there). He was so weak because of so much fasting that he could not come out of the river. He just remained there by the root of a tree.

He was so weak that he could not step out of the river! The thought came to his mind that if he had become so weak that he could not even cross a small river, then how could he cross the greater ocean of existence. So on that particular day, even the desire to achieve realization became futile. He said, "Enough!"

He came out of the water and sat under a tree (the Bodhi tree). That particular night the very desiring to achieve became futile. He had desired the world and found that it was just a dream. And not only a dream—a nightmare. For six years continuously he had desired enlightenment and that, too, proved to be only a dream. And not *only* a dream: it proved to be an even *deeper* nightmare.

He was completely frustrated; there was nothing left to

desire. He had known the world very well—he had known it *very* well—and he could not go back to it. There was nothing for him there. He had known the effort of so-called religions (of all the religions that were prominent in India); he had practiced all of their techniques, and nothing had come of it. There was nothing else to try now, no motivation remained, so he just dropped down on the ground near the Bodhi tree and for the whole night he remained there— without any desire. There was nothing left to desire; desiring, itself, had become futile.

In the morning when he awakened, the last star was setting. He looked at the star and for the first time in his life his eyes were without any mist because he was without any desire. The last star was setting . . . and as the star set, something in him withered with it: the self (because the self cannot exist without desiring). And he became enlightened!

This enlightenment came at a moment when there was no desire. And it had been prevented by six years of desiring. Really, the phenomenon happens only when you are out of the circle. So even Buddha, because of desiring enlightenment, had to wander uselessly for six years. This moment of transformation—this jumping out of the circle, out of the wheel of life—only comes, only happens, when there is no desire. Buddha said, "I achieved it when there was no achieving mind; I found it when there was no search. This happened only when there was no effort."

This, again, becomes a very difficult thing to understand because, with the mind, we cannot understand anything which is effortless. Mind means effort. The mind can tackle anything, can maneuver anything, which can be "done," but the mind cannot ever conceive of something which "happens" (and cannot be done). The faculty of the mind is to do something; it is an instrument for doing. The very faculty of mind is to achieve something, to gain some desire.

Just as it is impossible to hear with the eyes or to see

with the hands, it is impossible for the mind to conceive or to feel that which happens when you are not doing anything. The mind has no memory of such a thing. It knows only things that can be done and that cannot be done. It knows only things in which it succeeds and in which it fails. But it has not known anything which happens when *nothing* is done. So what to do?

Start with a desire. That desire is not going to lead you to the point of the happening, but that desire can lead you to the futility of that desire. One has to begin with desire; it is impossible to begin with "no desire." If you could begin with no desire, then the happening would happen this very moment. Then no technique, no method, would be needed. If you could begin with no desire, *this very moment* it happens! But that is impossible.

You cannot begin with no desiring. The mind will make this nondesiring also a desired object. The mind will say, "Okay, I will try not to desire." It will say, "Really, it looks fascinating. I will try to do something so that this no desiring happens." But the mind is bound to have some desire. It can begin only with desire, but it may not end in desire.

One has to begin with desiring something that cannot be achieved by desiring. But if you are aware of this fact—if you are aware of the fact that you are desiring something that cannot be desired—it helps. This awareness of the fact helps. Now, any moment, you can take the jump. And when you take the jump, there will be no desiring.

You have desired the world. Now, desire the divine. That is how one has to begin. The beginning is wrong, but you have to begin that way because of this built-in process of the mind. This is the only way to change it.

For example, I tell you that you cannot go through the wall to get to the outside. You have to go through the door. And when I say, "through the door," "door" means only the place where there is no wall. So when I say you have to go through the "no wall" to the outside, it is because you cannot go through the wall. The wall cannot be the door, and if you try to get out through the wall you will be frustrated.

But you have not known anything like a door. You have never been outside, so how can you know that there is a door? You have always been in this room (the room of the mind, the room of desires). You have always been in this room, so you have known only this wall, you have not known the door. Even if the door is there, it has appeared to you as a part of the wall. It has been a wall to you. Unless you open it, you cannot know it is a door.

So I say to you, "You cannot go outside through the wall. You cannot do anything with a wall; it will not lead you outside. You need the door." But you do not know anything about the door. You know only the wall. Even the door appears to you to be part of the wall. Then what is to be done?

I say, "Try from anywhere, but begin." You will be frustrated. You will go around the whole room, try every nook and corner—everywhere. You will be frustrated because the wall cannot open. But the door is somewhere, and you may stumble upon it. That is the only way: begin with the wall because that is the only beginning possible. Begin with the wall, and you will stumble upon the door. It is a fact that there is a door, that the door is not a wall, and that you cannot pass through the wall, you have to pass through the door. This very fact will make the stumbling easier. Really, whenever you are frustrated with the wall, the door becomes more of a possibility, more of a potential. Your search becomes deeper through this.

Mind *is* desiring. The mind cannot do anything without desire. You cannot transcend the mind through desiring because the mind *is* the desiring. So the mind has to desire even that which is found only when there is no desire. But begin with the wall. Know desire, and you will stumble upon the door. Even Buddha had to begin with a desire, but no one told him—the fact was not known to him—that the door opens only when there is no desire.

As I understand it, struggling with desire is the disease. Giving up the struggle is the freedom. That is the only real death: when you just give up. If you can just lie down and die with no struggle to live, without even an indication of struggle, that death can become a realization. If you just lie down and accept—with no movement inside, with no desire, with no help to be found, with no way to be sought—if you just lie down and accept, that acceptance will be a great thing.

It is not so easy. Even if you are lying down, the struggle is still there. You may be exhausted: that is another thing. That is not acceptance; that is not readiness. Somewhere in the mind you are still struggling. But, really, to lie down and die with no struggle makes death become ecstasy. Death becomes samadhi; death becomes realization. And then you say, "Of course!"

You may not have the desire to go out of this room. The desire to come out can come only in two ways. The first is that somehow you have had a glimpse of something of the outside from a hole in the wall or from the window (*somewhere* you have had a glimpse), or, somehow, in some mysterious way, in some moment, the door opened and you had a glimpse. This happens and goes on happening: in some mysterious moment, the door opens for just a single moment—like a flash of light—and then closes again. You have tasted something of the outside. Now the desire comes.

The desire comes: you are in the dark and there is a sudden flash of light. In a moment, in a single, simultaneous moment, everything becomes clear. The darkness is not there and then, again, the darkness is there. Everything is lost, but now you cannot be the same again. This has become part of your experience.

In some moments of silence, in some moments of love, in some moments of suffering, in some moments of sudden accidents—the door suddenly opens, and you have a taste

These things cannot be arranged; they are accidents. They *cannot* be arranged! When someone is in love, a door opens for a moment. This opening is really a happening.

In deep love, somehow your desire ceases. The very moment is enough; there is no desire for the future. If I love someone, then in that very moment of love the mind is not. This moment is eternity. For me, now, in this moment, there is no future. I am not concerned with the future at all. And there is no past. I am not bothered about it; the whole thought process has stopped at this moment of existence. Everything has stopped. And suddenly, in this nondesiring moment, a door opens.

So love has many glimpses of the divine. If you have really been in love, even for a moment, then you cannot remain "in this room" for long. Then you have tasted something that is of the beyond.

But, again, the mind begins to play tricks. It says, "This moment has happened because of this person whom I love. I must possess this person forever, otherwise this thing will not happen again." And the more you possess, the more you become concerned with the future. Then this moment will not come again. Even with this same person it is not going to come again because with expectation the mind is again tense. The moment happened when there were no expectations. And then the lovers go on condemning each other ("You are not loving me as much as you did before") because the moment is not happening.

This moment, this glimpse, is not in anyone's hand, and the lover cannot do anything about it. Whatever he tries to do will just be a destruction of the whole thing. He cannot *do,* because it was not his doing at all. It was just a spontaneous phenomenon. It happened, and the door opened!

It can happen in many ways. Someone whom you love has died and the death has struck like a dagger in your mind. The past and future are separated: death has become like a dagger in you. The whole past has stopped and, in your deep suffering, there is no future. Everything stops. You may get a taste of the divine, of the "outside."

But then your mind again begins to play tricks. It begins to weep, it begins to do something. It begins to think that "I am feeling suffering because someone has died." It becomes concerned with the other. But if, at the moment of death, you can remain *just in the moment*, then it sometimes happens. Then you can glimpse something of the beyond.

In some accident, it can happen. In a motor accident, it can happen. Things stop suddenly. Time stops. You cannot desire because there is no time/space to desire in. Your car is falling from a height. As it falls, you cannot remember the past, you cannot desire for the future. The moment has become *all*. In this moment, it can happen.

So there are two ways through which the desire to go beyond is created. The first is that somehow you have had a taste of the beyond. But this cannot be planned: you have it or you don't have it. Still, once you have had this taste, you begin to desire it. The desire can become a hindrance— it *becomes* a hindrance—but, still, that is how things begin. First you have to desire nondesiring.

Or it happens in another way. The other way is that you have *no* taste of the beyond—none! You have not known the beyond at all, but this room has become a suffering. You cannot tolerate it anymore. You do not know the beyond at all, but whatever it may be, you are ready to choose it (even though it is unknown) because this room, this very room, has become a misery, a hell. You do not know what is beyond—whether there is anything or not, whether the beyond exists or not—but you cannot remain in this room anymore. This room has become a suffering, a hell. Then you try . . . then you begin to desire the unknown, the beyond. Then, again, there is desire: the desire to escape from here. But you *have to* begin with a desire for that which cannot be desired, for that which cannot be attained by desiring.

Remember this fact continuously: go on doing whatever you are doing, constantly remembering that by *doing alone* it cannot be achieved. And there are so many methods to help you to do this. One is to remember that you cannot *get* it; only God can *give* it to you. This is simply a way to make you aware that your efforts are meaningless; only grace will do it. This is one way. It is just saying the same thing in a more metaphorical way, in a language that can be understood more easily: that you cannot do anything.

But that does not mean that you are not to do anything. You should do everything . . . but remember, it is not going to happen simply by your doing. Something happens to you, something unknown. Grace descends upon you. Your efforts will make you more receptive to the grace, that's all. But it is not as a direct result of your efforts that grace descends upon you.

This is how religious people have been trying to express this same phenomenon. A Buddha (or a type with a mind like Buddha) will express it more scientifically. Buddha would not have used the word "grace" because he would have said that you will even long for grace, desire grace. One can even desire grace, and go to the temple and cry and weep and *ask* for divine grace. So Buddha said, "It will not work. There is no such thing as grace. When you are in a nondesiring state of mind, it happens."

So it depends. It depends! It may be meaningful for someone as long as he understands that grace cannot be asked for, cannot be requested, cannot be demanded, cannot be persuaded (because if you can persuade then it is not grace; it has become part of your effort). Nothing can be done about grace; you just have to wait. If you can understand that grace comes only in waiting and you do not have to do anything, then go on doing anything and everything, knowing very well that nothing is going to happen by your doing—it will happen only in a non-doing moment.

Then, the very concept of grace can be helpful. But if

you begin to ask for grace and pray for grace, it will not happen at all. Then it is better to remember that we are in a vicious circle, which has to be broken from somewhere.

Begin by desiring, begin by doing. Remember constantly the fact that it cannot be done, and go on doing. . . .

Take an example: you are not feeling sleep descending on you. What to do? Sleep is not coming. Really, you cannot do anything because the very doing will be a disturbance. If you do something then, because of the doing, sleep will not come. Sleep needs a non-doing mind; it descends upon you only when you are not doing anything. But tell a person who is sleepless not to do anything and sleep will come, and then his very lying in the bed will be a tension. "Not to do anything" will become a doing. Tell him, "Relax and sleep will come," and he will try to relax, but it will be an effort and with effort there is no relaxation. Then what to do?

I use another method. I tell him to do everything he can do to bring sleep. "Do anything you want to do: jump, run, whatever you like. Do everything you can do." I tell him, "It is not going to come by your doing—but do!"

The very doing soon becomes futile. He runs, he goes on doing many automatic problems, he solves puzzles, he repeats mantras, he goes on doing, and I say, "Do it wholeheartedly." I know very well that the happening is not going to come about by his doing, but then the doing will be exhausted, and he will feel that it is just nonsense. In that moment, when doing has become futile, suddenly he will be asleep. This sleep has not come because of his doing at all, but the doing has helped in a way. It has helped because it made him aware that it was futile.

So go on desiring, doing something for the beyond, constantly remembering it is not going to come by your effort. But do not stop these efforts because your efforts are going to help in a way. They will make you so frustrated with the very fact of desiring that suddenly you will sit down and you will be *just sitting*—not doing. And the thing happens! And there is the jump . . . the explosion!

So I do something very contradictory: I know that with no technique can it be possible, and still I go on devising techniques. I know that you cannot do anything, and still I insist, "Do something!"

Do you understand me?

# ~ PART II ~

# QUESTIONS AND ANSWERS

## ~ 11 ~

## What Is the Soul?

QUESTION: "What is it that you call *atman* (soul)? Is this soul "consciousness," itself, or is it something individual?

Really, no matter what we call it, we will miss it. Any conceptualization is going to miss the real—*any* conceptualization—so whatever has been known as the self, the soul, the *atman,* is not the real thing. It cannot be! All those who have defined it have defined it with a condition: that they are trying something that is absurd. That which cannot be said, they are saying; that which cannot be defined, they are defining; that which cannot be known, they are making a theory about.

There have been three attitudes about it. First, there have been the mystics (the knowers) who have remained totally silent about it. They will not give any definition; they say definition is futile. Then there has been another group of mystics—the largest group—that says, "Even an effort that is futile can be helpful. Sometimes even untrue theory leads to Truth; sometimes even wrongs may become rights, sometimes even a false step may lead you to a right end. It may look false at the moment—or in the end it may even prove false—but, still, false devices can help."

This second group feels that by remaining silent you are

still saying something, that "nothing" *can* be said. And this second type of mystic has a point! Definitions belong to them. Then there is a third type who has been neither silent nor who has defined. They have just denied the whole thing in order that you will not be at all obsessed with it.

Buddha belongs to this third type. If you ask him whether there is a soul, whether there is God, whether there is an existence beyond life, he will just deny it. Even on the verge of death when someone asked him, "Will you *be*, beyond death?" he denied it.

He said, "No! I will not be. I will drop out of existence just like a flame that goes out. You can't ask where the flame is when it goes out. It just ceases." That is why Buddha says that *nirvana* means "cessation of the flame," not just *moksha* (not just liberation). Buddha says, "*This* is liberation: to cease completely. To *be* is to be somewhere, somehow, in slavery." This is the third type.

These three types all quarrel because one who speaks is bound to feel that those who have remained silent are not compassionate enough, that they should have said something for those who cannot understand silence. And those who have defined, have defined in so many ways that there are quarrels about it: quarreling is bound to be there.

All definitions are devices. One can define in any way. Mahavira defines in one way and Shankara is going to define in another way because all definitions are equally false or true. It makes no difference. How one defines depends on the type of person he is. There are so many definitions . . . and those definitions have become so many religions, so many philosophical systems. They have made man's mind so confused by now that, really, it sometimes appears that those who have remained silent were more compassionate. Definitions have become conflicts. One definition cannot allow the other—otherwise, it contradicts itself.

Mahavira tried to say that every definition has some truth in it, but only *some*. Then something remains false about every definition. But it was impossible for Mahavira to have a big following because if you do not define clearly, the confused mind becomes even more confused. If you say, "Every path is right," then, you are saying, "There is no path," and one who has come to find the path is just bewildered. You cannot get any help from me if I say, "Every path is right: wherever you go, you go to the divine. . . . Go anywhere, do anything, everything has some truth." It is true but, still, it is not helpful.

If you define in a particular way and make the definition absolute, all other definitions become false. Because Shankara has to define things exactly he may say, "Buddha is not right; he is wrong," but if Buddha is made to appear wrong, it just creates confusion. How can a Buddha be wrong? How can a Christ be wrong? Is only Shankara right? Then there are conflicts. . . .

Even the third attitude—the Buddhist attitude of denying—has not helped. It has not helped because by denying, the very search is lost . . . and without the search, there is no need of denying. Very few people are capable of understanding what total cessation is. The lust for life is so deep-rooted that we are even reaching for a God who is a part of our lust for life: we are searching for more life, really. Even if we are searching for *moksha*, we are not searching for total death. We want to *be* there somehow.

Buddha had been asked (and asked continuously for forty years) only one question: "If we are to cease completely, then why this whole effort?" It seems meaningless! Just to cease? Just to not be? Why this whole effort? And yet people around Buddha felt that he had not ceased. Really, he had become more. That was the feeling! Buddha had become something more, but still he went on denying and denying.

How can you define something that cannot be defined? But you will either have to be silent or you will have to define it.

As for me, I do not fall into any of these three groups. That is why I cannot be consistent. Each of these three types can be consistent, but I am not concerned with the concept of soul at all. I am always concerned with the questioner, the one who has asked. How can he be helped? If I think that he can be helped through positive faith, then I proclaim it; if I feel that he can be helped by silence, then I remain silent; if I feel he can be helped by definition, then I give the definition. To me, everything is just a device. There is nothing serious about it: it is just a device!

A definition may not be true. In fact, if I have to make it meaningful to you, it cannot be true really. You have not known what soul is; you have not known what this explosion is, which we call *Brahman* (the divine). You do not know the meaning; you know only the words. Words that you have not experienced are just meaningless sounds. You can create the sound "God," but unless you have known God it is just a sound.

"Heart" is a meaningful word, "cow" is a meaningful word, because you have, yourself, experienced what they mean. But "God" is just a word for you; 'soul" is just a word. If I have to help you, I can help you only with a false definition because you have no experience of God, no experience of the soul. And unless I can define it by something you know, a definition will be useless.

For a person who has never known a flower but has known a diamond, I must define flowers through diamonds. There is no other way. A flower has nothing to do with diamonds but, still, something can be indicated through it. I can say, "Flowers are living diamonds: *living* diamonds!" The whole thing is false—diamonds are irrelevant—but if I say, "Flowers are living diamonds, growing diamonds," I create a desire in you to experience them. A definition is there only to help you to move to the experience. All definitions are like that.

If you have not known diamonds, if you have not known anything positive for me to define through, then I have to define through negatives. If you do not have any positive feeling for anything, then I will define through negatives. I will say, "The misery that you have is not part of the soul. The *dukkha* (the anguish) that you are is not part of the soul . . . . I have to define negatively in terms of something with which you are crippled, from which you are dying . . . in terms of something with which you are burdened, which has become just a hell to you. I have to define negatively by saying, "It will not be this; it will be just the opposite."

So it depends with me. It depends! I have no absolute answers, I have only devices—only psychological answers. And the answer does not depend on me; it depends on you. Because of you, I have to give a particular answer.

That is why I cannot be a guru—never! Buddha can become one, but I never can. Because you are so inconsistent, every individual is so different, how can I become consistent? I cannot. And I cannot create a sect because for this, consistency is very needed. If you want to create a sect, you must be consistent—foolishly consistent. You must deny all inconsistencies. They are there, but you must deny them. Otherwise, you cannot attract followers. So I am less a guru and more like a psychiatrist (*plus* something). To me, *you* are meaningful. If you can understand this, then something more can be said. . . .

By "consciousness" I mean a movement toward total aliveness. You are never totally alive. Sometimes you are more alive—that you know—and sometimes you are less alive. And when you are more alive you feel happy. Happiness is nothing but an interpretation of your greater aliveness. If you love someone, then you become more alive with him and that greater aliveness gives you the feeling of happiness. Then you go on projecting the reasons for your happiness onto someone else. . . .

When you encounter nature you are more alive, when you are on a mountain you become more alive, and when you are just living with machines you are less alive because of the whole association. With trees you become more alive because you have once been trees. Deep down we are just walking trees—with roots in the air, not in the earth. And when you face the ocean you feel more alive because the first life was born in the ocean. In fact, in our bodies we still have the same composition of water as the ocean— the same salt quantity as the ocean has.

When you are with a woman—if you are of the opposite sex—you begin to feel more alive than with a man. With a man you feel less alive because nothing is pulling you out. You are enclosed; the opposite energy pulls you out. The flame flickers: you can be more alive. And whenever you begin to feel more alive, you begin to feel happy.

When we use the word "soul," we mean "total aliveness": total aliveness not with someone else, but with yourself; total aliveness with no outward causes. The ocean is not there and you become oceanic; the sky is not there and you become the whole space; the beloved is not there and you are just love, nothing else.

What I mean is that you begin to be alive independently. There is no dependence on anything or anyone: you are *liberated!* And with this liberation, this inner liberation, your happiness cannot be lost. It is total aliveness; it is total consciousness. It cannot be lost!

With this total aliveness many things happen that cannot really be understood *unless they have happened.* But tentatively, I can give you this definition of the soul as being "totally conscious . . . totally alive . . . totally blissful . . . without being bound by anything."

If you begin to love, or if you can be happy without a reason, then you are *soul,* not a body. Why then?

By body I mean the part of your soul that always exists in relation to the outside existence. You begin to feel sad when some cause for sadness is there, or you begin to feel good when some cause for happiness is there, but you never feel yourself without something else being there. That feeling—that state when nothing is there, but *you are* (in your total aliveness, in your total consciousness)—is the soul.

But this is a tentative definition. It just indicates; it doesn't define. It just shows. Much is there, but it is just a finger pointing to the moon. Never mistake the finger for the moon. The finger is not the moon; it is just an indication. Forget the finger and look at the moon. But all definitions are like that. . . .

You ask whether the soul is individual. It is a meaningless question, but it is pertinent because of you. It is like a question that a blind man would ask.

A blind man moves with his staff. He cannot move without it: he searches and gropes in the dark with it. If we talk to him about operating on his eyes to heal them so he can see, the blind man can ask, very pertinently, "When I have my eyes will I still be able to grope in the dark with my staff?"

If we say, "You will not need your staff," he cannot believe it.

He will say, "Without my staff I cannot exist, I cannot live. What you are saying is not acceptable. I cannot conceive of it. Without my staff, *I am not*. So what will become of my staff? First you tell me!"

Really, this individuality is like the blind man's staff. You are groping in the dark with an ego because you have no soul. This ego, this "I," is just a groping because you do not have eyes. The moment you have become totally alive, the ego is just lost. It was part of your blindness, part of your nonaliveness or partial aliveness, part of your unconsciousness, part of your ignorance. It just drops.

It is not that you are individual or you are not individual. Both things become irrelevant. Individuality is not relevant, but questions continue because the source of questioning remains the same.

When Moulinkyaputta came to Buddha for the first time, he asked many questions. Buddha said, "Are you asking in order to solve the questions or are you only asking to get answers?"

Moulinkyaputta said, "I have come to ask you—and you have begun to ask me! Let me ponder over it. I must think about it." He thought about it and the second day he said, "Really, I have come to solve them."

Buddha said to him, "Have you asked these same questions to anyone else as well?"

Moulinkyaputta said, "I have asked everyone, continuously, for thirty years."

Buddha said, "By asking for thirty years you must have gotten many answers—many, many. But have any proved to be *the* answer?"

Moulinkyaputta said, "None!"

Then Buddha said, "I will not give you any answers. In thirty years of questioning many answers have been given. I can add some more, but that is not going to help. So I will give you the solution, not the answer."

Moulinkyaputta said, "Okay, give it to me."

But Buddha said, "It cannot be given by me; it has to be grown in you. So remain for one year with me silently. Not a single question will be allowed! Be totally silent— be with me—and after one year you can ask. Then I will give you the answer."

Sariputra (the chief disciple of Buddha) was sitting nearby under a tree. He began to laugh. Moulinkyaputta asked, "Why is Sariputra laughing? What is there to laugh about?"

Sariputra said, "Ask right now if you have to ask. Do not wait for one year. We have been fooled—this happened to me, too!—because after one year we never ask. If you have remained totally silent for a year, then the very source of questioning drops. And this man is deceptive!

This man is very deceptive," Sariputra said. "After one year he will not give you any answers."

So Buddha said, "I will remain with my promise, Sariputra. I have remained with my promise with you, too. It is not my fault that you do not ask."

One year went by and Moulinkyaputta remained silent: silently doing meditation and becoming more and more silent outwardly and inwardly. Then he became a silent pool, with no vibrations, no waves. He forgot that the year had passed. The day that he was to ask had come but he, himself, forgot.

Buddha said, "There used to be a man called Moulinkyaputta here. Where is he? He has to ask some question. The year has passed, the day has come, so he must come to me." There were ten thousand monks there and everyone tried to find out who Moulinkyaputta was. And Moulinkyaputta also tried to find out where he was!

Buddha called to him and said, "Why are you looking around? *You* are the man. And I have to fulfill my promise. So you ask, and I will give you the answer."

Moulinkyaputta said, "The one who was asking is dead. That is why I was looking around to see who this man Moulinkyaputta is. I, too, have heard his name, but he is long since gone."

The original source must be transformed, otherwise we go on asking. And there are persons who will be supplying you with answers. You feel good in asking, they feel good in answering, but what goes on is only a mutual deception.

## ∽ 12 ∽

## LSD and Meditation

QUESTION: "Can LSD be used as a help in meditation?"

LSD can be used as a help, but the help is very dangerous. It is not so easy. If you use a mantra, even that can become difficult to throw, but if you use acid (LSD) it will be even more difficult to throw.

The moment you are on an LSD trip you are not in control. Chemistry takes control and you are not the master. And once you are not the master, it is difficult to regain that position. The chemical is not the slave now; *you* are the slave. Now how to control it is not going to be your choice. Once you take LSD as a help you are making a slave of the master and your whole body chemistry will be affected by it.

Your body will begin to crave LSD. Now the craving will not just be of the mind as it is when you get attached to a mantra. When you use acid as a help, the craving becomes part of the body; the LSD goes to the very cells of the body. It changes them, your inner chemical structure becomes different. Then all the body cells begin to crave acid and it will be difficult to drop it.

LSD can be used to bring you to meditation only if your body has been prepared for it. So if you ask if it can be used in the West, I will say that it is not for the West at all. It can be used only in the East—if the body is totally prepared for it. Yoga has used it, tantra has used it—there are schools of tantra and yoga that have used LSD as a help—but then they prepare your body first. There is a long process of purification of the body. Your body becomes so pure and you become such a great master of it that even chemistry cannot become your master now. So yoga allows it, but in a very specific way.

First your body must be purified chemically. Then you will be in such control of the body that even your body chemistry can be controlled. For example, there are certain yogic exercises. If you take poison, through a particular yogic exercise you can order your blood not to mix with it and the poison will pass through the body and come out in the urine without having mixed with the blood at all. If you can do this, if you can control your body chemistry, then you can use *anything* because you have remained the master.

In tantra (particularly in "leftist" tantra) they use alcohol to help meditation. It looks absurd; it is not. The seeker will take alcohol in a particular quantity and then will try to be alert. Consciousness must not be lost. By and by the quantity of alcohol will be raised, but the consciousness must remain alert. The person has taken alcohol, it has been absorbed in the body, but the mind remains above it. Consciousness is not lost. Then the quantity of alcohol is raised higher and higher. Through this practice a point comes when any amount of alcohol can be given and the mind remains alert. Only then can LSD be a help.

In the West there are no practices to purify the body or to increase consciousness through changes in body chemistry. Acid is taken without any preparation in the West. It is not going to help. Rather, on the contrary, it may destroy the whole mind.

There are many problems. Once you have been on an LSD trip you have a glimpse of something you have never known, something you have never felt. If you begin to practice meditation it is a long process, but LSD is not a process. You take it, and the process is over. Then the

body begins to work. Meditation is a long process—you
have to do it for years; only then will the results be forth-
coming—and when you have experienced a shortcut, it
will be difficult to follow a long process. The mind will
crave to return to using the drugs. So it is difficult to
meditate once you have known a glimpse through chemistry. To undertake something that is a long process will
be difficult. Meditation needs more stamina, more faith,
more waiting, and it will be difficult because now you can
compare.

Secondly, any method is bad if you are not in control all
the time. When you are meditating, you can stop at any
moment. If you want to stop, you can stop this very moment. You can come out of it. You cannot stop an LSD
trip: once you have taken LSD you have to complete the
circle. Now you are not the master.

Anything that makes a slave of you is ultimately not
going to help spiritually because spirituality basically means
to be the master of oneself. So I wouldn't suggest short-
cuts. I am not against LSD, I may sometimes be for it,
but then a long preliminary preparation is necessary. Then
you will be the master.

But then LSD is not a shortcut. It will take even longer
than meditation. Hatha yoga takes years to prepare a body.
Twenty years, twenty-five years—then a body is ready.
Now you can use any chemical help and it will not be
destructive to your being. But then the process is far longer.

Then LSD can be used; I am in favor of it then. If you
are prepared to take twenty years to prepare the body in
order to take LSD then it is not destructive, but the same
thing can be done in *two* years with meditation. Because
the body is more gross, mastery is more difficult. The mind
is more subtle so mastery is easier. The body is further
away from your being, so there is a greater gap; with the
mind the gap is shorter.

In India the primitive method to prepare the body to be
ready for meditation was hatha yoga. It took so long a time
to prepare the body that sometimes hatha yoga had to

invent methods to prolong life so that hatha yoga could be continued. It was such a long process that sixty years might not be enough, seventy years might not be enough. And there is a problem: if the mastery is not achieved in this life then in the next life you have to begin from ABC because you have a new body. The whole effort has been lost. You do not have a new mind in your next life (the old mind continues) so whatever is attained though the mind remains with you, but whatever is attained through the body is lost with every death. So hatha yoga had to invent methods to prolong life for two hundred to three hundred years so that mastery could be attained.

If the mastery is of the mind then you can change the body, but the preparedness of the body belongs to the body alone. Hatha yoga invented many methods so that the process could be completed, but then even greater methods were discovered: how to control the mind directly (raja yoga). With these methods the body can be a little helpful, but there is no need to be too concerned with it. So hatha yoga adepts have said that LSD can be used, but raja yoga cannot say LSD can be used because raja yoga has no methodology to prepare the body. Direct meditation is used.

Sometimes it happens—only sometimes, rarely—that if you have a glimpse through LSD and do not become addicted to it, that glimpse may become a thirst in you to seek something further. So to try it once is good, but it becomes difficult to know where to stop and how to stop. The first trip is good, to be on it once is good—you become aware of a different world and then you begin to seek, you begin to search, because of it—but then it becomes difficult to stop. This is the problem. If you can stop, then to take LSD once is good. But that "if" is a great one.

Mulla Nesrudin used to say that he never took more than one glass of wine. Many friends objected to his statement because they had seen him taking one glass after another. He said, "The second glass is taken by the first; 'I' take only one. The second is taken by the first and the third by the second. Then I am not the master. I am master only for the first, so how can I say that I take more than one? 'I' take only one—always only one!" With the first you are the master; with the second you are not. The first will try to take a second and then it will go on continuously. Then it is no longer in your hands.

To begin anything is easy because you are the master, but to end anything is difficult because then you are not the master. So I am not against LSD . . . and if I *am* against it, it is conditional. This is the condition: if you can remain the master, then okay. Use anything, but remain the master. And if you cannot remain the master, then do not enter into a dangerous road at all. Do not enter at all. It will be better.

## ∾ 13 ∾

## Intuition: A Non-Explanation

QUESTION: "Can intuition be explained scientifically? Is it a phenomenon of the mind?"

Intuition cannot be explained scientifically because the very phenomenon is unscientific and irrational. The very phenomenon of intuition is irrational. In language it looks okay to ask, "Can intuition be explained?" It means: can intuition be reduced to intellect? But intuition means something beyond the intellect, something not of the intellect, something coming from someplace where intellect is totally unaware. So intellect can feel it, but it cannot explain it.

The leap can be felt because there is a gap. Intuition can be felt by the intellect—it can be noted down that something has happened—but it cannot be explained because explanation means causality. Explanation means "from where does it come? why does it come? what is the cause?" And it comes from somewhere else—not from the intellect itself—so there is no intellectual cause. There is no reason, no link, no continuity in the intellect.

For example, Mohammed was an illiterate person. No one knew about him; no one ever felt that such a great thing as the Koran could come out of him. There was not a single act, not a single thought, that was special about him. He was just an ordinary man—absolutely ordinary.

No one ever felt that something extraordinary was possible in him. Then suddenly, this parable is recorded:

An angel appeared to Mohammed and said, "Read!"

Mohammed said to him, "How can I read? I do not know how. I cannot read; I am illiterate."

The angel repeated again, "Read!"

Mohammed again said, "But how can I read? I do not know anything about reading."

Then the angel said, "Read! By the grace of God, you will be able." And Mohammed began to read! This is intuition.

He returned to his house trembling, trembling because he could not conceive of what had happened. He could read . . . and he had read something inconceivable! The first *Ayat*[1] of the Koran had been given to him. He could not understand it because nothing in his whole past related to it. He could not feel the meaning of it; he had become the vehicle for something that was unrelated to his past, absolutely unrelated. Something from the unknown had penetrated him. It might have been related to something else, to someone else, but it did not relate to Mohammed at all. This is the penetration.

He came into his house trembling . . . he felt feverish. . . . He just went on thinking, "What has happened?" He was unable to understand what had happened, and for three days he was in deep fever, trembling, because there was no cause for what had occurred. He could not even gather the courage to say something to anyone. He was an illiterate: who was going to believe him? He, himself, could not believe what had happened. It was unbelievable!

After three days of deep fever, coma, unconsciousness, he gathered the courage to tell his wife, but only under the condition that she not tell anyone else. "It seems that I have gone mad," he said. But his wife was older than he was and more learned. (She was forty and Mohammed was twenty-six. She was a rich woman, a rich widow. . . .)

---

[1] A brief explanation of a longer teaching; a sutra.

She felt that something real had happened. And she was Mohammed's first convert.

Only then could Mohammed get up the nerve to speak to some friends and relatives. Whenever he would speak he would tremble, perspire, because what was happening was inconceivable. That is why Mohammed insisted (and this became a tenet, a foundational tenet, of Islam) that "I am not divine; I am nothing special. I am not extraordinary, I am just a vehicle."

This is what is meant by surrender and nothing else—nothing else! The postman just delivers the message to you. You, yourself, cannot even understand it.

This is intuition. It is a different realm of happening that is not related to the intellect at all although it can penetrate the intellect. It must be understood that a higher reality can penetrate a lower reality, but the lower cannot penetrate the higher. So intuition can penetrate intellect because it is higher, but intellect cannot penetrate intuition because it is lower. It is just like your mind can penetrate your body, but your body cannot penetrate the mind. Your being can penetrate the mind, but the mind cannot penetrate the being. That is why, if you are going into the being, you have to separate yourself from body and mind—both! They cannot penetrate a higher phenomenon.

As you go into a higher reality, the lower world of happenings has to be dropped. There is no explanation of the higher in the lower because the very terms of explanation are not existential there. They are meaningless. But the intellect can feel the gap, it can know the gap, it can come to feel that something has happened which is "beyond me." If even this much can be done, the intellect has done much.

But intellect can also reject. That is what is meant by a faithful mind or a faithless mind. If you feel that what cannot be explained by the intellect is *not*, then you are a nonbeliever. Then you will continue in this lower existence —tethered to it. Then you disallow mystery; then you disallow intuition to speak to you. This is what a rationalist mind means. The rationalist will not even see that something from beyond has come.

Mohammed was chosen. There were scholars around, many scholars, but Mohammed (a very illiterate person) was chosen *because he was faithful!* The higher could penetrate; he could allow the higher to enter into him. If you are rationally trained, you will not allow the higher. You will deny it, you will say, "It cannot be. It must be my imagination; it must be my dream. Unless I can prove it rationally, I will not accept it."

A rational mind becomes closed, closed within the boundaries of reasoning, and intuition cannot penetrate. But you can use the intellect without being closed. Then you can use reason as an instrument, but you remain open; you are receptive to the higher. If something comes, you are receptive. Then you can use your intellect as a help: it notes down that "something has happened that is beyond me." It can help you to understand this gap.

Beyond that, intellect can be used for expression. Not for explanation, for expression. A Buddha is totally non-explanatory. He is expressive, but non-explanatory. All the Upanishads are expressive without any explanations. They say, "This is such, this is so. This is what is happening. If you want, come in; do not stand outside. No explanation is possible from the inside to the outside, so come in. Become an insider." Even if you come inside, things will not be explained to you. You will come to know and feel them. Intellect can try to understand, but it is bound to be a failure. The higher cannot be reduced to the lower.

QUESTION: "Doesn't intuition come to one through thought waves that are just like radio waves?"

This, again, will be very difficult to explain. If intuition comes through some kind of waves, then sooner or later the intellect will be able to explain it.

It comes without any medium. That is the point! It comes

without a vehicle! It travels without any vehicle: that is why it is a jump; that is why it is a leap. If some waves are there and it comes to you through those waves, then it is not a jump, it is not a leap.

It is a jump from one point to another point, with no interconnection between the two. That is why it is a jump. If I come to you step by step, it is not a jump. Only if I come to you without any steps is it a jump. And a real jump is even deeper: it means that something exists on point A and then it exists on point B, and between the two there is no existence. That is a real jump!

Intuition is a jump. It is not something coming to you; that is a linguistic error. It is not something coming to you: it is something happening to you, not coming to you—something happening to you without any causality anywhere, without any source anywhere. This sudden happening means intuition.

If it is not sudden (not completely discontinuous with what went before) then reason will discover the path. It will take time, but it can be done. If some X-rays, some waves, or anything are carrying it to you, reason will be capable of knowing and understanding and controlling it. Then any day an instrument can be developed—just like radio or TV—in which intuitions can be received.

If intuition comes through rays or waves, then we can make an instrument to receive them. Then Mohammed is not needed. But as I see it, Mohammed will be needed. No instrument can "pick up" intuition because it is not a wave phenomenon. It is not a phenomenon at all. It is just a leap from nothing to being.

Intuition means just that. That is why reason denies it. Reason denies it because reason is incapable of encountering it. Reason can only encounter phenomenon that can be divided into cause and effect.

According to reason there are two realms of existence: the known and the unknown. And the unknown means that which is not yet known, but someday *will* be known. But religion says that there are three realms: the known, the unknown, and the unknowable. By "the unknowable" religion means that which can never be known.

Intellect is involved with the known and the unknown (not with the unknowable), and intuition works with the unknowable, with that which cannot be known. It is not just a question of time before it will be known; "unknow-ability" is its intrinsic quality. It is not that your instruments are not fine enough or your logic not up to date or your mathematics primitive. That is not the question. The intrinsic quality of the unknowable is unknowability. It will always exist as the unknowable. This is the realm of intuition.

When something from the unknowable comes to be known, it is a jump. *It is a jump!* There is no interlink; there is no passage; there is no going from one point to another point. But it seems inconceivable, so when I say, "You can feel it, but you cannot understand it," when I say such things, I know very well that I am uttering nonsense. Nonsense only means "that which cannot be understood by our senses." And mind is a sense, the most subtle . . . and wisdom is a sense.

Intuition is possible because the unknowable is there. Science denies the existence of the divine because it says, "There is only one division: the known and the unknown. If there is any God, we will discover Him through laboratory methods. If He exists, science will discover Him."

Religion, on the other hand, says, "Whatever you do, something in the very foundation of existence will remain unknowable—a mystery." And if religion is not right then I think that science is going to destroy the whole meaning of life. If there is no mystery, the whole meaning of life is destroyed and the whole beauty is destroyed. The unknowable is the beauty, the meaning, the aspiration, the goal. Because of the unknowable, life means something. When everything is known, then everything is flat. You will be fed up, bored. The unknowable is the secret; it is life itself.

I will say this: that reason is an effort to know the unknown and intuition is the happening of the unknowable.

To penetrate the unknowable is possible, but to explain it is not. The feeling is possible; the explanation is not.

The more you try to explain it the more closed you will become, so do not try. Let reason work in its own field, but remember continuously that there are deeper realms. There are deeper reasons which reason cannot understand, higher reasons that reason is incapable of conceiving.

## ∽ 14 ∽

## Consciousness, Witnessing, and Awareness

QUESTION: "What is the difference between awareness and witnessing?"

There is much difference between awareness and witnessing. Witnessing is still an act: you are doing it; the ego is there. So the phenomenon of witnessing is divided between the subject and the object.

Witnessing is a relationship between subject and object. Awareness is absolutely devoid of any subjectivity or objectivity. There is no one who is witnessing in awareness; there is no one who is being witnessed. Awareness is a total act, integrated. The subject and the object are not related in it; they are dissolved. So awareness doesn't mean that anyone is aware. Nor does it mean that anything is being attended to. Awareness is total—total subjectivity and total objectivity as a *single* phenomenon, while in witnessing a duality exists between subject and object.

Awareness is non-doing; witnessing implies a doer. But through witnessing, awareness is possible because witnessing means that it is a *conscious* act. It is an act, but conscious. You can do something and be unconscious—our ordinary activity is unconscious activity—but if you become conscious in it, it becomes witnessing. So from ordinary unconscious activity to awareness there is a gap that can be filled by witnessing.

Witnessing is a technique, a method, toward awareness. It is not awareness, but, as compared to ordinary activity, unconscious activity, it is a higher step. Something has changed: activity has become conscious; unconsciousness has been replaced by consciousness. But something more still has to be changed. That is, the activity has to be replaced by inactivity. That will be the second step.

It is difficult to jump from ordinary, unconscious action into awareness. It is possible but arduous, so a step in between is helpful. If one begins by witnessing conscious activity, then the jump becomes easier—the jump into awareness without any conscious object, without any conscious subject, without any conscious activity at all. This doesn't mean that awareness isn't consciousness. It is *pure* consciousness, but no one is conscious about it.

There is still a difference between consciousness and awareness. Consciousness is a quality of your mind, but it is not your total mind. Your mind can be both conscious and unconscious, but when you transcend your mind, there is no unconsciousness and no corresponding consciousness. There is *awareness*.

Awareness means that the total mind has become aware. Now the old mind is not there, but there is the quality of being conscious. Awareness has become the totality; the mind, itself, is now part of the awareness.

We cannot say that the mind is aware. We can only meaningfully say that the mind is conscious. Awareness means transcendence of the mind, so it is not the mind that is aware. It is only through transcendence of the mind, through going beyond mind, that awareness becomes possible. Consciousness is a quality of the mind; awareness is the transcendence. It is going beyond the mind.

Mind, as such, is the medium of duality, so consciousness can never transcend duality. It is always conscious of something, and there is always someone who is conscious. So consciousness is part and parcel of the mind, and mind, as such, is the source of all duality, of all divisions, whether they are between subject and object, activity or inactivity, consciousness or unconsciousness. Every type of duality is mental. Awareness is nondual, so awareness means the state of "no mind."

Then what is the relationship between consciousness and witnessing? Witnessing is a state, and consciousness is a means toward witnessing. If you begin to be conscious, you achieve witnessing. If you begin to be conscious of your acts, conscious of your day-to-day happenings, conscious of everything that surrounds you, then you begin to witness.

Witnessing comes as a consequence of consciousness. You cannot practice witnessing; you can only practice consciousness. Witnessing comes as a consequence, as a shadow, as a result, as a by-product. The more you become conscious, the more you go into witnessing, the more you come to be a witness. So consciousness is a method to achieve witnessing. And the second step is that witnessing will become a method to achieve awareness.

So these are the three steps: consciousness, witnessing, awareness. But where we exist is the lowest rank: that is, in unconscious activity. Unconscious activity is the state of our minds.

Through consciousness you can achieve witnessing, and through witnessing you can achieve awareness, and through awareness you can achieve "no achievement." Through awareness you can achieve all that is already achieved. After awareness there is nothing. Awareness is the end.

Awareness is the end of spiritual progress; unawareness is the beginning. Unawareness means a state of material existence. So unawareness and unconsciousness are not both the same. Unawareness means matter. Matter is not unconscious; it is unaware.

Animal existence is an unconscious existence; human existence is a mind phenomenon—99 percent unconscious and 1 percent conscious. This 1 percent consciousness means you are 1 percent conscious of your 99 percent unconsciousness. But if you become conscious of your own consciousness, then the 1 percent will go on increasing, and the 99 percent unconsciousness will go on decreasing.

If you become 100 percent conscious, you become a witness (a *sakshi*). If you become a *sakshi*, you have come to the jumping point from where the jump into awareness becomes possible. In awareness you lose the witness and only witnessing remains. You lose the doer, you lose the subjectivity, you lose the egocentric consciousness. Then consciousness remains, without the ego.

The circumference remains without the center. This circumference without the center is awareness. Consciousness without any center, without any source, without any motivation, without any source from which it comes—a "no source" consciousness—is awareness.

So you move from the unaware existence that is matter (*prakriti*) toward awareness. You may call it the divine, the godly, or whatever you choose to call it. Between matter and the divine, the difference is always of consciousness.

## ∽ 15 ∽

# The Difference Between Satori and Samadhi

QUESTION: "What is the difference in experience between satori (in Zen, a glimpse of enlightenment) and samadhi (cosmic consciousness)?"

Samadhi begins as a gap, but it never ends. A gap always begins and ends—it has boundaries: a beginning and an end—but samadhi begins as a gap and then is everlasting. There is no end to it. So if the happening comes as a gap and there is no end, it is samadhi, but if it is a complete gap—with a beginning and an end—then it is satori, and that is different.

If it is just a glimpse, just a gap, and the gap is again lost—if something is bracketed and the bracket is complete (you peep into it and come back; you jump into it and come back), if something happens and it is again lost—it is satori. It is a glimpse, a glimpse of samadhi, but not samadhi. Samadhi means the beginning of knowing, without any end.

In India we have no word that corresponds to satori, so sometimes, when the gap is great, one can misunderstand satori as samadhi. But it never is. It is just a glimpse. You have come to the cosmic and looked into it, and then everything is gone again. Of course, you will not be the same; now you will never be the same again. Something has penetrated into you, something has been added to you,

you can never be the same again, but, still, that which has changed you is not with you. It is just a remembrance, a memory. It is only a glimpse.

If you can remember it—if you can say, "I have known the moment"—it is only a glimpse because the moment samadhi has happened, you will not be there to remember it. Then you can never say, "I have known it," because with the knowing, the knower is lost. Only with the glimpse, the knower remains.

So the knower can keep this glimpse as a memory—he can cherish it, long for it, desire it, again endeavor to experience it—but *he* is still there. The one who has had a glimpse, the one who has looked, is there. It has become a memory. And now this memory will haunt you, will follow you, and will demand the phenomenon again and again.

The moment samadhi has happened, you are not there to remember it. Samadhi never becomes a part of memory because the one who *was* is no more. As they say in Zen, "The old man is no more and the new one has come . . ." and these two have never met, so there is no possibility of there being any memory. The old has gone and the new has come, and there has been no meeting between the two because the new can come only when the old has gone. Then it is not a memory. There is no haunting and no hankering after it. There is no longing for it. Then, as you are, you are at ease and there is nothing to desire.

It is not that you have killed the desire—no! It is desire-lessness in the sense that the one who could desire is no more. It is not a state of no desire; it is desirelessness because the one who could desire is no more. Then there is no longing, there is no future, because the future is created through our longings; it is a projection of our desires.

If there is no desire, there is no future. And if there is no future, there is no need of the past because the past is always a background against which, or through which, the future is longed for.

If there is no future, if you know that this very moment

you are going to die, there is no need to remember the past. Then there is no need to even remember your name because the name has a meaning only if there is a future. It may be needed. But if there is no future, you just burn all your bridges of the past. There is no need of them. The past has become absolutely meaningless. It is only against the future or for the future that the past is meaningful.

The moment samadhi has happened, the future becomes nonexistential. It is not, only the present moment is. It is the only time. There is not even any past. The past has dropped and the future also and a single, momentary existence becomes the total existence. You are in it, but not as an entity that is different from it. You cannot be different because you only become different from the total existence due to your past or your future. The past and future, crystallized around you, is the only barrier between you and the present moment that is happening. So when samadhi happens, there is no past and no future. Then it is not that you are in the present, but you *are* the present, you *become* the present.

Samadhi is not a glimpse, samadhi is a death; but satori is a glimpse, not a death. And satori is possible through so many ways! An aesthetic experience can be a possible source for satori; music can be a possible source for satori; love can be a possible source for satori. In any intense moment in which the past becomes meaningless—in any intense moment when you are existing in the present (a moment of either love or music or poetic feeling, or of any aesthetic phenomenon in which the past doesn't interfere, in which there is no desire for the future)—satori becomes possible. But this is just a glimpse.

This glimpse is meaningful because, through satori, you can feel for the first time what samadhi can mean. The first taste, or the first distinct perfume of samadhi, comes through satori. So satori is helpful. But anything that is helpful can be a hindrance if you cling to it and you feel that it is everything. Satori has a bliss that can fool you; it has a bliss of its own.

The Difference Between Satori and Samadhi 171

Because you have not known samadhi, this is the ultimate that comes to you, and you cling to it. But if you cling to it, you can change that which was helpful, that which was friendly, into something that becomes a barrier and an enemy. So one must be aware of the possible danger of satori. If you are aware of this, then the experience of satori will be helpful.

A single, momentary glimpse is something that can never be known by any other means. No one can explain it. No words, no communication, can even be a hint to it. Satori is meaningful, but just as a glimpse, as a breakthrough, as a single, momentary breakthrough into the existence, into the abyss.

You have not even known the moment, you have not even become aware of it before it becomes closed to you. Just a click of the camera—a click—and everything is lost. Then a hankering will be created; you will risk everything for that moment. But do not long for it; do not desire it. Let it sleep in the memory. Do not make a problem out of it; just forget it. If you can forget it and do not cling to it, these moments will come to you more and more, the glimpses will be coming to you more and more.

A demanding mind becomes closed, and the glimpse is shut off. It always comes when you are not aware of it, when you are not looking for it—when you are relaxed, when you are not even thinking about it, when you are not even meditating. Even when you are meditating the glimpse becomes impossible, but when you are not meditating, when you are just in a moment of let go—not even doing anything, not even waiting for anything—in that relaxed moment, satori happens.

It will begin to happen more and more, but do not think about it; do not long for it. And never mistake it for samadhi.

QUESTION: "What kind of preparations are necessary to experience satori?"

Satori becomes possible for a great number of people because sometimes it needs no preparations; sometimes it happens by chance. The situation is created, but unknowingly. There are so many people who have known it. They may not know it as satori, may not have interpreted it as satori, but they have known it. A great surging love can create it.

Even through chemical drugs, satori is possible. It is possible through mescaline, LSD, marijuana, because through a chemical change the mind can expand enough so that there is a glimpse. After all, all of us have chemical bodies—the mind and the body are chemical units—so through chemistry, too, the glimpse can be possible.

Sometimes a sudden danger can penetrate you so much that the glimpse becomes possible . . . sometimes a great shock can bring you so much into the moment that the glimpse becomes possible. And for those who have some aesthetic sensibility, who have a poetic heart, who have a "feeling" attitude toward reality (not an intellectual attitude), the glimpse can be possible.

For a rational, logical, intellectual personality, the glimpse is impossible. Sometimes it can happen to an intellectual person, but only through some intense, intellectual tension—when suddenly the tension is relaxed. It happened for Archimedes. He was in satori when he came out into the street, naked from his bathtub, and began to cry, "Eureka, I've found it!" It was a sudden release of the constant tension he had concerning a problem. The problem was solved, so the tension that existed because of the problem was suddenly completely released. He ran out naked into the streets and cried, "Eureka, I've found it!"

For an intellectual person, if a great problem that has demanded his total mind and brought him to the peak of intellectual tension is suddenly solved, it can bring him to a moment of satori. But for aesthetic minds it is easier.

QUESTION: "You mean even intellectual tension can be a way to achieve satori?"

It may be; it may not be. If you become intellectually tense during this discussion and the tension is not brought to the extreme, it will be a hindrance. But if you become totally tense and then suddenly something is understood, that understanding will be a release and satori can happen.

Or, if this discussion is not at all tense, if we are just chitchatting—totally relaxed, totally nonserious—even this discussion can be an aesthetic experience. It is not only that flowers are aesthetic; even words can be. It is not only that trees are aesthetic; human beings can also be. It is not only when you are watching clouds floating by that satori becomes possible; even if you participate in a dialogue, it becomes possible. But either a relaxed participation is needed or a very tense participation. You can either be relaxed to begin with or relaxation can come to you because your tension has been brought to a peak and then released. When either happens, even a dialogue, a discussion, can become a source of satori.

Anything can become a source of satori; it depends on you. It never depends on anything else. You are just passing through a street: a child is laughing . . . and satori can happen!

There is a haiku that tells a story something like this: a monk is crossing a street and a very ordinary flower is peeking out from a wall—a very ordinary flower, a day-to-day flower, which is everywhere. He looks at it. It is the first time he has ever really looked at it because it is so ordinary, so obvious. It is always to be found somewhere, so he never bothered to really look at it before. He looks into it . . . and satori happens!

An ordinary flower is never looked at. It is so common that you forget it. So the monk has never really seen this flower before. For the first time in his life he has *seen* it, and the event became phenomenal. This first meeting with the flower, with this very ordinary flower, becomes unique.

Now he feels sorry for it. It has always been there waiting for him, but he has never looked at it. He feels sorry for it, asks its pardon . . . and the thing happens!

The flower is there, and the monk is standing there dancing. Someone asks, "What are you doing?"

He says, "I have seen something uncommon in a very common flower. The flower was always waiting. I never looked at it before, but today a meeting has happened." The flower is not common now. The monk has penetrated into it, and the flower has penetrated into the monk.

An ordinary thing, even a pebble, can be a source. For a child a pebble is a source, but for us it is not a source because it has become so familiar. Anything uncommon, anything rare, anything that has come into your sight for the first time, can be a source for satori, and if you are available—if you are there, if your presence is there—the phenomenon can happen.

Satori happens to almost everyone. It may not be interpreted as such, you may not have known it to be satori, but it happens. And this happening is the cause of all spiritual seeking. Otherwise spiritual seeking would not be possible. How can you be in search of something of which you have not even had a glimpse? First something must have come to you, some ray must have come to you (a touch . . . a breeze . . .), something must have come to you that has become the quest.

A spiritual quest is only possible if something has happened to you without your knowing. It may be in love, it may be in music, it may be in nature, it may be in friendship. It may be in any communion. Something has happened to you that has been a source of bliss and it is now just a remembering, a memory. It may not even be a conscious memory; it may be unconscious. It may be waiting like a seed somewhere deep within you. This seed will become the source of a quest, and you will go on searching for something that you do not know. What are you searching for? You do not know. But still, somewhere, even unknown to you, some experience, some blissful moment, has become part and parcel of your mind. It has become a seed, and now that seed is working its way through, and you are in quest of something which you cannot name, which you cannot explain.

What are you seeking? If a spiritual person is sincere and honest he cannot say, "I am seeking God," because he does not know whether God is or not. And the word "god" is absolutely meaningless unless you have known. So you cannot seek God or *moksha* (liberation). You cannot.

A sincere seeker will have to fall back upon himself. The seeking is not for something outward; it is for something inward. Somewhere something is known which has been glimpsed at, which has become the seed, and which is compelling you, pushing you, toward something unknown.

Spiritual seeking is not a pulling from without; it is a push from within. It is always a push. And if it is a pull, the seeking is insincere, unauthentic. Then it is nothing but a search for a new sort of gratification, a new turn to your desires.

Spiritual seeking is always a push toward something deep inside you of which you have had a glimpse. You have not interpreted it; you have not known it consciously. It may be a childhood memory of satori that is deep down in the unconscious. It may be a blissful moment of satori in your mother's womb, a blissful existence with no worry, with no tension, with a completely relaxed state of mind. It may be a deep, unconscious feeling, a feeling that you have not known consciously, that is pushing you.

Psychologists agree that the whole concept of spiritual seeking comes from the blissful experience in the mother's womb. It is so blissful, so dark; there is not even a single ray of tension. With the first glimpse of light, tension begins to be felt, but the darkness is absolute relaxation. There is no worry, nothing to do. You do not even have to breathe; your mother breathes for you. You exist exactly as it is interpreted that one exists when *moksha* is achieved. Everything just is . . . and to be is blissful. Nothing has to be done to achieve this state; it just is.

So it may be that there is a deep, unconscious seed inside you that has experienced total relaxation. It may be
some childhood experience of aesthetic blissfulness, a
childhood satori. Every childhood is "satori-ful," but we
have lost it. Paradise is lost, and Adam is thrown out of
Paradise. But the remembrance is there, the unknown remembrance that pushes you on.

Samadhi is different from this. You have not known
samadhi, but through satori there is the promise that something greater is possible. Satori becomes a promise that
leads you toward samadhi.

QUESTION: "What should we do to achieve it?"

You should not do anything. Only one thing: you must
be aware; you must not resist. There must not be any resistance to it. But there *is* resistance. That is why there is
suffering. There is an unconscious resistance. If something
begins to happen to the *brahma-randhra*,[1] it just begins to
make ego death come nearer. It seems so painful that there
is inner resistance. This resistance can take two forms:
either you will stop doing meditation or you will ask what
can be done to transcend it, to go beyond it.

Nothing should be done. This asking, too, is a sort of
resistance. Let it do what it is doing. Just be aware, and
accept it totally. Be with it; let it do whatever it is doing,
and be cooperative with it.

QUESTION: "Should I just be a witness to it?"

Don't be just a witness because to be just a witness to
this process will create barriers. Do not be a witness. Be
cooperative with it; be one with it. Just cooperate with it.
Totally surrender to it—surrender yourself to it—and say
to it, "Do anything, do whatsoever is needed," and you just
be cooperative.

Do not resist it and do not be attentive to it because
even your attention will be a resistance. Just be with it and

[1] See page 76.

let it do whatever is needed. You cannot know what is
needed and you cannot plan what is to be done. You can
only surrender to it and let it do whatever is necessary.
The *brahma-randhra* has its own wisdom, every center has
its own wisdom, and if we become attentive to it, a disturbance will be created.

The moment you become aware of any of the inner
workings of your body you create a disturbance because
you create tension. The whole working of the body, the
inner working, is unconscious. For example, once you have
taken your food you must not be attentive to it. You must
let your body do whatever it likes. If you become attentive
to your stomach, then you will disturb it. The whole working will become disturbed and the whole stomach will be
diseased.

Likewise, when the *brahma-randhra* is working, do not
be attentive to it because your attention will work against
it, *you* will work against it. You will be face to face with
it, and this facing, this encountering, will be a disturbance.
Then the process will be unnecessarily prolonged.

So starting from tomorrow, just be with it, move with it,
suffer with it, and let it do whatever it wants to do. You
must be totally surrendered, wholly given to it.

This surrender is *akarma* (nonactivity). It is more
*akarma* than being attentive because your attention is
karma (action); it is an activity.

So just be with whatever is happening. It is not that by
being with it you will not be aware, but only that you will
not be attentive. You will be aware and that is different.
While being with it there will be awareness, a diffused
awareness. You will be knowing all the time that something is happening, but now you will be with it, and there
will be no contradiction between your awareness and the
happening.

QUESTION: "Will meditation lead to samadhi?"

In the beginning effort will be needed. Unless you are
beyond the mind, effort will be needed. Once you are

beyond the mind there is no need of effort, and if it is still
needed that means you are not beyond the mind. A bliss
that needs effort is of the mind. A bliss that does not need
any effort has become natural; it is of the being. Then it
is just like breathing. No effort is needed—not only no
effort, but no alertness is needed. It continues. Now it is
not something added to you; it *is* you. Then it becomes
samadhi.

*Dhyan* (meditation) is effort; samadhi is effortlessness.
Meditation is effort; ecstasy is effortlessness. Then you do
not need to do anything about it. That is why I say that
unless you come to a point where meditation becomes
useless, you have not achieved the goal. The path must
become useless. If you have achieved the goal, if you have
come to the goal, the path is useless.

## ~ 16 ~

## Sexual Energy and the Awakening
## of the *Kundalini*

QUESTION: "How does one overcome the pull toward sex
so that the *kundalini* can go upward?"

Energy has been going downward through the sex center
continuously for many births, so when any energy is created
it will first try to move downward. That is why meditation
sometimes will create more sexuality in you than you have
ever felt before. You will feel more sexual because you
have generated more energy than you previously had. When
you have conserved something, the old, habitual passage is
ready to release it. The mechanism is ready: the old
passage is ready. Your mind only knows one passage—the
lower one, the sexual passage—so when you are meditating
the first movement of your life energy will be downward.
Just be aware of it.

Do not struggle with it; just be aware of it. Be aware of
the habitual passage; be aware of sexual images. Let them
come. Be aware of them, but do not do anything about the
situation. Just be aware of it. The sexual passage cannot
operate without your cooperation, but if you cooperate with
it even for a single moment, it can start functioning. So
do not cooperate with it: just be aware of it.

The mechanism of sex is so much a momentary phenomenon that it *only* functions momentarily. If you do not cooperate at the right moment, it stops. At the right moment your cooperation is needed, otherwise it cannot work. It is only a momentary mechanism, and if you do not cooperate with it, it will stop by itself.

Time and time again, energy is created through meditation. It continues to move downward, but now you are aware of it. The old passage is cut—*not* suppressed! Energy is there, and it needs to be released, but the lower door is closed. Not suppressed: closed. You have not cooperated with it, that's all. You have not *positively* suppressed it, you have only *negatively* not cooperated with it.

You have just been aware of what is happening to your mind, to your body. You are just aware. Then energy is conserved. Then the quantity of the energy becomes more and more intense and an upward thrust becomes necessary. Now the energy will go upward. By its very force, a new passage will be thrown open.

When energy goes upward you will be more sexually attractive to others because life energy going upward creates a great magnetic force. You will become more sexually attractive to others, so you will have to be aware of this. Now you will attract persons unknowingly. And the attraction will not only be physical; the attraction will be etheric.

Even a repulsive body, a nonattractive body, will become attractive with yoga. The attraction is etheric. And it is so magnetic that one has to be constantly aware of it, constantly aware. You will be attractive . . . and the opposite sex will be irresistibly drawn to you. There are subtle vibrations that are created by your etheric body: you have to be aware of them. The type of attraction that will be felt by the opposite sex will differ—it will take so many different forms—but basically it will be sexual. At its root, it will be sexual.

But you can help these people. Even if they are attracted to you sexually, they have become attracted to a sexual

energy that is moving upward. And they, too, are not ordinary sexual beings. Upward-moving sexual energy has
become an attraction, a magnet. So you can help them. If
you do not become involved, then you can help them.

QUESTION: "In the awakening of the *kundalini,* in the opening of the passage, isn't there an increase in sexual power?"

The increase in sexual power and the opening of the
*kundalini* passage are simultaneous . . . not the same, but
simultaneous. The increase in sexual power will be the
thrust to open up the higher centers. So sexual power will
increase. If you can be aware of it and not use it sexually—
if you do not allow it to be released sexually—it will become so intense that the upward movement will begin.

First the energy will try its best to be released sexually
because that is its usual outlet, its usual center. So one must
first be aware of one's downward "doors." Only awareness
will close them; only noncooperation will close them. Sex
is not so forceful as we feel it to be. It is forceful only
momentarily: it is not a twenty-four-hour affair; it is a
momentary challenge.

If you can be noncooperative and aware, it goes. And
you will feel more happiness than when sexual energy is
released from the downward passage. Conservation of
energy is always blissful. Wastage of energy is only a relief;
it is not blissful. You have unburdened yourself; you have
alleviated something that was troubling you. Now you have
become unburdened, but you have also become emptied.

That is why depression follows sex. You have unburdened yourself and now you are empty: something has been
lost, exhausted. But by conserving the energy there is an
upward thrust. You feel enriched. You feel an inner growth;
you feel an inner richness. You feel something is there
within you. You are not emptied.

The feeling of emptiness that is overtaking the whole
Western mind is just because of sexual wastage. Life seems
to be empty. Life is never empty! But it seems to be empty

because you have been simply unburdening yourself, just
relieving yourself. If something is conserved it becomes a
richness: if your upward door is open and energy goes upward, not only do you feel relieved, not only is the strain-
ing point relieved, but now it is not vacant. In a way it is
fulfilled; it is overflowing.

The energy has gone upward, but the basic center has
not become empty. It is overflowing, and the overflowing
energy goes upward, up toward the *brahma-randhra.* Then,
near the *brahma-randhra,* there is neither an upward movement nor a downward movement. Now the energy goes to
the cosmic: it goes to the All; it goes to the *Brahman*
(the ultimate reality). That is why the seventh chakra
is known as the *brahma-randhra*—the door to the Brahman, the door to the divine. Then there is no "up" and no
"down." It will feel like something is penetrating, thrust-
ing upward . . . and a moment will come when one will
feel as though that something is no longer there, that it has
gone. Now it is overflowing into the passage.

The "petals" of the *sahasrar* are just a symbol for the
feelings that occur when energy overflows. The overflowing
is a flowering, just like a flower, itself, is an overflowing.
You will feel that something has become a flower. The door
is open, and it will go outward.

It will not be felt inwardly; it will be felt outwardly.
Something has opened like a flower, like a flower with a
thousand petals. It is just a feeling, but the feeling corresponds to the truth. The feeling is a translation and interpretation. The mind cannot conceive of it, but the feeling
is just like a flowering. The closest, the nearest, thing that
we can say is that it is like a bud opening. It is felt like
that. That is why we have conceived of the opening of the
*sahasrar* as "a thousand-petaled lotus."

So many petals—so many! And they go on opening . . .
they go on opening. The opening is endless. It is a fulfill-
ment; it is a flowering of the human being. Then you be-

come just like a tree, and everything that was in you has flowered.

Then all you can do is to offer this flower to the divine. We have been offering flowers, but they are broken flowers. Only *this* flower can be a real offering.

## ❧ 17 ❧

# The Manifestations of Prana in the
# Seven Bodies

QUESTION: "What is prana and how is it manifested in
each of the seven bodies?"

Prana is energy—the living energy in us, the life in us.
This life manifests itself, as far as the physical body is concerned, as the incoming and the outgoing breath. These
are two opposite things. We take them as one—we say,
"breathing"—but breathing has two polarities: the incoming breath and the outgoing breath. Every energy has
polarities, every energy exists in two opposite poles. It cannot exist otherwise. The opposite poles, with their tension
and harmony, create energy—just like magnetic poles.

The incoming breath is quite contrary to the outgoing,
and the outgoing is quite contrary to the incoming. In a
single moment the incoming is just like birth and the outgoing is just like death. In a single moment both things are
happening: when you take breath in, you are born; when
you throw breath out, you die. In a single moment there
is birth and death. This polarity is life energy coming up,
going down.

In the physical body, life energy takes this manifestation.
Life energy is born, and after seventy years it dies. That,

too, is a greater manifestation of the same phenomenon: the incoming breath and the outgoing breath . . . the day and the night.

In all of the seven bodies (the physical, the etheric, the astral, the mental, the spiritual, the cosmic, and the nirvanic) there will be a corresponding incoming and outgoing phenomenon. As far as the mental body is concerned, thought coming in and thought going out is the same kind of phenomenon as breath coming in and breath going out. Every moment a thought comes in your mind and a thought goes out. . . .

Thought, itself, is energy. In the mental body the energy manifests as the coming of thought and the going of thought; in the physical body it manifests as breath coming and breath going. That is why you can change your thinking with breathing. There is a correspondence.

If you stop your breath from coming in, thought will be stopped from coming in. Stop your breath in your physical body and in the mental body thought will stop. And as the physical body becomes uneasy, your mental body will become uneasy. The physical body will long to breathe in; the mental body will long to take thought in.

Just as breath is taken in from the outside and the air exists outside you, likewise an ocean of thought exists outside you. Thought comes in, and thought goes out. Your breath can become my breath at another moment and your thought can become my thought. Every time you throw your breath out you are likewise throwing your thought out. Just as air exists, so thought exists; just as air can be contaminated, so thought can be contaminated; just as air can be impure, so thought can be impure.


The breath, itself, is not prana. "Prana" means the vital energy that manifests itself by these polarities of coming in and going out. The *energy* that takes the breath in is prana, not the breath itself. The energy that takes breath

in, which asserts it, that energy that is taking the breath in
and throwing it out, is prana.

The energy that takes thought in and throws thought out:
that energy, too, is prana. In all of the seven bodies, this
process exists. I am only talking now of the physical and
the mental because these two are known to us; we can
understand them easily. But in every layer of your being
the same thing exists.

Your second body, the etheric body, has its own incoming and outgoing process. You will feel this process in each
of the seven bodies, but you will feel it to be just like the
incoming breath and outgoing breath because you are only
acquainted with your physical body and its prana. Then
you will always misunderstand.

Whenever any feeling comes to you of another body or
its prana you will first understand it as the coming in and
the going out of breath because this is the only experience
you know. You have only known this manifestation of
prana, of vital energy. But on the etheric plane, there is
neither breath nor thought, but influence (simply influence) coming in and going out.

You come into contact with somebody without having
known him before. He has not even talked with you, but
something about him comes in. You have either taken him
in or thrown him out. There is a subtle influence: you may
call it love or you may call it hatred—the attractive or
the repulsive.

When you are repulsed or attracted, it is your second
body. And every moment the process is going on; it never
stops. You are always taking influences in and then throwing them out. The other pole will always be there. If you
have loved someone, then in a certain moment you will
be repulsed. If you have loved someone the breath has been
taken in: now it will be thrown out and you will be repulsed. So every moment of love will be followed by a
moment of repulsion.

The vital energy exists in polarities. It never exists at one pole. It cannot! And whenever you try to make it do so, you try the impossible.

You cannot love someone without hating him at some time. The hatred will be there because the vital force cannot exist at a single pole. It exists at opposite polarities, so a friend is bound to be an enemy . . . and this will go on. This coming in and going out will happen up to the seventh body. No body can exist without this process— this coming in and going out. It cannot; just as the physical body cannot exist without the incoming and outgoing breath.

As far as the physical body is concerned, we never take these two things as opposites, so we are not disturbed about it. Life makes no distinction between the incoming breath and the outgoing breath. There is no moral distinction. There is nothing to be chosen; both are the same. The phenomenon is natural.

But as far as the second body is concerned, hatred *must not* be there and love *must* be there. Then you have begun to choose. You have begun to choose, and this choice will create disturbances. That is why the physical body is ordinarily more healthy than the second, the etheric, body. The etheric body is always in conflict because moral choosing has made a hell out of it.

When love comes to you, you feel a well-being, but when hatred comes to you, you feel diseased. But it is bound to come . . . so a person who knows, a person who has understood the polarities, is not disappointed when it comes. A person who has known the polarities is at ease, at equilibrium. He knows it is bound to happen, so he neither tries to love when he is not loving nor does he create any hatred. Things come and go: he is not attracted to the incoming nor repulsed by the outgoing. He is just a witness. He says, "It is just like breath coming in and breath going out."

The Buddhist meditation method of Anapana-sati Yoga[1] is concerned with this. It says to just be a witness to your incoming and outgoing breath. Just be a witness. And begin from the physical body. The other six bodies are not talked about in Anapana-sati because they will come by themselves, by and by.

The more you become acquainted with this polarity (with this dying and living simultaneously, with this simultaneous birth and death), the more you will become aware of the second body. Toward hatred, then, Buddha says, "Have *upeksha*" ("Be indifferent"). Whether it is hatred or it is love, be indifferent. And do not be attached to anyone because if you are attached, what will happen to the other pole? Then you will be at a "dis-ease." Disease will be there; you will not be at ease.

Buddha says, "The coming of the beloved one is welcomed, but the going of the beloved one is wept over. The meeting with the one who is repulsive is a misery, and the departing of a repulsive one is bliss. But if you go on dividing yourself into these polarities, you will be in hell, living in a hell."

If you just become a witness to these polarities, then you say, "This is a natural phenomenon. It is natural to the 'body' concerned (i.e., one of the seven bodies). The body exists because of this; otherwise, it cannot exist." And the moment you become aware of it, you transcend the body. If you transcend your first body, then you become aware of the second. If you transcend your second body, then you become aware of the third. . . .

Witnessing is always beyond life and death. The breath coming in and the breath going out are two things, and if you become a witness, then you are neither. Then a third force has come into being. Now you are not the manifestations of prana in the physical body. Now you *are* the prana, the witness. Now you see that life manifests on the physical

[1] See pages 201–205 for a discussion of Anapana-sati Yoga.

level because of this polarity, and if this polarity stops the physical body will not be there, it cannot exist. It needs tension to exist—this constant tension of coming and going, this constant tension of birth and death. It exists because of this. Every moment it moves between the two poles. Otherwise, it would not exist.

In the second body, "love and hate" is the basic polarity. It is manifested in so many ways. The basic polarity is this "liking and disliking," and every moment your liking becomes disliking and your disliking becomes liking. Every moment! But you never see it. When your liking becomes disliking, if you suppress your disliking and continue fooling yourself that you will go on liking the same things always, you are only fooling yourself doubly. And if you dislike something, you go on disliking it, never allowing yourself to see the moments when you have liked it. We suppress our love for our enemies, and we suppress our hatred for our friends. We are suppressing! We allow only one movement (only one pole), but, because it comes back again, we are at ease. It returns, so we are at ease. But it is discontinuous; it is never continuous. It never can be.

The vital force manifests itself as like and dislike in the second body. But it is just like breath: there is no difference. Influence is the medium here; air is the medium in the physical body. The second body lives in an atmosphere of influences. It is not simply that someone comes in contact with you and you begin to like him. Even if no one comes in and you are alone in the room, you will be liking/disliking, liking/disliking. It will make no difference: the liking and disliking will go on alternating continuously.

It is through this polarity that the etheric body exists. It is its breath. If you become a witness to it, then you can just laugh. Then there is no enemy and no friend. Then you know it is just a natural phenomenon.

If you become aware and become a witness to the second body (to the liking and disliking) then you can know the third body. The third is the astral body. Just like the "in-fluences" of the etheric body, the astral body has "mag-netic forces." Its magnetism is its breath. One moment you are powerful and the next moment you are powerless; one moment you are hopeful and the next moment you are hopeless; one moment you are confident and the next mo-ment you lose all your confidence. It is a coming in of magnetism to you and a going out of magnetism from you. There are moments when you can defy even God, and there are moments when you fear even a shadow.

When the magnetic force is in you (when it is coming into you), you are great; when it has gone from you, you are just a nobody. And this is changing back and forth, just like day and night. The circle revolves, the wheel revolves. So even a person like Napoleon had his impotent moments and even a very cowardly person has his moments of bravery.

In judo there is a technique to know when a person is powerless. That is the moment to attack him. When he is powerful you are bound to be defeated, so you have to know the moment when his magnetic power is going out and attack him then. And you should incite him to attack you when your magnetic force is coming in.

This coming in and going out of the magnetic force corresponds to your breathing. That is why, when you have to do something difficult, you will hold your breath in. For example, if you are to lift a heavy stone, you cannot pick it up when the breath is going out. You cannot do it! But when the breath is coming in, or when the breath is held in, you can do it. Your breath corresponds to what is happening in the third body. So when the breath is going out (unless the person has been trained to fool you), that is the moment when his magnetic force is going out. That is the moment to attack! And this is the secret of judo. Even a stronger person than you can be defeated if you know the secret of when he is fearful and powerless. When the magnetic force is out of him, he is bound to be power-less.

The third body lives in a magnetic sphere, just like air. There are magnetic forces all around: you are breathing them in and breathing them out. But if you become aware of this magnetic force that is coming and going, then you are neither powerful nor powerless. You transcend both.

Then there is the fourth body, the mental body: thought pulling in and thought pulling out. But this "thought coming in" and "thought going out" has parallels, too. When thought comes to you while you breathe in, only in those moments is original thinking born. When you breathe out, those are moments of impotency; no original thought can be born in those moments. In moments when some original thought is there, the breathing will even stop. When some original thought is born, then the breath stops. It is only a corresponding phenomenon.

In the outgoing thought, nothing is born. It is simply dead. But if you become aware of thoughts coming in and thoughts going out, then you can know the fifth body.

Up to the fourth body, things are not difficult to understand because we have some experience which can become the basis to understand them. Beyond the fourth, things become very strange . . . but still, something can be understood. And when you transcend the fourth body you will understand it more.

In the fifth body—how to say it? The atmosphere for the fifth body is *life*, just as thought, as breath, as magnetic force, as love and hatred, are atmospheres for the lower bodies.

For the fifth body, life, itself, is the atmosphere. So in the fifth, the coming in is a moment of life, and the going out is a moment of death. With the fifth, you become aware that life is not something that is in you. It comes into you and goes out from you. Life, itself, is not in you. It simply comes in and goes out, just like breath.

That is why breath and prana became synonymous, because of the fifth body. In the fifth body, the word "prana" is meaningful. It is life that is coming and life that is going. And that is why the fear of death is constantly following us. You are always aware that death is nearby, waiting at the corner. It is always there, waiting. This feeling of death always waiting for you—this feeling of insecurity, of death, of darkness—is concerned with the fifth body. It is a very dark feeling, very vague, because you are not completely aware of it.

When you come to the fifth body and become aware of it, then you know that life and death both are just breaths to the fifth body (coming in and going out). And when you become aware of this, then you know that you cannot die because death is not an inherent phenomenon. Nor is life. Both life and death are outward phenomena happening to you. You never have been alive, you never have been dead. You are something that completely transcends both. But this feeling of transcendence can only come when you become aware of the life force and the death force in the fifth body.

Freud said somewhere that he somehow had a glimpse of this. He was not an adept in yoga, otherwise he would have understood it. He called it "the will to die" and he said every man sometimes is longing for life and sometimes is longing for death. There are two opposing wills in men: a will to live and a will to die. To the Western mind it was absolutely absurd: how could these contradictory wills exist in one person? But Freud said that because suicide is possible, there must be a will to die.

No animal can commit suicide because no animal can become aware of the fifth body. Animals cannot commit suicide because they cannot become aware, they cannot know, that they are alive. To commit suicide, one thing is necessary—to be aware of life—and they are not aware of life. But another thing is also necessary: to commit suicide you must also be unaware of death.

Animals cannot commit suicide because animals are not aware of life, but we *can* commit suicide because we are aware of life but not aware of death. If one becomes aware of death, then one cannot commit suicide. A Buddha cannot commit suicide because it is unnecessary; it is nonsense. He knows that you cannot really kill yourself, you can only pretend to. Suicide is just a pose because, really, you are neither alive nor dead.

Death is on the fifth plane, in the fifth body. It is a going out of a particular energy and a coming in of a particular energy. You are the one in which this coming and going happens. If you become identified with the first, you can commit the second. If you become identified with living, and if life becomes impossible, you can say, "I will commit suicide." This is the other aspect of your fifth body asserting itself. There is not a single human being who has not thought at sometime to commit suicide because death is the other side of life. This other side can become either suicide or murder: it can become either.

If you are obsessed with life, if you are so attached to it that you want to deny death completely, you can kill another. By killing another you satisfy your death wish ("the will to die"). By this trick you satisfy it, and you think that now you will not have to die because someone else has died.

All those persons who have committed great murders— Hitler, Mussolini—are still very much afraid of death. They are always in fear of death, so they project this death on others. The person who can kill someone else feels that he is more powerful than death. He can kill others. In a "magical way," with a "magical formula," he thinks that because he can kill he transcends death, that a thing he can do to others cannot be done to him. This is a projection of death. But it can come back to you. If you kill so many persons that in the end you commit suicide, it is the projection coming back to you.

In the fifth body, with life and death coming to you— with life coming and going—one cannot be attached to anyone. If you are attached, you are not accepting the polarity in its totality, and you will become ill.

Up to the fourth body it was not so difficult, but to conceive of death and to accept it as another aspect of life is the most difficult act. To conceive of life and death as parallel—as just the same, as two aspects of one thing—is the most difficult act. But in the fifth, this is the polarity. This is pranic existence in the fifth.

With the sixth body, things become even more difficult because the sixth is no longer life. For the sixth body—what to say? After the fifth, the "I" drops, the ego drops. Then there is no ego; you become one with the All. Now it is not *your* "anything" that comes in and goes out because the ego is not. Everything becomes cosmic, and because it becomes cosmic, the polarity takes the form of creation and destruction (*srishti* and *pralaya*). That is why it becomes more difficult with the sixth: the atmosphere is "the creative force and the destructive force." In Hindu mythology they call these forces "Brahma" and "Shiva."

Brahma is the deity of creation, Vishnu is the deity of maintenance, and Shiva is the deity of the great death—of destruction or dissolution (where everything goes back to its original source). The sixth body is in that vast sphere of creativity and destructivity: the force of Brahma and the force of Shiva.

Every moment the creation comes to you, and every moment everything goes into dissolution. So when a yogi says, "I have seen the creation, and I have seen the *pralaya* (the end) . . . I have seen the coming of the world into being and I have seen the returning of the world into nonbeing," he is talking about the sixth body. The ego is not there: everything that is coming in and going out is you. You become one with it.

A star is being born: it is *your* birth that is coming. And the star is going out: that is *your* going out. So they say in Hindu mythology that one creation is one breath of Brahma—only one breath! It is the cosmic force breathing. When he, Brahma, breathes in, the creation comes into existence: a star is born . . . stars come out of chaos . . .

everything comes into existence. And when his breath goes out, everything goes out, everything ceases: a star dies . . . existence moves into nonexistence.

That is why I am saying that in the sixth body it is very difficult. The sixth is not egocentric; it becomes cosmic. And in the sixth body, everything about creation is known —everything that all of the religions of the world talk about. When one talks about creation, he is talking about the sixth body and the knowledge concerned with it. And when one is talking of the great flood (the end), one is talking about the sixth body.

With the great flood of Judeo-Christian or Babylonian mythology, or Syrian mythology, or with the *pralaya* of the Hindus, there is one out breath—that of the sixth body. This is a cosmic experience, not an individual one. This is a cosmic experience! You are not there!

The person who is in the sixth body—who has reached to the sixth body—will see everything that is dying as his own death. A Mahavira cannot kill an ant, not because of any principle of nonviolence, but because it is his death. Everything that dies is his death.

When you become aware of this, of the creation and the destruction, of things coming into existence every moment and things going out of existence every moment, the awareness is of the sixth body. Whenever a thing is going out of existence, something else is coming in: a sun is dying; another is being born somewhere else . . . this earth will die; another earth will come. We become attached even in the sixth body ("Humanity must not die!"), but everything that is born must die, even humanity must die. Hydrogen bombs will be created to destroy it. And the moment we create hydrogen bombs, the very next moment we create a longing to go to another planet because the bomb means that the earth is near its death. Before this earth dies, life will begin to evolve somewhere else.

The sixth body is the feeling of cosmic creation and destruction (creation: destruction . . . the breath coming in: the breath going out). That is why "Brahma's breath" is used. Brahma is a sixth-body personality; you become Brahma in the sixth body. Really, you become aware of both Brahma and Shiva, the two polarities. And Vishnu is beyond the polarity. They form the *tri-murti*, the trinity: Brahma, Vishnu, and Mahesh (or Shiva).

This trinity is the trinity of witnessing. If you become aware of the Brahma and Shiva (the creator and the destroyer)—if you become aware of those two—then you know the third, which is Vishnu. Vishnu is your reality in the sixth body. That is why Vishnu became the most prominent of the three. Brahma is remembered, but—although he is the god of creation—he is worshipped in perhaps only one or two temples. He *must* be worshipped, but he is not really worshipped.

Shiva is worshipped even more than Vishnu because we fear death. The worship of him comes out of our fear of death. But hardly anyone worships Brahma, the god of creation, because there is nothing to be fearful of: you are already created. So you are not concerned with Brahma. That is why not a single great temple is dedicated to him. He is the creator, so every temple *should* be dedicated to him, but it is not.

Shiva has the greatest number of worshippers. He is everywhere because so many temples were made as a dedication to him. Just a stone is enough to symbolize him. (Otherwise it would have been impossible to create so many idols of him!) So just a stone is enough. . . . Just put a stone somewhere and Shiva is there. Because the mind is so fearful of death you cannot escape from Shiva. He must be worshipped! And he *has* been worshipped.

But Vishnu is the more substantial divinity. That is why Ram is an incarnation of Vishnu, Krishna is an incarnation of Vishnu, every avatar (divine incarnation) is an incarnation of Vishnu. And even Brahma and Shiva worship Vishnu. Brahma may be the creator, but he creates for Vishnu; Shiva may be the destroyer, but he destroys for Vishnu. These are the two breaths of Vishnu (the incoming and the outgoing): Brahma is the incoming breath and

Shiva is the outgoing one. And Vishnu is the reality in the sixth body.

In the seventh body things become even more difficult. Buddha called the seventh body the *Nirvana Kaya* (the body of enlightenment) because the Truth, the absolute, is in the seventh body. The seventh body is the last body, so there is not even creation and destruction but, rather, Being and non-Being. In the seventh, creation is always of something else, it is not of you. Creation will be of something else and destruction will be of something else (not of you), while Being is of you, and non-Being is of you.

In the seventh body, Being and non-Being—existence and nonexistence—are the two breaths. One should not be identified with either. All religions are started by those who have reached to the seventh body, and at the end language can be stretched, at the most, to two words: Being and non-Being. Buddha speaks the language of non-Being (of the outgoing breath), so he says, "Nothingness is the reality," while Shankara speaks the language of Being and says that the Brahman is the ultimate reality. Shankara uses positive terms because he chooses the incoming breath, and Buddha uses negative terms because he chooses the outgoing breath. But these are the only choices as far as language is concerned.

The third choice is the reality, which cannot be said. At the most we can say "absolute Being" or "absolute non-Being." This much can be said because the seventh body is beyond this. Transcendence is still possible.

I can say something about this room if I go out. If I transcend this room and reach another room, I can recollect this one, I can say something about it. But if I go out of this room and fall into an abyss, then I cannot say anything about even this room. So far, with each body, a third point could be caught into words, symbolized, because the body beyond it was there. You could go there and look backward. But only up to the seventh is this possible.

Beyond the seventh body nothing can be said because the seventh is the last body. Beyond it is "bodilessness."

With the seventh, one has to choose Being or non-Being —either the language of negation or the language of positivity. And there are only two choices. One is Buddha's choice: he says, "Nothing remains," and the other is Shankara's choice: he says, "Everything remains."

In the seven dimensions (in the seven bodies), as far as man is concerned and as far as the world is concerned, life energy manifests into multidimensional realms. Everywhere, wherever life is to be found, the incoming and the outgoing process will be there. Wherever life is, the process will be. Life cannot exist without this polarity.

So prana is energy—cosmic energy—and our first acquaintance with it is in the physical body. It manifests first as breath, and then it goes on manifesting as breath in other forms: influences, magnetism, thoughts, life, creation, Being. It goes on, and if one becomes aware of it, one always transcends it to reach to a third point. The moment you reach this third point, you transcend that body and enter the next body. You enter the second body from the first, and so on.

If you go on transcending, up to the seventh, there is still a body, but beyond the seventh there is "bodilessness." Then you become pure. Then you are not divided; then there are no more polarities. Then it is *adwait* ("not two"): then it is Oneness.

# ~ PART III ~

# THE TECHNIQUES

## ~ 18 ~

## Traditional Techniques

### ANAPANA-SATI YOGA

A flower that has never known the sun and a flower that has encountered the sun are not the same. They cannot be. A flower that has never known the sunrise has never known the sun to rise within itself. It is dead. It is just a potentiality. It has never known its own spirit. But a flower that has seen the sun rise has also seen something arise within itself. It has known its own soul. Now the flower is not just a flower. It has known a deep, stirring innerness.

How can we create this innerness within ourselves? Buddha invented a method, one of the most powerful methods, for creating an inner "sun" of awareness. And not only for creating it: the method is such that it not only creates this inner awareness but simultaneously allows the awareness to penetrate to the very cells of the body, to the whole of one's being. The method that Buddha used is known as Anapana-sati Yoga—the yoga of incoming and outgoing breath awareness.

We are breathing, but it is unconscious breathing. Breath is prana, breath is the *élan vital* ("the vitality, the very life"), and yet it is unconscious. You are not aware of it. And if you had to be aware of breathing in order to breathe, you would die. Sooner or later you would forget. You cannot continuously remember anything.

Breathing is a link between our voluntary and our involuntary systems. We can control our breathing to a certain extent, we can even stop our breathing for a while, but we cannot stop it permanently. It goes on without us; it does not depend on us. Even if you are in a coma for months, you will go on breathing. It is an unconscious mechanism.

Buddha used breath as a vehicle to do two things simultaneously: one, to create consciousness, and another, to allow that consciousness to penetrate to the very cells of the body. He said, "Breathe consciously." This does not mean to do *pranayama* (yogic breathing). It is just to make breath an object of awareness, without changing it.

There is no need to change your breath. Leave it as it is —natural. Do not change it. But when you breathe in, breathe consciously. Let your consciousness move with the ingoing breath. And when the breath goes out, let your consciousness move out with it.

Move with the breath. Let your attention be with the breath. Flow with it. Do not forget even a single breath. Buddha is reported to have said that if you can be aware of your breath for even a single hour, you are already enlightened. But not a single breath should be missed!

One hour is enough. It looks like such a small fragment of time, but it is not. When you are trying to be aware, an hour can seem like a millennium because ordinarily you cannot be aware for more than five or six seconds. Only a very alert person can be aware for even that long. Most of us miss every second. You may start by being aware as the breath is going in, but no sooner has it gone in when you are somewhere else. Suddenly you remember that the breath is going out. It has already gone out, but you were somewhere else.

To be conscious of the breath means that no thoughts can be allowed because thoughts will distract your attention. Buddha never says, "Stop thinking." He says, "Breathe consciously." Automatically, thinking will stop. You cannot both think and breathe consciously. When a thought comes into your mind, your attention is withdrawn from the breathing. A single thought and you have become unconscious of the breathing process.

Buddha used this technique. It is a simple one, but a very vital one. He would say to his *bikkhus* (his monks), "Do whatsoever you are doing, but do not forget a simple thing: remember the incoming and the outgoing breath. Move with it; flow with it."

The more you try to do it, the more you endeavor to do it, the more conscious you will become. It is arduous, it is difficult, but once you can do it, you will have become a different person, a different being in a different world.

This works in another way, too. When you consciously breathe in and out, by and by you come to your center because your breath touches the very center of your being. Every moment that the breath goes in, it touches the center of your being.

Physiologically you think that breath is just for the purification of the blood, that it is just a bodily function. But if you begin to be aware of your breath, by and by you will go deeper than physiology. Then one day you will begin to feel your center, right near your navel.

This center can be felt only if you move with the breath continuously because the nearer you reach to the center, the more difficult it will be to remain aware. You can start when the breath is going in. When it is just entering your nose, begin to be aware of it. The more inward it moves, the more difficult awareness will become. A thought will come, or some sound, or something will happen, and you will move away.

If you can go to the very center, for a brief moment breath stops and there is a gap. The breath goes in, the breath goes out: between the two there is a subtle gap. That gap is your center.

Only after practicing breath awareness for a long time
—when you are finally able to remain with the breath, to
be aware of the breath—will you become aware of the gap
when there is no movement of breath. Breath is neither
coming in nor going out. In the subtle gap between breaths,
you are at your center. So breath awareness was used by
Buddha as a means of coming nearer and nearer to the
center.

When you breathe out, remain conscious of the breath.
Again there is a gap. There are two gaps: one gap after
the breath has come in and before it goes out again, and
another gap after the breath has gone out and before it
comes in again. This second gap is more difficult to be
aware of.

Between the incoming breath and the outgoing breath is
your center. But there is another center, the cosmic center.
You may call it "God." In the gap between when the breath
goes out and when it comes in is the cosmic center. These
two centers are not two different things. First, you will
become aware of your inner center and then you will become aware of the outer center. Ultimately, you will come
to know that both these centers are one. Then "out" and
"in" will lose their meaning.

Buddha says, "Move consciously with the breath and you
will create a center of awareness within you." Once this
center is created, awareness begins to move to your very
cells because every cell needs oxygen, every cell breathes,
so to speak.

Now scientists say that even the earth breathes. When
the whole universe is breathing in, it expands. When the
whole universe breathes out, it contracts. In old Hindu
mythological scriptures (*puranas*) it is said that creation
is Brahma's one breath—incoming breath—and destruction
(*pralaya*), the end of the world, will be the outgoing
breath. One breath is one creation.

In a very miniature way, in a very atomic way, the same
thing is happening in you. And when your awareness becomes one with breathing, breathing takes your awareness

to your very cells. Then your whole body becomes the universe. Really, then you have no material body at all. You are just Awareness.

## TWENTY-ONE-DAY EXPERIMENT IN SILENCE AND SECLUSION

It is helpful to practice breath awareness for twenty-one days in total seclusion and silence. Then, much will happen.

During the twenty-one-day experiment, practice Dynamic Meditation once a day and constant awareness of breathing for twenty-four hours a day. Do not read, do not write, do not think, because all these acts are of the mental body. They are not concerned with the etheric body.

You can go for a walk. This helps because walking is part of the etheric body. All manual actions are concerned with the *prana sharira* (the etheric body). The physical body does these things, but it is for the etheric body. Everything concerned with the etheric body should be done, and everything concerned with another body must not be done. You can also have a bath once or twice a day. It is concerned with the etheric body.

When you go for a walk, just walk. Do not do anything else: just be concerned with your walking. And while walking, keep your eyes half-closed. Half-closed eyes cannot see anything other than the path, and the path itself is so monotonous that it will not give you something new to think about.

You must remain in a monotonous world, just in one room, seeing the same floor. It must be so monotonous that you cannot think about it. Thinking needs stimuli; thinking needs new sensations. If your sensory system is constantly bored, there will be nothing outside of you to think about.

During the first week you may feel less need of sleep. Do not be concerned about it. Because you are not thinking, because you are not doing many of the things that you ordinarily do, you will need less sleep. And if you are constantly aware of your breathing, so much energy will be generated in you, you will become so vital, that you will not feel sleepy. So if sleep comes it is all right. If it doesn't come, it is all right. If you do not sleep, it will not be harmful.

There are many reasons why awareness of breath will create more energy in you. First, when you watch the breathing, the breathing becomes rhythmic. It will follow its own rhythm. A harmony will be created and the whole of the being will become musical. This "rhythmic-ness" this rhythm, conserves energy.

Ordinarily our breathing is not rhythmic. It is haphazard. This causes an unnecessary leakage of energy. Rhythm, harmony, creates a storage of energy. And because you are constantly aware, breath awareness, itself begins to take only a minimal amount of energy. You are not doing anything; it is a non-doing. You are just aware.

The moment you begin to do something, even to think, doing has come in. Now energy will be wasted. If you move your body, doing has come in; energy will be wasted. Twenty-four hours of constant awareness means a minimal wastage of energy, so energy is conserved. You become a storehouse of energy. This energy will be used in *kundalini*.

Ordinarily, so much energy is wasted during the day that there is not enough energy left to raise *kundalini*. Not much energy is needed in order for the energy to move downward, but to raise energy upward you need a great storage of energy. Only then can the gates open upward; otherwise not. So those who have little energy left only have sex as an outlet for it.

We usually think of a sexual person as being very vital, but that is not so. A very vital person is not sexual because when energy is overflowing, it moves upward. Sexuality requires energy, but only a very small quantity of it. When there is very little energy, it cannot move upward. Then moving down—toward the sex center—is the only possibility.

Energy needs to move continually. It cannot be static.

it must move. If it cannot move upward, it will move downward. There is no choice then. But if it can move upward, then the downward passage will eventually stop by itself. It is not that you will stop energy from being released through the sex center, but it will stop by itself because the energy is moving upward.

If you are constantly watching your breath, all doing stops and energy is conserved. But there is another point to be made, and that is that the very observation—the awareness, the alertness—also helps the life force to become more vital within you. It is as if someone is watching you. If someone is watching you, you become more vital; laziness disappears.

That is why leaders feel vital. The crowd is always there to observe, and the very observation makes them vital. The moment the crowd has forgotten them—no sooner are they forgotten—then they are dead. The happiness of being a leader, of being a public man, a crowd-watched personality, is because of the feeling of vitality that comes through people's observation. The vitality does not come because of the observation itself, but because, with so many people observing you, you become more alert about yourself. And this alertness becomes vitality.

So when you become aware of your breathing, when you begin to observe yourself, the innermost source of vitality is touched. Therefore, if sleep is lost, do not become anxious about it. It is natural.

If there are upheavals in your mind—if things come to your mind which you have never thought about before (images . . . stories . . .)—then, too, do not become anxious. Just watch them. So much that is in the unconscious is being released. Before it is thrown out, it must come to the conscious mind. If you suppress these things, they will become unconscious again. On the other hand, if you are too concerned with them, you will waste unnecessary energy. So just go on watching your breath, and at the periphery (in the background) go on watching indifferently everything that happens.

Just be indifferent to these things. Do not be concerned at all; just go on witnessing your breathing. You will be witnessing your breathing, but on the periphery things will be happening. Thoughts will be there, vibrations will be there, but only on the periphery—not at the center. At the center you are just watching your breath.

So much will come to you: things that are absurd, illogical, unimaginable, inconceivable, fantastic, night-marish. You must go on watching your breath. Let these things come and go. Just be indifferent to them. (It is as if you are going for a walk. The street is full of people. They pass by, but you are indifferent to them; you are not concerned with them.) Then these images and fantasies will be released, and, by the end of the first week, a new silence will come to you. The moment the unconscious is unburdened, there will be no more inner noise. Silence will come to you, a deep inner silence.

You may experience moments of depression. If a deep-rooted feeling of depression has been suppressed in the unconscious, it will come and overwhelm you. It will not be a thought; it will be a mood. Not only thoughts will be coming to you, but moods, too, will be coming. Sometimes you will feel exhilarated, sometimes you will feel depressed or bored, but be as indifferent to these moods as you are indifferent to thoughts. Let them come and go. They will go by themselves, so do not be concerned with them. Moods, too, have been suppressed in the unconscious. During the twenty-one days of the experiment they will be released, and then you will experience something that you have never experienced before—something new, something unknown.

Each individual will experience something different. There are many possibilities, but whatever happens, don't be afraid. There is no need to be. Even if you feel that you are dying, no matter how strong that feeling is, no matter how sure you are of it, accept it. Thoughts, feelings, moods,

will be so acute, so real. Just accept them. If you feel that
death is coming, then welcome it—and go on watching your
breath!

It is hard to be indifferent to feelings, but if you can be
indifferent to your thoughts and moods, it will happen. You
may feel as if death is coming. Within a moment you will
die; there is no other possibility. There is nothing you can
do about it, so accept it, welcome it . . . and the moment
you have welcomed it, you have become indifferent to it.
If you fight it, you distort everything.

You may feel as if death is coming, or you may feel that
you have become ill. You have not become ill. The feeling
of being ill (or of dying) is just part of your unconscious
that is being released. Many illnesses will be felt that were
unknown a moment before. Be indifferent to any illness
and go on doing what you are doing: go on watching your
breath. The breath must be watched no matter what you
are thinking, no matter what you are feeling, no matter
what is happening.

After the first week you will begin to have some psychic
experiences. The body may become very big or very small.
Sometimes it will disappear, it will evaporate, and you will
be bodiless. Do not be afraid. There will be moments when
you cannot find where your body is (it is "not") and moments when you will see your body lying or sitting at a
distance away from you. Again, do not be afraid.

You may feel electrical shocks. Everytime a new chakra
is penetrated, there will be shocks and tremblings. The
whole body will be in a turmoil. Do not resist; cooperate
with these reactions. If you resist, you will be fighting
against yourself. Shocks, trembling, a feeling of electricity,
heat, cold—anything felt on your chakras you must cooperate with. You, yourself, have invited it, so do not resist it.
If you resist it, your energies will be in conflict. So cooperate with any psychic experiences that you may have.

Sometimes you may not feel that you are breathing. It is not that breath has stopped, but that it has become so natural, so silent, so rhythmic, that it is not felt. We only feel disease. When you have a headache, you feel that you have a head, but when there is no headache you don't feel your head. The head is there, but you cannot feel it. And in the same way, when our breathing is discordant, unnatural, we feel it, but when it has become natural it is not felt. It is not felt, but it is there.

As you continue to watch your breath, the breath will become more and more subtle. But awareness, too, will become more subtle because you will be continuing to watch this subtle breath. And when there is no breath, you will be aware of this "no breathness," you will be aware of this harmony. Then awareness will penetrate even more deeply. The more subtle the breath is, the more aware you will have to become so that you can be aware of it.

Go on being aware, and if you feel that there is no breath, then be aware of your "no breath." Do not try to breathe; just be aware of "no breathness." This will be a very blissful moment.

The more subtle the awareness, the more it goes into the etheric body. When you are watching your breath, first there is an awareness of your physical breath. You are aware of your physical body and the breathing mechanism. When the breath becomes subtle and harmonious, then you become aware of your etheric body. Then you may feel that now there is no breath, but the breath is still there. It may not be as much there as it was because your needs are not so great now, but it is still there.

You may have noticed that if you are in anger then you need more oxygen, and if you are not in anger you do not need so much. If you are in sexual passion you need more breath. So the quantity of breath will go down or up with your needs. If you are completely silent, then only a very small quantity of air will be enough. Just enough to be alive.

Just be aware of this situation. You were aware of

breathing; now be aware of a situation where no breath is felt. Whatever happens, be aware of it. Awareness must be there. If nothing is felt, then you must be aware of your "no feeling." Nothing is being felt . . . but awareness must be there.

Do not go to sleep now because this is the very moment for which you were longing. If you go to sleep, you have wasted the time that has been spent bringing you to this point. Now be aware of what is happening. There is no breath; be aware of it. In total stillness the breath is almost nonexistent. Very little is needed, and only that much comes to you. The quantity has fallen much and the harmony has risen much, so you do not feel it.

If you go on watching your breath and being indifferent to everything that is happening, then the third week will be a week of complete nothingness. It will be as if everything has died, as if everything has gone into nonexistence, and only nothingness remains.

Do not stop the experiment before the twenty-one days are over. After the first week you may want to stop it. Your mind may say, "This is nonsense. Leave." Do not listen to it. Just tell yourself once and for all that for twenty-one days there is nowhere else to go.

After the third week you may not want to leave. If your mind is so blissful that you do not want to disturb it, if only nothingness, blissfulness is there—if you are just a vacuum —then you can prolong the experiment for two or three or four more days. But do not break it before the twenty-one days are over.

Anything that you want to make a note of you must do after you have come out of seclusion, not before that. Then if you want to, sit down for a day or two and write down everything. But within these twenty-one days, nothing should be written. Do not even try to remember anything.

All that has happened will be there . . . and will be clearer because the mind is not trying to remember it.

You can forget a thing if you have tried to remember it, but you cannot forget a thing that you have not tried to remember. Then it comes to you totally. And if it is not coming, it means it is useless—so let it go.

Everything that is nonuseful remains with you. You try to remember much that is useless and do not understand that it is useless. But the mind works automatically: all that is worth remembering is always remembered. So do not try to remember anything; there is no need. You will remember whatever has happened to you. Whatever is worth remembering will be with you when the experiment is finished.

So go and begin it as soon as you can.

## MIRROR GAZING

The unconscious is not really unconscious. Rather, it is only less conscious. So the difference between the conscious and the unconscious is a difference only of degree. They are not polar opposites; they are related, joined.

Because of our false system of logic we divide everything into polar opposites. Logic says, "either yes or no, either light or darkness." As far as logic goes there is nothing in between. But life is neither white nor black. Rather, it is a great expanse of gray.

So when I say "conscious" and "unconscious," I do not mean that the two are in opposition to each other. For Freud, conscious is conscious and unconscious is unconscious—it is the difference between black and white, between yes and no, between life and death—but when I say "unconscious" I mean "less conscious"; when I say "conscious" I mean "less unconscious." They overlap each other.

How can we encounter the unconscious? As far as Freud is concerned the encounter is impossible. If you had asked

Freud how to encounter the unconscious he would have said, "It is nonsense; you cannot encounter it. And if you encounter it, it is conscious because encountering is a conscious phenomenon." But if you ask me how to encounter the unconscious I will say, "There are ways to encounter it." For me, the first thing to be noted is that unconscious simply means "less conscious." So if you grow more conscious, you can encounter it.

Secondly, conscious and unconscious are not fixed boundaries. They change every moment—just like the pupil of your eye. If there is more light, the pupil is narrowed; if there is less light, it widens. It constantly creates an equilibrium with the light outside. And your consciousness is constantly changing in the same way. Really, to understand the phenomenon of consciousness by the analogy of the eye is very relevant because consciousness is the inner eye, the eye of the soul. So, just like your eye, your consciousness is constantly expanding or shrinking.

For example, if you are angry you become more unconscious. Unconsciousness is now more widespread, and only a very small part of you remains conscious. Sometimes even that part is not there and you have become completely unconscious. On the other hand, in a sudden accident—if you are on the road and suddenly you feel that an accident is going to occur, you are on the verge of death—you become completely conscious, and there is no unconsciousness at all. Suddenly the whole mind is conscious. So this change is continuously taking place.

When I say conscious and unconscious, I do not mean that there are any fixed boundaries between the two. There are none. It is a fluctuating phenomenon. It depends on you whether you are less conscious or more conscious. You can create consciousness: you can train and discipline yourself for more consciousness or for less consciousness.

If you train yourself for less consciousness you will never be able to encounter the unconscious. Really, you will become incapable of encountering it. When someone takes drugs or an intoxicant, he is training his mind to be totally unconscious. When you go to sleep, or if you are hypnotized or you hypnotize yourself, you lose consciousness. There are many ways, and many of the ways that help you to be more unconscious are even known as religious practices. Anything that creates boredom creates unconsciousness.

There are many methods to help you to encounter the unconscious. I will suggest a simple exercise that will help you to encounter it.

At night, before you go to bed, close the doors of your room and put a big mirror in front of you. The room must be completely dark. Then put a small flame by the side of the mirror in such a way that the flame is not directly reflected in the mirror. Just your face should be reflected in the mirror, not the flame.

Stare constantly into your own eyes in the mirror. Do not blink. This is a forty-minute experiment, and within two or three days you will be able to keep your eyes from blinking for the whole forty minutes. Even if tears come, let them come. But, still, do not blink, and go on staring into the eyes.

Within two or three days you will become aware of a very strange phenomenon: your face will begin to take on new shapes. You may even be scared! The face in the mirror will begin to change. Sometimes a very different face will be there—one which you have not known as yours. But all the faces that come to you belong to you. Now the subconscious mind is beginning to explode. These faces, these masks, are yours. And sometimes you may even see a face that belonged to you in a past life.

After one week of constant practice—staring for forty minute every night—your face will be a constant flux. Many fa es will be coming and going constantly. After three weeks you will not be able to remember which one is *your* face. You will not be able to remember your own face because you have seen so many different faces coming and going.

If you continue, then one day—after three weeks or so—the strangest thing will happen: suddenly there will be no face in the mirror! The mirror will be vacant! You are staring into emptiness; there will be no face there at all.

This is the moment! Close your eyes, and encounter the unconscious. When there is no face in the mirror, just close the eyes. This is the most significant moment. Close the eyes, look inside, and you will face the unconscious. You will be naked, completely naked—as you *are*. All deceptions will fall.

This is your reality, but society has created so many layers in order that you will not be aware of it. And once you know yourself in your nakedness, your total nakedness, you will begin to be a different person. Then you cannot deceive yourself. Now you know what you are.

Unless you know what you are you can never be transformed. Only this naked reality can be transformed. And, really, just the will to transform it will effect the transformation.

As you are, you cannot transform yourself. You can change one false face to another false face—a thief can become a monk, a criminal can become a saint—but these are not really transformations. Transformation means becoming *that which you really are*.

The moment you face the unconscious, encounter the unconscious, you are face to face with your reality, with your authentic being. The false societal being is not there. Your name is not there; your form is not there; your face is not there. Only the naked reality of your nature is there, and with this naked reality transformation is possible.

This mirror-gazing technique is a very powerful method —very powerful—to know one's own abyss and to know one's own naked reality. And once you have known it, you have become the master of it.

## TRATAK

When doing *tratak* you are to stare continuously, without blinking, for thirty to forty minutes.[1] Your whole consciousness must come to the eyes. You must *become* the eyes. Forget everything; forget the rest of your body. Just be the eyes and continually stare without blinking.

When the whole of your consciousness is centered in the eyes you will come to a peak of tension, a climax of tension. Your eyes are the most delicate part of you. That is why they can become more tense than any other part. And with tension in the eyes, the whole mind will be tense. The eyes are just doors to the mind. When you become the eyes and the eyes reach a peak of tension, the mind, too, reaches a climax of tension. When you fall down from that climax you fall effortlessly into the abyss of relaxation. *Tratak* creates one of the most tense peaks possible in the consciousness. From that peak the opposite will happen spontaneously, relaxation will happen spontaneously.

When you are doing *tratak*, thinking will stop automatically. By and by your consciousness will become more cen-

---

[1] Mirror gazing is a form of *tratak*, the ancient yogic technique of fixed gazing or staring.

Another powerful form of *tratak* is to gaze at a photo of one's guru or the photo of a spiritual master toward whom one feels a great affinity. The photo should be full-faced, with the eyes of the master looking directly ahead.

Place the photo about an arm's length away with the eyes of the master at the same height as your own eyes. Fix your gaze on the eyes of the guru or at the space between the two eyes. Like mirror gazing, this technique should be done for thirty to forty minutes and practiced on a daily basis for a minimum of twenty-one days.

*Tratak* can also be done with another person: each gazing into the eyes of the other for thirty to forty minutes. If the other person is either one's lover or a person toward whom one has a strong feeling (either positive or negative), another dimension will be added. Again, it is good to do this on a daily basis—with the same person—for at least twenty-one days.

tered in the eyes. You will just be aware; there will be no thinking. Eyes cannot think. When the whole consciousness is centered in the eyes, the mind had no energy left for thinking. There is no mind—only the eyes exist—so there is no thinking.

The moments when your eyes want to blink are the moments to watch out for. The mind is trying to get energy back to think; it is trying to divert consciousness away from the eyes and back to the mind. That is why constant staring, fixed staring, is needed. Even a single movement of the eyes gives energy to the mind, so do not move the eyes at all. Your gaze must remain absolutely fixed.

When you are staring with no movement of the eyes, the mind is also fixed. The mind moves with the eyes. Eyes are the doors: doors that belong to the inside mind and also to the outside world. If the eyes are totally fixed, the mind stops. It cannot move.

This technique begins from the eyes because to begin from the mind is difficult. It is hard to control the mind, but eyes are outer things; you can control them. So keep your gaze absolutely fixed, staring without blinking. When your eyes are still, your mind will become still.

## MANTRA REPETITION

You can use a mantra to still the mind, to make the mind totally silent. You go on repeating some name: Ram, Krishna, or Jesus. The mantra can help to make you unoccupied with other words, but once the mind has become silent and still, then this name, Ram, Krishna, or Jesus, will become a hindrance. It becomes a replacement, a substitute. All other words are thrown away, but then this word continues in a crazy way. You become attached to it; you cannot drop it. It has become a habit, a deep occupation.

So begin with *japa* (mantra repetition), but then come to a state where *japa* is not needed and can be thrown. Use

"Ram" to dispel all other words from the mind, but when all other words have been dispelled, do not retain this word. It is also a word, so throw it.

This throwing becomes difficult. One begins to feel guilty about discarding the mantra because it has helped so much. But now this help has become a hindrance. Throw it! Means must not become the end.

QUESTION: "When I meditate I usually repeat a mantra or a *namokar* (a rather lengthly Jain mantra). But the mind remains restless. How can one best occupy one's mind while meditating?"

The need to occupy time is the need of the nonmeditative mind, so you should first understand why you have this need. Why can't you be unoccupied, what is this need to be occupied constantly? Is it just an escape from yourself?

The moment you are unoccupied you have only yourself, you fall back on yourself. That is why you have to be occupied. This need to be occupied is just an escape. But this is a necessity for the nonmeditative mind.

The nonmeditative mind is constantly occupied with others. When others are not there, then what is to be done? You do not know how to be occupied by yourself! You are not even aware that you can live with yourself. You have always lived with others and others and others, so now (in meditation) when you are not with others and you are alone—though it is not really being alone—you begin to feel lonely. Loneliness is the absence of others; aloneness is the presence of oneself.

You begin to feel lonely, and you have to be filled with something. A *namokar* can do that; anything can do that. But unless you have a meditative mind, if you continue a *namokar* or any other repetition it is just a crutch and it has to be thrown.

If you are doing something of this sort, it is better to use a one-word mantra (such as *ram* or *aum*) than something long like a *namokar*. With one word you will feel less occupied than with many words because with the changing of words, the mind also changes. With one word you will be bored, and boredom is good because then it is easy to drop the whole thing at some point. So rather than using a *namokar*, it is better to use one word, and if you can use a word that is meaningless, it is still better because even the meaning becomes a distraction.

When you have to throw something out, then you should be aware that you have to throw it. You must not be too attached to it. So use one word, one thing—something that is meaningless. For example: *hoo!* It has no meaning. *Aum* is basically the same, but it has begun to have meaning now because we have been associating it with something divine.

The sound should be meaningless, just a meaningless word. It must not convey anything because the moment something is conveyed the mind is fed. The mind is fed not by words but by meanings. So use some word like *hoo*. It is a meaningless sound.

And, really, *hoo* is more than a meaningless sound because with *hoo* an inner tension is created. With the sound *hoo* something is being thrown out. So use a word that is throwing something out, which is throwing *you* out, not one which is *giving* you something.

Use *hoo*. With *hoo* you will feel that something is being thrown out. Use the word when the breath is going out and make the incoming breath the gap. Balance it: *hoo* . . . then the incoming breath as the gap . . . then, again, *hoo*. . . . The word should be meaningless; it should be a sound rather than a word. And emphasize the outgoing breath. The word (the sound) has to be thrown in the end, so it should not be taken with the ingoing breath.

This is very subtle. Just throw the sound out as if you are throwing out some excreta, as if you are throwing something out of you. Then it cannot become food. Remember always, and remember deeply, that anything which goes in with the ingoing breath becomes food—anything, even a sound, becomes food—and everything which goes out with the outgoing breath is excreta. It is just thrown out. So with the ingoing breath, always be vacant, empty. Then you are not giving the mind any new food.

The mind is taking in subtle foods even with sounds, words, and meanings—with everything. Experiment with this. When you are feeling sexual, when you are in a sexual fantasy, use this *hoo* with the outgoing breath. Within moments you will feel beyond sex because something is being thrown out, a very subtle thing is being thrown out. If you are angry then use this sound, and within seconds there will be no anger.

If you are feeling sexual and you use this same sound with the ingoing breath, you will feel more sexual. If you are feeling angry and you use this same *hoo* with the ingoing breath, you will feel more angry. Then you will become aware of how even a simple sound affects your mind and how it affects it differently with the ingoing breath or the outgoing breath.

When you see someone beautiful, lovely, someone who is your beloved, and you want to touch her body, touch it with the outgoing breath and you will feel nothing . . . but touch her with the ingoing breath and you will feel a fascination. With the ingoing breath the touch becomes a food, but with the outgoing breath it is not a food at all. Take someone's hand in yours and only feel the hand with the ingoing breath. Let the outgoing breath be empty. Then you will know that touch is a food.

That is why a child who has been raised without a mother or who has not been touched and fondled by his mother is lacking something. He will never be able to love anyone if he has not been touched and fondled and cuddled by his mother because that subtle touch is food for the child. It creates many things in him. If no one has touched him lovingly, he will not be able to love anyone because he doesn't know what "food" is lacking, that some vital thing is lacking.

So I do not say not to touch a woman. I say, "Touch,

but with the outgoing breath." And when the ingoing
breath is coming, just be aware; be in the gap. Do not feel
the touch. Go on touching, but do not feel the touch.

Be aware of the sensation when the breath is going out
and then you will be aware of the secret of breath—why it
has been called prana, the vital force. Breath is the most
vital thing. If you eat your meal with an emphasis on the
outgoing breath, then no matter how good the food is it
will not be a food for your body. Even if you eat very
much, there will be no nutrition if your emphasis is on the
outgoing breath. So eat with the ingoing breath and let
there be a gap when the breath is going out. Then, with a
very small quantity of food, you can be more alive.

Remember this sound *hoo* with the outgoing breath. It
destroys the restlessness of the mind. But this, too, is a
crutch and soon, if you are doing meditation regularly,
you will feel that there is no need for it. And not only is
there no need, but it will become a disturbance, a positive
disturbance.

To be unoccupied is one of the most beautiful things in
the world . . . to be unoccupied is the greatest luxury.
And if you can afford to be unoccupied, you will become
an emperor. It is out of those moments when we are occupied that sometimes there will come a moment when we
are *un*occupied—totally unoccupied. It is not only unnecessary to go on being occupied all the time; in the end, it
becomes harmful.

It is madness to destroy an unoccupied state because that
is the very moment that you enter into timelessness. With
occupation you can never transcend time, with occupation
you can never transcend space, but if you are unoccupied,
totally unoccupied—not even occupied with yourself, not
even meditating (you just *are*)—that is the moment that is
the peak moment of spiritual existence, of bliss. That is
*satchitananda*.

The first part of the word is *sat*. It means existence;

you are just existing. Then you become conscious of this existence—not only conscious, you become consciousness (*chit*) and existence both. Existence becomes consciousness . . . and bliss (*ananda*) follows.

It is not just a feeling. You become bliss, existence, and consciousness simultaneously. We use three words because we cannot express it in one word. You are all three simultaneously.

So look forward to the unoccupied moments. You can use crutches (such as a mantra), but do not be happy about it. And know that, ultimately, they must be thrown.

## A TECHNIQUE OF VISUALIZATION

Mind, itself, means projection, so unless you transcend the mind whatever you come to experience is projection.[1] Mind is the projecting mechanism. If you experience any visions of light, of bliss, even of the divine, these are all projections. Unless you come to a total stopping of the mind you are not beyond projections: you are projecting. When mind ceases, only then are you beyond the danger. When there is no experience, no visions, nothing objective —the consciousness remaining as a pure mirror with nothing reflected in it—only then are you beyond the danger of projections.

Projections are of two types. One type of projection will lead you to more and more projection. It is a positive projection; you can never go beyond it. The other type of projection is negative. It is a projection, but it helps you to go beyond projections.

[1] At a meditation camp held in spring 1972, Bhagwan Shree led participants in this technique. First he told them to see light, without any object; then, to feel bliss, without any object; and finally, to feel *divine presence*. A questioner asked about the dangers of projection in using such a technique.

In meditation you use the projecting faculty of the mind as a negative effort. Negative projections are good: it is just like one thorn being pulled out by another thorn or one poison being destroyed by another poison. But you must be constantly aware that the danger remains until *everything* ceases, even these negative projections, even these visions. If you are experiencing something, I will not say it is meditation. It is still contemplation; it is still a thought process. However subtle, it is still thinking. When only consciousness remains with no thought—just an unclouded, open sky—when you cannot say what "I" am experiencing, this much can be said: *I am.*

The famous maxim of Descartes (*Cogito ergo sum*— "I think; therefore, I am") in meditation becomes *Sum cogito sum*—"I am; therefore, I am." This "I am–ness" precedes all thinking. You *are* before you think. Thinking comes later on, your being precedes it, so being cannot be inferred from thinking. You can be without thinking, but thinking cannot be without you, so thinking cannot be the basis upon which your existence can be proved.

Experiences, visions, anything felt objectively, is part of thinking. Meditation means total cessation of the mind, of thinking, but not of consciousness. If consciousness also ceases, you are not in meditation but in deep sleep. That is the difference between deep sleep and meditation.

In *deep* sleep projection also ceases. Thinking will not be there, but, simultaneously, consciousness will also be absent. In meditation projections cease, thinking ceases, thoughts are no more there—just like in deep sleep—but there is consciousness. You are aware of this phenomenon: of total absence around you, of no objects around you. And when there are no objects to be known, felt and experienced, for the first time you begin to feel yourself. This is a nonobjective experience. It is not something that you experience; it is something you are.

So even if you feel the divine existence, it is a projection.

These are negative projections. They help—they help, in a way, to transcend—but you must be aware that they are still projections, otherwise you will not go beyond them. That is why I say that if you feel you are encountering bliss you are still in the mind because duality is there: the duality of the divine and the nondivine, the duality of bliss and nonbliss. When you really reach to the ultimate you cannot feel bliss because nonbliss is impossible; you cannot feel the divine as divine because the nondivine is no more.

So remember this: mind is projection, and whatever you do with the mind is going to be a projection. You cannot do anything with the mind. The only thing is how to negate the mind, how to drop it totally, how to be mindlessly conscious. That is meditation. Only then can you know, can you come to know, that which is other than projection.

Whatever you know is projected by you. The object is just a screen: you go on projecting your ideas, your mind, upon it. So any method of meditation begins with projection—with negative projection—and ends with nonprojection. That is the nature of all meditation techniques because you have to begin with the mind.

Even if you are going toward a state of no mind, you have to begin with the mind. If I am to go out of this room, I have to start by going *into* the room. The first step must be taken in the room. This creates confusion. If I am just going in a circle in the room, then I am walking in the room. If I am going out of the room, then, again, I have to walk in the room—but in a different way. My eyes must be on the door and I must travel in a straight line, not in a circle.

Negative projection means walking straight out of the mind. But first, you have to take some steps within the mind.

For example, when I say "light," you have never really seen light. You have only seen lighted objects. Have you ever seen light itself? No one has seen it; no one can see it. You see a lighted house, a lighted chair, a lighted person, but you have not seen light itself. Even when you see the sun you are not seeing light. You are seeing the light returned.

You cannot see light itself. When light strikes something, comes back, is reflected, only then do you see the lighted object, and because you can see the lighted object, you say there is light. When you do not see the lighted object, you say it is dark.

You cannot see pure light, so in meditation I use it as a first step—as a negative projection. I tell you to begin to feel light without any object. Objects are dropped; there is just light. Begin to feel light without any objects. . . . One thing has been dropped (the object), and without the object you cannot continue to see light for a long time. Sooner or later the light will drop because you have to be focused on some object.

Then I tell you to feel bliss. You have never felt bliss without any object. Whatever you know as happiness, bliss, is concerned *with* something. You have never known any moment of bliss that is unconcerned with anything. You may love someone and then feel blissful, but that someone is the object. You feel blissful when you listen to some music, but then that music is the object. Have you ever felt a blissful moment without any object? Never! So when I say to feel blissful without any object, it seems to be an impossibility. If you try to feel blissful without any object sooner or later the bliss will stop because it cannot exist by itself.

Then I say to feel divine presence. I never say, "feel God," Because then God becomes an object. Have you ever felt *presence* without someone being present there? It is always concerned with someone: if someone is there, then you begin to feel the presence.

I drop that someone totally. I simply say: feel the divine presence. This is a negative projection. It cannot continue for long because there is no ground to support it. Sooner or later it will drop. First I drop objects and then, by and by, projection itself will drop. That is the difference between positive and negative projection.

In positive projection the object is significant and the feeling follows, while in negative projection the feeling is important and the object is simply forgotten, as if I am taking the whole ground from under your feet. From within you, below you, from everywhere, the ground has been taken and you are left alone with your feeling. Now that feeling cannot exist. It will drop. If objects are not there, then the feelings that are directly connected to objects cannot continue any longer. For a while you can project them; then they will drop. And when they drop, you alone remain there . . . in your total aloneness. That point is the point of meditation, from there meditation begins. Now you are out of the room.

So meditation has a beginning in the mind, but that is not real meditation. Begin in the mind, so that you can move toward meditation, and when mind ceases and you are beyond it, then real meditation begins. We have to begin with the mind because we are in the mind. Even to go beyond it, one has to use it. So use the mind negatively, never positively, and then you will achieve meditation.

If you use the mind positively, then you will only create more and more projections. So whatever is known as "positive thinking" is absolutely antimeditative. Negative thinking is meditative; negation is the method for meditation. Go on negating to the point where nothing remains to be negated, and only the negator remains. Then you are in your purity, and then you know what *is*. Everything that is known before that is just the mind's imaginings, dreamings, projections.

## TO DIE CONSCIOUSLY

Meditation means surrender, total letting go. As soon as someone surrenders himself he finds himself in the hands of divinity. If we cling to ourselves, we cannot be one with the almighty. When the waves disappear, they become the ocean itself.

Let us try some experiments in order to understand what is meant by meditation. . . .

Sit in such a way that no one touches you. Close your eyes slowly, and keep your body loose. Relax completely so that there is no strain, no tension in the body at all.

Now imagine that a river is flowing very fast, with tremendous force and sound, between two mountains. Observe it and dive in . . . but do not swim. Let your body float without any movement. Now you are moving with the river—just floating. There is nowhere to reach, no destination, so there is no question of swimming. Feel as if a dry leaf is floating effortlessly in the river. Experience it clearly so that you can know what is meant by "surrender," by "total letting go."

If you have understood how to float, now discover how to die and how to be dissolved completely. Keep your eyes closed, let your body become loose, and relax completely. Observe that a pyre is burning. There is a pile of wood-sticks that have been set afire and the flames of the pyre seem to be reaching toward the sky. And remember one more thing: you are not just observing the burning pyre, you have been placed on it. All your friends and relatives are standing around.

It is better to experience this moment of death consciously, as one day or the other it is sure to come. With the flames growing higher and higher, feel that your body is burning. Within a short while the fire will be put out by itself. People will disperse and the cemetery will be empty and silent again. Feel it, and you will see that everything has become quiet and nothing but the ashes remains. You have dissolved completely. Remember this experience of being dissolved because meditation is also a kind of death.

Keep your eyes closed now and relax completely. You do not have to do anything. There is no necessity to do anything: before you were, things were as they are, and they will be the same even after you die.

Now feel that whatever is happening *is happening!* Feel the "suchness" of it. It is so: it can only be this way; there is no other way possible. So why resist? By "suchness" is meant "no resistance." There is no expectation that anything be other than what is. The grass is green, the sky is blue, the waves of the ocean roar . . . birds sing, crows are crowing. . . . There is no resistance from you because life is *such.* Suddenly a transformation takes place! What was normally considered to be a disturbance now seems to be amiable. You are not against anything; you are happy with everything as it is.

So the first thing you had to do was to float, rather than swim, in the ocean of existence. For one who is ready to float, the river, itself, takes him to the ocean. If we do not resist, life itself takes us to the divinity.

Secondly, you had to dissolve yourself, rather than save yourself, from death. What we want to save is sure to die, and what is going to be there eternally will be there without our effort. The one who is ready to die is able to open his doors to welcome the divinity, but if you keep your doors closed—because of the fear of death—you do so at the cost of not attaining divinity. Meditation is to die!

The last thing you had to experience was "suchness." Only an acceptance of both the flowers *and* the thorns can bring you peace. Peace, after all, is the fruit of total acceptance. Peace will come only to him who is ready to accept even the absence of peace.

So close your eyes, let your body be loose, and feel as if there is no life in the body. Feel as if your body is relaxing. Go on feeling this, and within a short time you will know that you are not the master of the body. Every cell, every nerve of the body, will feel relaxed—as if the body does not exist. Leave the body alone as if it is floating on the river. Let the river of life take you anywhere it wants to, and float upon it just like a dry leaf.

Now feel that your breath is gradually becoming quiet,

silent. As your breathing becomes silent, you will feel that you are being dissolved. You will feel as if you are on the burning pyre, and you have been burnt completely. Not even ashes have remained.

Now feel the sound of the birds, the sun's rays, the waves of the ocean, and just be a witness to them—receptive and yet aware, watchful. The body is relaxed, breathing is silent, and you are in "suchness." You are just a witness to all this.

Gradually you will feel a transformation within, and then suddenly something will become silent inside. The mind has become silent and empty. Feel this: be a witness to it, and experience it. The river has taken away your floating body, the pyre had burnt it, and you have been a witness to it. In this nothingness, a blissfulness enters, which we call divinity.

Breathe slowly two or three times now, and with each breath you will feel freshness, peace, . . . and a blissful pleasure. Now open your eyes slowly and come back from meditation.

Try to do this experiment nightly before going to bed and go to sleep right afterward. Gradually, your sleep will turn into meditation.

## ENTERING SLEEP CONSCIOUSLY

The moment you are dropping into sleep is the moment to encounter the unconscious. You have been sleeping every day, but you have not encountered sleep yet. You have not seen it: what it is, how it comes, how to drop into it. You have not known anything about it. You have been going into sleep every night and awakening from sleep every morning, but you have not felt the moment when sleep comes, you have not felt what happens. So try this experiment, and after three months, suddenly, one day, you will enter sleep knowingly.

Drop on your bed, close your eyes, and then remember— remember!—that sleep is coming and you are to remain awake when it comes. This exercise is very arduous. The first day it will not happen, the next day it will not happen, but if you persist every day, constantly remembering that sleep is coming and you are not to allow it to come without being aware of it—you must feel *how* sleep takes over, *what* it is—then one day, sleep will be there and you will still be awake.

That very moment you become aware of your unconscious! And once you become aware of your unconscious, you will never be asleep again. Sleep will be there, but you will be awake. A center in you will go on knowing. All around you there will be sleep, and the center will go on knowing.

When this center is knowing, dreams become impossible. And when dreams become impossible, daydreams also become impossible. Then you will be asleep in a different sense. A different quality happens because of the encounter.


## WORDLESS COMMUNICATION
## WITH EXISTENCE

You are looking at a flower: look at the flower, feel the beauty of it, but do not use the word "beauty," not even in the mind. Look at it: let it be absorbed in you, go deeply into it, but do not use words. Feel the beauty of it, but do not say, "It is beautiful." Not even in the mind! Do not verbalize and gradually you will become capable of feeling the flower as beautiful without using the word. Really, it is not difficult; it is natural.

You feel first and then the word comes, but we are so habituated to words that there is no gap. The feeling is there, but you have not even felt it before suddenly a word comes. So create a gap. Just feel the beauty of the flower, but do not use the word.

If you can disassociate words from feelings, you can disassociate feelings from existence. Then let the flower be there and you be there—as two presences—but do not allow the feeling to come in. Do not even feel now that the flower is beautiful. Let the flower be there and you be there, in a deep embrace, without any ripple of feeling. Then you will feel beauty without feeling. You will *be* the beauty of the flower. It will not be a feeling: you will *be* the flower. Then you have existentially felt something.

When you can do this, then you will feel that everything has gone: thoughts, words, feelings. And then you can feel . . . existentially.

## ∽ 19 ∽

## Techniques Devised by Bhagwan Shree

### DYNAMIC MEDITATION
#### (or, "Chaotic" Meditation)

Dynamic Meditation is Bhagwan Shree's major technique
and the technique upon which many of his other meditations are based.[1] For a complete discussion of Dynamic
Meditation see chapters 3 and 4.

[1] These meditation techniques, devised by Bhagwan Shree are
all active, dynamic. They start with activity, doing, to lead you
to a state of total non-doing. Some meditation techniques are
for those who are body-oriented, others for those who are heart-
oriented, and still others for those who are mind-oriented.
Bhagwan Shree's techniques are for all three types. They start
with the body, work through the heart, and take you to the
silence, the stillness, of a "no mind" consciousness.
   It is suggested that you try whatever technique appeals to you
for twenty-one days in order to be able to best feel its effects.
If the technique suits, try to practice it (play with it) every day,
at the same time, for three months. After three months its
effects upon you will be self-evident. Then there will no longer
be the need to discipline yourself to do it. It will either drop
spontaneously or it will become a part of your life, a part of
you.
   Bhagwan Shree has said that it is helpful to practice an
active meditation in the morning and a silent meditation at

The technique can be practiced individually or in a group.[2] If group meditation is possible, the energy will be particularly powerful and the results particularly potent. It should be done on an empty stomach, with eyes closed or blindfolded, and with a minimum of clothing worn.

*First Stage:* Ten minutes of deep, fast breathing through the nose. Let the body be as relaxed as possible; then begin with deep, fast, chaotic breathing—as deep and as fast as possible. Go on breathing intensely for ten minutes. Don't stop; be total in it. If the body wants to move while you are breathing, let it; cooperate with it completely.

*Second Stage:* Ten minutes of catharsis, of total cooperation with any energy that breathing has created. Let the emphasis be on catharsis and total letting go. Just let whatever is happening happen. Do not suppress anything. If you feel like weeping, weep; if you feel like dancing, dance. Laugh, shout, scream, jump, shake—whatever you feel to do, *do it!* Just be a witness to whatever is happening within you.

*Third Stage:* Ten minutes of shouting *hoo-hoo-hoo*. Raise your arms above your head and jump up and down as you continue to shout *hoo-hoo*. As you jump, land hard on the souls of your feet so that the sound reaches deep into the sex center. Exhaust yourself completely.

*Fourth Stage:* Ten minutes of stopping dead, *as you are*. Now freeze. In whatever position you are in, stop com-

---

night. As you move from day to night, you move from the outer to the inner, from the active to the passive.

So move into these techniques totally, with the whole of your being, but in a nonserious attitude. There is nothing to be expected, nothing to be achieved, so you can just play with it. Play with it and enjoy it. And enjoy yourself in it.—Ed.

[2] It is very helpful if appropriate music be used as an accompaniment to many of the following techniques. Tapes of the music for these meditations are available through the Rajneesh Foundation, 17 Koregaon Park, Poona, Maharastra, India.

pletely. Energy has been awakened through breathing, cleansed through a catharsis, and raised through the Sufi mantra *hoo*. Now allow it to work deeply within you. Energy means movement. If you are no longer throwing it out, it will begin to work within.

*Fifth Stage:* Ten to fifteen minutes of dancing, of celebration, of thanksgiving for the deep bliss you have experienced.

An alternate form of Dynamic Meditation has been introduced by Bhagwan Shree for those who are unable to make noise in the location where they do the meditation. In this alternative technique, the energy is kept inside, all sound is kept inside, rather than being thrown out. For those who can enter into it fully, it is a very deep form of meditation, as the energy is kept inside and thus can move deeply within.

The stages are the same as above. Allow your body to explode into catharsis in the second stage, without making any sounds. The release, the purging, will be done totally through body movement. Don't suppress anything. If you want to scream, allow the scream to be expressed *through the body*. Then, in the third stage, hammer the sound *hoo* deep inside. Keep the sound inside, but be total with it, intense with it.

## GIBBERISH

Like the Dynamic Meditation, gibberish is a highly cathartic technique. It is said to have first been used hundreds of years ago by a Sufi mystic named Gibbere. Bhagwan Shree has updated it for modern usage.

Either alone or in a group, close your eyes and begin to say nonsense sounds—gibberish. For fifteen minutes move totally into the gibberish. Allow yourself to express whatever needs to be expressed within you. Throw everything out. The mind thinks, always, in terms of words. Gibberish helps to break up this pattern of continual verbalization. Without suppressing your thoughts, you can throw them out—in gibberish. Let your body likewise be expressive.

Then, for fifteen minutes, lie down on your stomach and feel as if you are merging with mother earth. With each exhalation, feel yourself merging into the ground beneath you.

If this is done outside, a slight variation is suggested. Rather than closing your eyes, let them remain open and throw your gibberish out to the sky above you. Don't focus on anything. Just look deeply into the sky and throw out everything that is within you. Begin by sitting, but then, if you want to stand or lie down or move in any way, allow your body to do so.

In the second fifteen-minute stage, sit or lie down on your back and look deeply into the sky. Feel as if you are merging with the sky.

## DEVAVANI

*Devavani* means "the divine voice." When practicing this technique, just imagine that the divine is speaking through you, the divine is moving through you. You are just a channel, an empty vessel, through which the divine speaks and moves.

Each of the four stages is for fifteen minutes and the eyes are to remain closed throughout. The technique may be practiced either alone or in a group.

*First Stage:* Just sit quietly and listen to music. Nothing is to be done.

*Second Stage:* After fifteen minutes, when the music stops, allow yourself to become a channel for the divine voice. Start by saying softly *la . . . la . . . la* until unfamiliar words come to your lips. After a few days of doing this meditation the words will become an unaccustomed language, and you will find that you are speaking whole sentences in an unknown tongue.

This is to be a "Latihan" of the tongue, so do not cry, shout, laugh, or scream, as this will show that it has become meaningful. The words need to come from the part of the brain that you used as a child—before you could talk—not from the part that thinks and talks all day. The words are to come from the unfamiliar part of the brain. In the Old Testament this speaking in tongues is called "Glossolalia."

Latihan is to be distinguished from the gibberish described in the previous technique. It is not a catharsis. It is not to "get out" what is inside you. Rather, it is to allow yourself to be a vehicle for the divine energy. Gibberish is a doing; Latihan is an allowing. Gibberish allows things to be released from *inside* you; Latihan allows something to pass *through* you.

If words stop coming, start the *la . . . la . . . la* again until the words once again begin to fall from your tongue.

*Third Stage:* For fifteen minutes, stand, continue speaking in tongues, but now allow the divine to move through the body as well. Allow a total Latihan to happen. If you allow your body to be soft and loose, soon you will feel subtle energies moving inside. Let these energies move your body—slowly, gently. Don't you do the moving. Let the energies move you.

*Fourth Stage:* Simply lie down and be perfectly still.

*Note:* The second stage of this meditation can be done almost anywhere, anytime—driving, bathing, working . . . "and it is more powerful than any prayer," Bhagwan Shree says.

## THE PRAYER MEDITATION

Bhagwan Shree has spoken about four levels of communion: sex, love, prayer, and meditation. The lowest is sex. It is a communion between two bodies. Love is higher. It is a communion between two minds, two souls. Next comes prayer. Prayer is a deep communication, a deep love, between you and the whole of existence. But, still, a duality exists. In meditation this duality ceases. You are not in communion with something outside of yourself, you are not in communication with the divine or with existence. Rather, you have become one with it, one with the All.

Bhagwan Shree has spoken elsewhere on how sex can be used to lead you to meditation and how love can be used to lead you to meditation.[3] Here he speaks on how prayer can be used.

"To me, a prayer is a feeling, a flowing with nature. If you want to talk, talk, but remember, your talk is not going to affect the existence. It will affect you, and that may be good, but prayer is not going to change God's mind.

"It may change you, but if it is not changing you then it is a trick. You can go on praying for years, but if it doesn't change you, drop it, throw it, it is rubbish; don't carry it anymore.

"Prayer is not going to change God. You always think that if you pray, God's mind will change, He will be more favorable, He will be a little partial to your side of things. No! The vast sky, the totality, can be with you only if you can be with it. There is no other way to pray.

"I also suggest praying, but praying should be an energy phenomenon—not a 'devotion to God' phenomenon, but an energy phenomenon.

---

[3] See *The Book of the Secrets*, vols. 1–5, for an extensive discussion of techniques of sex and love.

"You simply become silent, you simply open yourself.
You raise both hands, palms uppermost, head up, toward
the sky, just feeling existence flowing in you. As the energy
(or prana) flows down your arms, you will feel a gentle
tremor. Be like a leaf in the breeze, trembling. Allow it,
help it. Then let your whole body vibrate with energy. Just
let whatever happens, happen.

"After two or three minutes, or whenever you feel completely filled by the energy, lean down and kiss the earth.
You simply become a vehicle to allow the divine energy to
unite with the earth. You feel again a flowing with the
earth: heaven and earth, above and below, yin and yang,
male and female. You float, you mix, you drop yourself
completely. You are not. You become one, you merge.

"These two stages should be repeated six more times, so
that each of the chakras can become unblocked. It may be
done more than that, but it should never be done for *les*.
than seven times or you will feel restless and unable to
sleep.

"It is best to do this prayer at night, in a darkened room,
going to sleep immediately afterward. Or, it can be done
in the morning, but then it must be followed by fifteen
minutes of rest. This rest is necessary; otherwise you will
feel as if you are drunk, in a stupor.

"This merging with energy is prayer. It changes you.
And when you change, the whole existence changes."


## THE MASS PRAYER

This technique can be done with a minimum of three
people, but it is most effective when done in a large group.
It is best done in the evening.

Stand in a circle, with your eyes closed, holding hands.
Begin to slowly chant, as loudly as you can with comfort,
"Holy . . . holy . . . holy . . ." Allow a silence—the
valley—to descend between the words (the peaks). After

three or four minutes a natural harmony and rhythm will develop between the participants.

As you chant, feel that everything is holy. Every object is holy, every person is holy, you are holy. Everything is holy and everything is a part of the wholeness. Feel the reality of the holiness and wholeness of yourself and all that surrounds you. Let your ego dissolve and become unified in the chant.

Bhagwan Shree has said, "Those who have eyes will see a pillar of energy arising from the group. One individual cannot do much alone, but imagine five hundred meditators joining hands in this prayer!"

After ten minutes or so, or at the dropping of hands initiated by the leader, all kneel down, kiss the earth, and allow the energy to flow into the earth, to return to the source from which it has come.

## THE MANDALA

"Mandala" in Hindi means circle. Every circle contains a center. The aim of this technique is to create a circle of energy so that *centering* results naturally. The technique is divided into four fifteen-minute stages. It starts out with intense activity and each stage gets progressively more still so that in the fourth stage one is left in absolute stillness, absolute silence—and meditation can happen.

*First Stage:* For fifteen minutes, jog in place. Start off slowly and then gradually begin to jog faster and faster. It is helpful if music is played that increases in intensity throughout the fifteen minutes. The breath should be even and regular, deep and relaxed.

It is important to keep going during this stage—to forget the mind, forget the body, and just pay attention to the jogging. Starting with the lowest portion of your body, an upsurge of energy will be created that will circulate in the body. Those who find the jogging impossible can alternate between jogging and "cycling"—or, "cycle" throughout the entire first stage. The cycling is done lying down on the back, with hips on the floor and the legs rotating in a circular motion as if riding a bicycle. Whether jogging or cycling, the legs should be moving in a circular fashion.

*Second Stage:* For fifteen minutes, sit with the eyes closed and rotate your body from side to side in a circular motion. Just feel as if you are a reed, blowing in the wind. Surrender to the wind. Let it move you from side to side, back and forth, around and around. The swaying should be slow, gentle, relaxed, natural.

Energy is moving up through the body. You will feel it concentrated now at the navel.

*Third Stage:* Lie on your back, open your eyes, and for fifteen minutes rotate them clockwise, in as wide a circle as possible. Start slowly and then gradually move the eyes faster and faster.

Many tensions accumulate in the muscles in the back of the eyes. In this stage those muscles become relaxed. Energy that has been moving up through the body is drawn now to the third eye (the space between the two eyes). You become centered at the third eye (the "inner eye").

*Fourth Stage:* Now close your eyes, lie perfectly still, and relax completely. All tensions will have been released from the body and an abundance of energy will be there. The energy, no longer blocked by tensions, will be able to work within you: cleansing you, bathing you.

*Note:* It is important to allow one's lower jaw to drop open and remain loose throughout this entire technique, particularly in the second and third stages. Many tensions are collected and concentrated in the jaw. If you keep the jaw relaxed in this technique, these tensions can easily be released.

## *KUNDALINI* MEDITATION

One of Bhagwan Shree's most popular (and potent) techniques. Much *kundalini* energy will be awakened in you. You will feel yourself alive with it, vibrating with it. After the energy has been awakened, dancing is used in order to disperse the energy, in order to return it to the universe, to the existence. Then silence follows, stillness follows.

The technique is divided into four fifteen-minute stages. Music should be used as an accompaniment to the first three stages, but the final stage should be done in complete silence.

*First Stage:* For fifteen minutes, let your whole body shake. Let the shaking start from your hands and your feet, where all the nerve endings in the body are located. Keep your eyes relaxed, the muscles of your face relaxed. Let everything shake, everything vibrate. In the beginning you will have to do it, but after a few minutes the shaking will take over. If you keep your whole body loose, the shaking will move from your hands, from your feet, from your head, until it takes you over completely, until you *become* the shaking.

*Second Stage:* Now, for fifteen minutes, allow the energy that has been awakened to be expressed through dance. You will be alive with energy; allow this energy to be dispersed through dance. The dancing is important. More energy has been awakened in you than your body is accustomed to. Without the dancing you will feel a certain disturbance, a certain restlessness, a certain uneasiness. So move totally into the dance. Express whatever energy has been awakened in you through dance, through celebration. Enjoy!

*Third Stage:* Standing or sitting, remain perfectly still for fifteen minutes. Mellow music should be playing. Allow yourself to merge with it.

*Fourth Stage:* For fifteen minutes, lie down and *be*. There is nothing but silence, nothing but stillness, within and without.

*Note:* Eyes remain either opened or closed in the first two stages and, of course, closed in the last two.

## WHIRLING

Whirling is originally a Sufi (dervish) meditation exercise said to have first been done about seven hundred years ago. No food or drink should be taken for several hours before the meditation. Loose clothing and bare feet are best.

Try to center yourself just above the navel. Begin to turn in place, moving in a counterclockwise direction. (If you begin to feel any nausea, try turning in a clockwise direction instead.) Keep your eyes open, your body loose, and your arms extended out comfortably from your side. Your right arm should be held high, with the palm turned upward, and the left arm held low, palm downward. Try not to focus the eyes on anything. Just surrender to the constant blur that your motion creates. Or, focus your vision on your extended right hand.

Start turning slowly, building up speed as you go. If you are centered just above the navel, you will soon begin to feel that you are a wheel, rotating around its center. On the periphery the body will be turning. At the hub, at the center, there will be stillness.

The music to use as an accompaniment to the whirling should be constant, rhythmic, and alive, picking up gradually in tempo without becoming frantic. As you spin faster and faster you will find that at your center there will be more and more stillness.

Keep turning around and around until the body some-how finds that, by itself, it has fallen to the ground. There is no set time for this stage of the meditation. You are to continue spinning until, spontaneously, you drop to the ground. Dervish dancers have been known to continue well into the night, although generally the whirling will last anywhere from twenty minutes to three hours. In group situations, forty-five minutes of whirling is suggested.

At whatever point you fall to the ground, stay there. Don't get up and begin whirling again. Lie on your stomach, close your eyes, and let your bare navel touch the ground. Feel yourself sinking into the ground as if it were your mother's breast. Stay in this second stage for a minimum of fifteen minutes.

## NATARAJ
### ("The Dancing Meditation")

Bhagwan Shree has spoken often about dance as a technique. It has been used by many. When the dance is there, the dancer is not. Only the dance exists.

Many of these techniques use dance. The *Nataraj* is *only* dance. It is dance as a total meditation.

*First Stage:* Forty minutes of dancing. Let your unconscious completely take over. Dance as if possessed. Do not plan or have any control over your movements. Forget witnessing, observing, awareness—just be totally in the dance. The dance will start at the sex center and then move upward. Let it happen.

*Second Stage:* When the music stops, stop dancing immediately, lie down, and, for twenty minutes, be perfectly silent, perfectly still. Vibrations of the dancing, of the music, will continue inside. Allow them to penetrate to your most subtle layers.

*Third Stage:* Stand up, and for five minutes, dance in celebration. Enjoy.

# GOURISHANKAR

Bhagwan Shree has said that if we do the breathing correctly in the first stage of this meditation, we will get so much oxygen in our bloodstream that we will feel as high as if we were on the top of Gourishankar (Mount Everest).

The meditation is in four parts. Each part is fifteen minutes long.

*First Stage:* Sit with your eyes closed and inhale as deeply as you can through the nose. Hold the breath for as long as you can, then exhale gently through the mouth. Hold the exhalation until you can't hold it any longer and then breathe in again through the nose. Repeat this for fifteen minutes.

*Second Stage:* Return to normal breathing and stare at a candle flame or a flashing light. If possible, use a blue strobe light. Let your gaze be soft and gentle, as if you are looking lovingly at someone. Keep your body still.

*Third Stage:* Stand up, close your eyes, and let "Latihan" happen. In Latihan you let your body be soft and loose and soon subtle energies will be felt moving inside the body. Allow those energies to move your body—slowly, gently. Don't you do the moving; let the moving move you.

These first three stages should be accompanied by music —a combination of soothing background music and a steady beat that is seven times as fast as a normal heartbeat. (The first sound that any of us ever heard was the sound of our mother's heart.) The fourth stage is done in total silence.

*Fourth Stage:* Lie down in silence and remain perfectly still.

## NADABRAHMA

*Nadabrahma* is an old Tibetan technique. It was originally done early in the morning. Meditators would awake
between two and four, practice the technique, and then
return to sleep.

Bhagwan Shree has suggested that it be done either at
night before going to sleep or during the morning. If it is
not done at night, it should be followed by at least fifteen
minutes of rest.

*Nadabrahma* can be done both as a mass meditation and
individually. It can even be done at work, particularly if
you do any kind of manual work. It is good to do it on an
empty stomach as, otherwise, the inner sound will not be
able to go so deep. When doing it alone, it will be helpful
to use earplugs.

*First Stage:* For a minimum of thirty minutes, sit in a
relaxed position with the eyes closed. With lips together,
begin to hum, loudly enough to create a vibration throughout your entire body. The humming should be loud enough
so that people around will be able to hear it.

You can alter the pitch as you like, humming, then in-
haling, at your own pace. If the body wants to move, allow
it, but the movement should be very slow, very graceful.

Visualize your body as a hollow tube, an empty vessel
filled only with the vibrations of the humming. After a
while a point will come where you are just the listener: the
humming will be happening by itself. This activates the
brain, cleansing every fiber. It is also particularly helpful
in healing.

*Second Stage:* With your eyes still closed, begin to move
your hands (palms up) outward in a circular motion—the
right hand moving to the right and the left hand moving to
the left. Make the circles large and move as slowly as
possible, the slower the better. You may even feel some-

times that they are not moving at all. If your body wants to move, allow it, but, again, keep the movement slow, soft, and graceful.

After seven and a half minutes, move the hands in the opposite direction: palms down and hands moving, circularly, inward toward your body. Move your hands in this direction for another seven and a half minutes. As your hands move inward, imagine that you are taking energy in. As they move outward again, away from the body, imagine energy going out.

*Third Stage:* Stop your hand movements and sit silently for fifteen minutes, with no movement anywhere in the body.

Bhagwan Shree has given a slight variation of this technique for couples: sit facing one another, with your hands crossed, and holding your partner's two hands. Cover yourself with a bedsheet so that the two bodies are completely covered. It is best if no clothing be worn at all. The room should be fairly dark, with four small candles providing the only light. Burn incense. The same incense should be burning every night, and this particular incense should be used *only* when this technique is being practiced.

Facing one another, with your hands crossed and clasped, close your eyes and begin humming. Continue your humming for a minimum of thirty minutes. The humming should be done together. After a minute or two, your breathing will begin to be in union and the humming in unison. As you hum feel your energies merging with one another, uniting.

## SHIVA-NETRA
### ("The Third Eye Meditation")

A blue light must be used for this meditation, as blue is the color of the third eye. For group meditation, a five-hundred-watt bulb is recommended, as is a dimming switch to regulate the intensity of the light. If the meditation is done at home, an ordinary blue light can be used, without regulating the intensity of it.

The meditation lasts for an hour and has two stages of ten minutes each—repeated three times.

*First Stage:* Sit perfectly still and look at the blue light. Your eyes should be soft and relaxed. It doesn't matter if there is any blinking. The light should be started in the dim position and then slowly and gently the light should be increased to its full intensity. Then slowly, gently, it should again be dimmed. This brightening and dimming should be done three times in *each* of the three ten-minute light stages.

*Second Stage:* Close your eyes and slowly, gently, sway from side to side. As you shift from side to side, the energy from each of the two eyes will move to the third eye. Sway gently—as if you are a tree, blowing in the breeze.

*Third Stage:* Repeat the first stage.
*Fourth Stage:* Repeat the second stage.
*Fifth Stage:* Repeat the first stage.
*Sixth Stage:* Repeat the second stage.

*Note:* This technique, as well as the others mentioned in this section, are most effective when accompanied by appropriate music. Tapes of the music used for these meditations are available through the Shree Rajneesh Foundation, 17 Koregaon Park, Poona, Maharastra, India.


## LAUGHING

We are so attached to our suffering that laughing happens, generally, only as a release of tension. Only rarely, very rarely, does laughing happen without cause. We cannot laugh, we cannot be happy; even in our laughing there is pain.

But laughing is so beautiful, such a deep cleansing, a deep purification. Bhagwan Shree has devised a "laughing technique." Practiced every morning upon awakening, it will change the whole nature of your day. If you wake up laughing, you will soon begin to feel how absurd life is. Nothing is serious: even your disappointments are laughable, even your pain is laughable, even *you* are laughable.

When you wake up in the morning, before opening your eyes, stretch like a cat. Stretch every part of your body. Enjoy the stretching; enjoy the feeling of your body becoming awake, alive. After three or four minutes of stretching, with your eyes still closed, *laugh*. For five minutes just laugh. At first you will be doing it, but soon, the sound of your very attempt to laugh will cause a genuine laughter. Lose yourself in laughter.

This technique may take several days before you are able to do it. We are not accustomed to laughing; we have forgotten how. But soon it will be spontaneous. And then, every morning, *enjoy*.

## An Invitation

As Bhagwan Shree is constantly devising new techniques, and revising old ones, it is impossible to keep up to date with all his techniques. He may tell one person to suck on a pacifier for ten hours a day, another to make faces at himself in the mirror for an hour a day, another to "kill a pillow" (a pillow effigy of one of his parents). He may tell one person to laugh for an hour, another to cry all night. He says, "I tailor the pants; I don't ask you to cut off your legs."

But there is more to a master than his techniques. A master creates situations that, left to yourself, you might avoid —the very situations through which you will grow. Everything he does is a technique, a device.

Whoever is interested in sharing in the unique experience that being with an enlightened master is, is invited to visit Shree Rajneesh Ashram, 17 Koregaon Park, Poona, Maharastra, India.

# About the Author

Bhagwan Shree Rajneesh is one of India's most widely known and widely respected spiritual teachers. He is a Tantric, a Taoist, a Zen Buddhist, a Sufi, a yogi, a Christian mystic, and a Hasid. Belonging to no one particular tradition, he incorporates in his teachings what is most valid for the modern seeker from each of the ancient traditions.

Born on December 11, 1931, in a small village in Madhya Pradesh, India, he achieved his own realization (his enlightenment) at the age of twenty-one. He had no guru, no spiritual master. For nine years he served as a professor of philosophy at two colleges, resigning from his professorship in 1966 in order to devote his life totally to the spiritual awakening of others. As he traveled around India delivering revolutionary discourses on a variety of subjects, many people came to recognize his level of consciousness and spontaneously began surrendering themselves to him. Although he has always claimed that he is not a guru, he soon had thousands of disciples. "I am not a guru," he says, "but I do not deny your need to be a disciple. My every effort is to awaken the guru within you."

Although Bhagwan Shree has never been outside of India, thousands of Westerners have been attracted to his rapidly growing ashram in Poona (about one hundred miles outside of Bombay). Many of these Westerners have become disciples of Bhagwan Shree and within the last two years numerous Rajneesh Meditation Centers have opened up in Europe, North America, South America, and Asia, where hundreds practice his meditation techniques daily.

Over a hundred books by Bhagwan Shree (including approximately thirty in English), as well as numerous scholarly critiques of his teachings, have been published in India.

This is the first American publication of his work.